G000150767

MUSCLE CAR MANIA

An Advertising Collection 1964-1974

MITCH FRUMKIN

Motorbooks International
Publishers & Wholesalers Inc
Osceola, Wisconsin 54020, USA

© Mitch Frumkin, 1981

ISBN: 0-87938-153-1
Library of Congress Catalog Card Number: 81-14123

All rights reserved. No part of this publication may be reproduced without prior written permission from the publisher: Motorbooks International Publishers & Wholesalers, Inc., P.O. Box 2, Osceola, Wisconsin 54020, U.S.A.

Motorbooks International is a certified trademark, registered with the United States Patent Office.

Printed and bound in the United States of America.

1 2 3 4 5 6 7 8 9 10

Cover illustration by Roger Boehm, Minneapolis, Minnesota.

Cover design by William F. Kosfeld.

Motorbooks International books are also available at discounts in bulk quantity for industrial or sales-promotion use. For details write to Marketing Manager, Motorbooks International, P.O. Box 2, Osceola, Wisconsin 54020.

Library of Congress Cataloging in Publication Data

Frumkin, Mitch, 1943-
  Muscle car mania.

  1. Automobiles—Miscellanea. 2. Automobiles—
Pictorial works. I. Title.
TL15.F74   629.2'222'0973   81-14123
ISBN 0-87938-153-1 (pbk.)   AACR2

Preface

A muscle car is a "Howitzer with windshield wipers," or so says a 1965 Buick magazine ad.

Plymouth had a different opinion. It advertised that a muscle car is a cartoon bird that goes "BEEP-BEEP" and possesses a 426-cubic-inch hemi-head heart.

During the years 1964-1974 almost every American auto manufacturer took up the challenge of creating the ideal muscle car. Their goal, it seemed, was to build the best high-performance car in the industry.

This is the era I affectionately call Muscle Car Mania.

The auto companies battled it out by continually increasing the horsepower and making available more exotic speed equipment with each new year. They then proceeded to bolt their bored-out engines into gutsy new body designs, and began calling these models by bizarre, sometimes comical, names.

Packed in this book are some of the wackiest auto artwork and terminology ever used. The text within these ads serves as a written history of the American auto philosophy during its wildest period.

Sit back and, with each ad, relive Muscle Car Mania.

Mitch Frumkin
September 1981

For their love
and "High Performance" enthusiasm,
I dedicate this book
to my wife Vivi
and son Kristian.

Contents

Chapter One
American Motors

RAMBLER AMERICAN ROGUE

343 CUBES

We don't build them the way we used to.

For American Motors to stuff a 343 cube Typhoon V-8 into an innocent-looking Rambler American is guaranteed to cause news. But 1967 is a driver's year like no other, and American Motors has risen to the occasion.

Witness this Rogue hardtop. Its 343 cubes are fed by a 4-barrel Carter to develop 280 horses, and this mill winds up to higher rpm's faster and pays off in quicker shifts.

The 4-speed stick is mandatory (as you'd expect in a machine of this caliber), and you can opt for a fat pile of goodies including Hi-Performance Cam kit, a 4.44 rear axle, Twin-Grip differential, special handling package, power disc brakes, electric tach, shoulder belts, and extra-wide-profile red line nylons mounted on 5.5" rims.

So you see, we don't build them the way we used to.

That's our message. With this added plus: American Motors believes any driver's year must be a safe driver's year. So you get an energy-absorbing steering column, deep-dish wheel, Double-Safety brake system, shoulder belt anchors, and many other built-in safety features.

See what a 343-CID Typhoon looks like in any of seven Rambler Americans, at your American Motors/ Rambler Dealer.

Drive one. It just might end up that you don't build them the way you used to, either!

American Motors builds your kind of car
AMBASSADOR · MARLIN · REBEL · RAMBLER AMERICAN

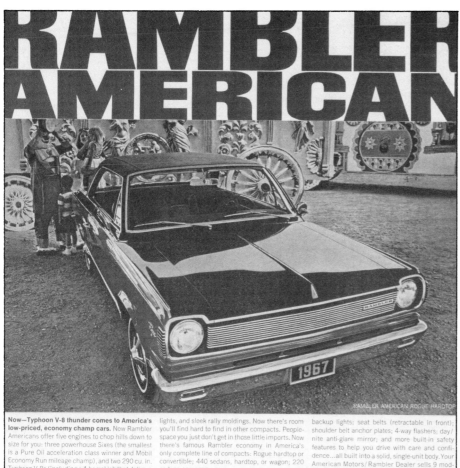

RAMBLER AMERICAN

RAMBLER AMERICAN ROGUE HARDTOP

Now—Typhoon V-8 thunder comes to America's low-priced, economy champ cars. Now Rambler Americans offer five engines to chop hills down to size for you: three powerhouse Sixes (the smallest is a Pure Oil acceleration class winner and Mobil Economy Run mileage champ), and two 290 cu. in. Typhoon V-8s (including a 4-barrel job that delivers 225 hp). Now there are five Rambler American transmissions—including a 4-speed floor stick—plus power disc brakes and a specially tuned suspension that turns bad roads into good roads.

Now there's styling that matches the performance —starting with straight-line grilles, concave tail-

lights, and sleek rally moldings. Now there's room you'll find hard to find in other compacts. People-space you just don't get in those little imports. Now there's famous Rambler economy in America's only complete line of compacts: Rogue hardtop or convertible; 440 sedans, hardtop, or wagon; 220 sedans or wagon.

Now every Rambler American gives you these standard safety features: 153.8 sq. in. brakes on Sixes (167.5 on V-8s); Double-Safety brake system; warning signal light to monitor both brake line systems; energy-absorbing steering column and three-spoke deep-dish wheel; padded dash, visors;

backup lights; seat belts (retractable in front); shoulder belt anchor plates; 4-way flashers; day/ nite anti-glare mirror; and more built-in safety features to help you drive with care and confidence...all built into a solid, single-unit body. Your American Motors/Rambler Dealer sells 9 models of Rambler Americans. See him. He's the only Now Car dealer in town.

THE 1967 AMERICAN MOTORS

AMBASSADOR · MARLIN · REBEL · RAMBLER AMERICAN

Quality built in—so the value stays in. Read new 5-year or 50,000-mile warranty...see opening page. 5/50,000

THE NOW CARS

1967

Wind up Rebel's 343 cube 4-bbl. Typhoon V-8 — and you'll wind up owning the first Excitement Machine in the intermediate class! Okay, drivers, here's how one of the Now Cars looks from your end. Three of Rebel's five engines are optional Typhoon V-8s: slim-wall cast-iron, mass balanced beauties with the lightest reciprocating weight of any industry V-8s. 280 horses are on tap in the big bore, high-compression 343 job. There's a road-gripping wide stance, a 4-link trailing arm rear suspension (the first ever in a single-unit body), and optional handling hardware like heavy-duty shocks and springs, extra-wide-profile red-line tires for high-performance driving, and power disc brakes.

A machine? Of the first order. But Rebel SST is also a car for the groovy gal next to you (even if you married her). She can get bucket seats with headrests, Shift-Command

Transmission with stick or automatic control (unless you've vetoed that for a 4-speed floor stick, and tach), and an SST convertible that seats three in back easily. She also gets a lot of Rebel safety for Now: energy-absorbing steering column and deep-dish wheel, a signal light that monitors both Double-Safety brake line systems, anchor plates for shoulder belts, and plenty more features to help her drive with care and confidence. The place for you to wind up this machine is your Now Car dealer. Your American Motors/Rambler Dealer. That's right, your American Motors/Rambler Dealer.

THE 1967 AMERICAN MOTORS

AMBASSADOR · MARLIN · REBEL · RAMBLER AMERICAN

NEW WARRANTY—IN ADDITION TO 2-YEAR OR 24,000-MILE WARRANTY ON THE ENTIRE AUTOMOBILE. American Motors Corporation warrants the engine block, head and internal parts, water pump, intake manifold, transmission case and internal parts (except manual clutch), torque converter, drive shaft, universal joints, rear axle, differential and rear wheel bearings of its 1967 cars to be free from defects in material or 5-YEAR OR 50,000 MILE WARRANTY workmanship for 5 years or 50,000 miles, whichever comes first. The owner must change the engine oil and install new oil filter every six (6) months or 4,000 miles, whichever comes first, clean oil filler cap (filtered type) and carburetor air cleaner element every 4,000 miles and replace it every 24,000 miles and furnish evidence of this service to an Authorized American Motors Dealer every six (6) months and have him certify its receipt and the car's mileage. Further, American Motors Corporation so warrants the remainder of the car for 2 years or 24,000 miles, which ever comes first, except tires (warranted by tire manufacturer). Any part so defective, will be repaired or replaced, in accordance with the applicable portion of the warranty, without ON THE ENGINE AND DRIVE TRAIN charge at an Authorized American Motors Dealership. Owners are responsible for deterioration, misuse and normal maintenance. QUALITY BUILT IN—SO THE VALUE STAYS IN.

REBEL

Rebel SST: The Excitement Machine

Equipment for a Sunday afternoon.

Sunday afternoon.
The wife and kids want to go over the river and through the woods to grandmother's house. Fine.
But why should the drive be a drag? With the Rebel SST shown above, you can turn a prosaic trip into a grand touring experience.
Just order your SST with the 290 cubic inch Typhoon V-8; or the bigbore 343-CID version. Feed it with a Holley 2-bbl or a Carter 4-bbl (with 10.2:1 compression ratio). Add a hi-performance Camshaft Kit and 3.54 or 4.44 rear axle ratio. Pick a few options like dual exhausts, power

discs, electric tach, shoulder belts, extra-wide profile rubber, and a special handling package.
Your wife will be so impressed with all the standard safety features she'll never even notice you're taking the long way around. Check out a Rebel SST hardtop or convertible at your American Motors/Rambler Dealer. Next week maybe you'll be the one to say, "Let's go to grandma's."

THE **NOW** CARS FROM THE
1967 AMERICAN MOTORS
AMBASSADOR · MARLIN · REBEL · RAMBLER AMERICAN

Test Drag a Javelin.

Don't laugh. The Javelin SST is even faster than it looks.
When equipped with a 343 cube/280-BHP 4-barrel V-8, and a 4-speed manual transmission with a 3.54 rear axle, it will move from a standstill to 60 in about 7.86 seconds and pin your backbone to the bucket in the process.
The engine pumps out a tough 365 lb.-ft. of torque at 3000 RPM. This SST in pure stock form will cover a standing quarter in 15.8.
But performance just begins there.
The real surprise comes in the Javelin's handling.
The Javelin can be equipped with front disc brakes, and a special handling suspension that includes a larger diameter sway bar and heavy-duty springs and shocks.
You'll notice the Javelin's phenomenal control in tight turns and high speed cornering.
Popular Science Monthly wrote that "The Javelin reacts almost the same at high speed as it does during low-speed maneuvers. Steering ratio was 18.1 to 1 overall and it felt just right for this car. Not too slow, not too fast. I particularly liked the action of the power steering. Aside from handling, the ride is excellent – tight and firm, yet comfortable enough for long-distance or everyday driving."
That's what the experts say.
And they say it better than we do.

American Motors
Ambassador · Rebel · Rambler American · And the new Javelin

The AMX.
It takes more than money to get one.

If you can find an AMX, we'll sell you one. But as this message goes to press, less than 2,000 AMX's have been produced.

And we, American Motors, will only make about 8,000 more this year.

You see the difficulty.

Even if you have the $3,245[1] necessary to buy an AMX, you may get a lot of exercise before you ever get close enough to pay for one.

Ah, but the thrill of being the first man in your state to own one will surely be surpassed by the thrill of being the first man in your state to drive one.

A two-seater, the AMX gives you the ease of maintenance associated with a family sedan, combined with the sheer fun and maneuverability of a foreign sports car.

In fact, its incredibly *uncomplex* design means that, once the optional 390 engine is broken in, you could roll right onto a race track and be ready to do about 130 mph.

In pure stock form—without special engine modifications.

Specially equipped AMX's with modified engines broke 106 USAC speed records.

And while there are cars on the road that are faster than the AMX, we hasten to add that beating other drivers isn't the AMX's main appeal.

It's the way the car reacts to you *as you drive*, not the usual dull split second later. You get out of lane, pass the car in front and get back in lane in one sure motion.

Because the AMX offers one of the fastest steering wheel ratios of any U.S.-built car, it turns, corners, follows your direction *simultaneously*.

Being a sports car, the AMX is sports-car sized.

So, while the inside isn't much of a place to hold meetings, it will hold a lot of other things.

The trunk is a lot bigger than you'd expect a sports car trunk to be. Because we didn't fill it with a big spare tire.

We gave you The Airless Spare.

When you need it, it "wwwhhhooossshh!" inflates.

The Airless Spare is nice because it doesn't fill up your trunk with air that you don't need.

It's something every car should have.

But then, every car should have a lot of things.

Things like a short throw, all-syncromesh 4-on-the-floor, fiberglass belted wide-profile tires, shoulder harness seat belts, tachometer, aircraft-type instrument panel, energy-absorbing steering column, heavy-duty springs and shocks.

To mention only a few of the AMX's standard features.

Another un-standard standard feature is the production number that will be set in the AMX dash when you (if you find one) buy it.

AMX 00001 through AMX 10,000.

While this number may mean a lot to collectors in the years ahead, we do want to point out one thing.

All AMX's are made with the same attention and quality.

And while possessing a lower number may have a sentimental or prestige value, it does not in any way make one AMX better than another.

Just as possessing an AMX does not make one man better than another.

Just luckier.

American Motors

Ambassador · Rebel · Rambler American · Javelin · And the new AMX

1. Based upon manufacturer's suggested retail price, federal taxes included. State and local taxes, destination charges, options, excluded.

Mr. and Mrs. Breedlove went for a nice, long, Sunday drive in an AMX.

They drove right into Monday and 3,380 miles later they broke 77 speed records.

On Thursday and Saturday they came back and broke 13 more records.

And on the following Tuesday, they broke 16 more. All in all the Breedloves set a total of 106 records in the 1968 AMX.

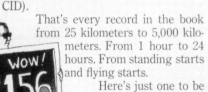

90 Class C records were broken (with a modification of the standard AMX 290 CID engine bored out to 304 CID).

That's every record in the book from 25 kilometers to 5,000 kilometers. From 1 hour to 24 hours. From standing starts and flying starts.

Here's just one to be specific: in Class C the

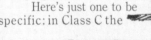

AMX's average speed for 24 hours was 140.790 m.p.h. The old mark was 102.310.

The AMX also broke 16 records in Class B (with a modification of the optional 390 CID engine bored out to 397 CID).

For 1,000 kilometers standing start the AMX averaged 156.548 m.p.h. The old record was 148.702.

For 75 miles flying start it averaged 174.295 m.p.h. The old record was 172.160.

Every record set by the specially prepared and modified AMX's was sanctioned by USCA and FIA.

And this is just the beginning.

American Motors

Ambassador · Rebel · Rambler American · Javelin · And the new AMX

Some people like it for what it is.

Some like it for what it can be.

We think the Javelin SST manages to do one very important thing more successfully than any other sporty car.

It unites the two worlds of speed and comfort without allowing one to completely dominate the other.

Yet it lists for less money than any other American made sporty car.

We give you a bigger standard engine *and* a bigger trunk than Mustang and Camaro.

We scoop out a little more room for legs in the front than our competitors do.

We include reclining bucket seats as standard equipment and a nylon carpet nice enough to have impressed Motor Trend magazine (see March issue).

Of course, you can get options like the 390 engine, a 4-speed transmission with Hurst shifter, disc brakes and mag wheels.

But even without a single option the Javelin is very easy to like.

Just the way it is.

Recently, however, word has gotten back to us that some people are making our hot sporty Javelin even hotter.

That comes as no surprise. We've been doing the same thing ourselves.

In last season's Trans-Am road races, specially prepared and modified Javelins often outran far more seasoned competition.

And in our first year, we were the only factory team who never failed to finish a race.

This year, in addition to SCCA Trans-Am, we'll be represented by two factory sponsored teams on the NASCAR GT circuit.

But you don't have to be a pro to be competitive in a Javelin, because pros are making custom parts specifically for it.

Here are just a few: Hurst shifters.

Doug's headers. "Isky" cams. Edlebrock and Offenhauser intake manifolds. Schiefer clutches and flywheels.

Order them through your American Motors dealer or your favorite speed shop ...and who knows?

Driving the Javelin could become a career.

American Motors' Javelin

The first American sports car for under $3,500 since 1957.

The last of the two-seater T-Birds was priced at $4,015.[1]

It was 1957, the same year that Corvette listed at $3,465.[1]

In the 10 years that followed, Corvette was the only remaining American sports car, and it got progressively more costly.

Then, in 1968, along came the AMX. We introduced it with dual exhausts, fiberglass belted wide-profile tires, energy absorbing steering column, heavy-duty springs and shocks, a short throw all-synchromesh 4-on-the-floor. A standard 290 CID engine, and optional 343 and high performance 390 CID's.

Now, though the AMX isn't quite a year old, we have some changes to report:

A 140 m.p.h. speedometer and a big new tach are standard for 1969.

Leather upholstery is available as an option.

So are new dealer installed rear axle ratios from 3.73:1 up to 5.00:1.

Famous names are making custom parts specifically for the AMX:

Hurst shifters. Doug's headers. "Isky" cams. Edelbrock and Offenhauser intake manifolds. Grant Industries' piston rings. Schiefer clutches and flywheels.

These are just a few. But the point is you have a choice.

You can have a lot of fun in a basic AMX for only $3,297.[1]

Or you can spend more and modify an AMX. Who knows, you just might break some speed records with it.

Craig Breedlove did.

American Motors AMX

1 Based on manufacturer's suggested retail prices for models named, federal taxes included. State and local taxes, if any, destination charges and optional equipment extra.

An unfair comparison between the AMX and...what?

You see the problem.

American Motors is in the unique position of having built a limited edition, two-seater sports car which, in modified form, smashed 106 American, national and international speed and endurance records in February, 1968.

Including everything in the FIA/USAC book from 25 to 5,000 kilometers, and from one to 24 hours.

In the 24 hour, Class C run, the AMX's average speed was 140.790 mph. The old record was 102.310.

So the AMX can be a very fast racing car.

But it was really intended for the road.

And you can get it on the road for $3,297.*

That includes an AMX with the following:

A 290 cubic inch V-8 with a 4-barrel carburetor, rated at 225 HP. Short throw, all synchromesh 4-speed stick. Dual exhausts. Fiberglass belted wide profile tires.

Slim shelled reclining bucket seats. 8,000 rpm tach. Padded aircraft-type instrument panel with deep-set controls. Energy-absorbing steering column. Heavy-duty springs and shocks. Large diameter sway bar. Rear traction bars.

And a production number set in the dash.

A low number, because we don't intend to make millions of AMX's.

When you drive one, you won't see yourself coming and going.

Which is a bit sad, because the AMX is a great car to look at.

We wish we could say the same for the car on the right.

American Motors

Ambassador · Rebel · Rambler · Javelin · AMX

The 1969 AMX.

*Based upon manufacturer's suggested retail price. Federal taxes included. State and

A Rambler that does the quarter mile in 14.3.

American Motors and Hurst have collaborated on the custom-built SC/Rambler.

It's a limited production car; only 500 units are planned at this time.

Enough to qualify the SC/Rambler for stock classes in drag racing.

The price is $2,998: Which is very little money when you see what it buys.

1. 390 cubic inch AMX V-8 Engine.
2. 4-speed all-synchromesh close-ratio transmission.
3. Special Hurst 4-speed shift linkage with T-handle.
4. A Sun tach mounted on the steering column.
5. Dual Exhaust system with special-tone mufflers and chrome extensions.
6. Functional Hood Scoop for cold-air induction.
7. Twin-Grip differential.
8. 10½" diameter clutch.
9. 3.54:1 axle ratio.
10. Power disc brakes (front).
11. Rear axle torque links.
12. Handling package (heavy-duty front sway bar plus heavy-duty springs and shocks).
13. Heavy-duty cooling system (heavy-duty radiator, power-flex fan and fan shroud).
14. A 20:1 manual steering ratio.
15. Special application of new Red, White and Blue exterior colors.
16. Two hood Tie-Downs with locking safety pins and cables.
17. Custom Tear-Drop racing mirrors (one each side).
18. Custom Grille.
19. Custom SC/Rambler-Hurst emblem on front fenders/rear panel.
20. Mag styled wheels, 14" x 6", painted specially to complement exterior color scheme.
21. Five E 70 x 14 Goodyear Polyglas™ Wide-Tread tires.
22. Sports steering wheel.
23. Custom-upholstered head restraints in Red, White and Blue vinyl.
24. All-vinyl charcoal seat upholstery with full carpeting.
25. Individually adjustable reclining seats.

There's more, but you get the idea. With this car you could make life miserable for any GTO, Roadrunner, Cobra Jet or Mach 1.

American Motors'/Hurst SC/Rambler

1. Manufacturer's suggested retail price includes all items listed and federal taxes. State and local taxes, if any, and destination charges excluded.

Big Bad Javelin

Optional Big Bad Orange, Big Bad Blue or Big Bad Green paint—includes painted front and rear bumpers.

Optional Twin-Grip differential.

Optional dual exhausts. (Standard with 390 engine.)

Optional Adjust-O-Tilt steering wheel.

Optional "Go" Package. (Includes 343 or 390 V-8, dual exhausts, power disc brakes, E70 X 14 Red Line tires, handling package and black fiberglass hood scoops.)

Optional roof spoiler.

Optional 140 mph speedometer and big faced tach.

Optional "C" rally stripe.

Optional exhaust-style trim panels.

Optional E70 X 14 Goodyear Polyglas™ Red Line tires.

Optional AMX 390 cu. in. engine. (High-performance dealer installed AM parts plus "Isky," Edelbrock, Offenhauser and Doug's Headers parts available for this engine, if you want to modify it.)

Optional power disc brakes.

Optional mag-style wheels.

Optional air-conditioning.

Optional 4-speed close-ratio gear box with Hurst shifter.

Optional Airless Spare.

Optional 8-track stereo tape with AM radio.

Optional handling package. (Includes heavy-duty springs and shocks plus beefed up anti-sway bar.)

American Motors

Introducing the Rebel "Machine."

Standing before you is the car you've always wanted.

And, if you like everything about it, except for the paint job, which admittedly looks startling, you can order the car painted in the color of your choice.

You may be wondering why a company like American Motors would paint a car red, white and blue.

And that's what we keep asking ourselves: Why would a company like American Motors paint a car red, white and blue?

But we have nothing to be embarrassed about under the hood, which is all you should be concerned about.

The Machine has a 390 CID engine as standard equipment and develops a horsepower the equivalent of 340 horses all pulling in unison, which is no mean feat.

Next, and this will be particularly impressive to those people who have buried their heads in hot rod magazines since they were old enough to say "zoom . . . zoom . . . lookee it's a car," the Machine has a 4-speed all-synchromesh close-ratio transmission with special Hurst shift linkage and a 3.54:1 standard rear axle ratio (or an optional 3.91:1).

To feed air to your engine, and it will be your engine once you buy the car, we have bolted on a ram-air hood scoop. And in the hood scoop, we mounted a tach that's lighted and registers 8000 rpm's.

Heavy-duty shocks and springs raise the rear end a bit and give the Machine, a raked, just mowed the lawn look.

And our dual exhaust system uses special low back pressure mufflers and larger exhaust pipes.

We will make the description of the rest of the Machine's features mercifully short. Front and rear sway bars, high-back bucket seats, 15 inch tires with raised white letters, mag styled steel wheels, power disc brakes, and racing stripes that glow in the dark.

Incidentally, if you have delusions of entering the Daytona 500 with the Machine, or challenging people at random, the Machine is not that fast. You should know that.

For instance, it is not as fast on the getaway as a 427 Corvette, or a Hemi, but it is faster on the getaway than a Volkswagen, a slow freight train, and your old man's Cadillac.

In short, in order to fully make up your mind about the Machine, you will have to see it in person at your American Motors dealer.

And when you're introduced to it, a simple "How do you do?," "Nice meeting you," or something friendly like "How are your pipes?," will suffice.

Up with The Rebel Machine

For a set of four "Up with the Rebel Machine" decals send 25¢ and your name and address to: Machine Decal Offer, American Motors Sales Corporation, 14250 Plymouth Road, Detroit, Michigan 48232.

MOTOR TREND AND *CAR CRAFT:* DECEMBER '69. IN ITS CONTINUOUS ATTEMPT TO SHED THE MOM AND POP CAR IMAGE FROM THE 1950'S, WITH THE PERFORMANCE NAME-TAG OF SIMPLY 'THE MACHINE.'

We made the AMX look tougher this year because it's tougher this year.

The 1970 AMX comes with a new 360 cu. in. engine as standard equipment.

It develops 290 horsepower, 65 more than we had last year.

And this year we've added to our list of standard items.

To go with our completely redesigned instrument panel, we offer contoured high-back bucket seats with integral head restraints.

Mag style wheels.

A new air scoop system in the front bumper to aid brake cooling.

And the Corning safety windshield is also available. It's an American Motors exclusive.

Of course, an all-synchromesh 4-on-the-floor with Hurst shifter is standard for '70 just as it was for '69.

So are dual exhausts, fiberglass belted wide profile tires, an energy absorbing anti-theft steering column, heavy duty shocks and springs, rear torque links, a 140 m.p.h. speedometer, and a big tach.

As for optional extras, a 390 cu. in. engine and a functional Ram-Air hood scoop top a long list.

But rather than elaborate any further, we'll rest our case on the standard AMX.

It's tough enough.

American Motors

Donohue puts his mark on the Javelin.

Starting now you can buy a Javelin with a spoiler designed by Mark Donohue.

You couldn't before this, but an exciting development has changed everything.

Mark Donohue and Roger Penske, the most successful driver-manager team in road racing, recently signed a three year contract with American Motors.

Together they've won two straight Trans-Am championships. They'll go for a third with the Javelin.

One of the modifications in their Trans-Am Javelin is a spoiler designed by Donohue.

This means that according to Trans-Am rules, the spoiler has to be homologated.

In other words we must incorporate the spoiler into 2,500 Javelins that the public can buy.

And that's just what we've done. But the Donohue designed spoiler isn't the only extra these Javelin SST's will have.

Dual exhausts, power front discs, E70 x 14 white lettered wide profile tires, 14 x 6 wheels, handling package, and a Ram-Air induction system with an AMX hood are also part of the deal.

And you can choose between a 360 or a 390 CID engine. Console shift automatic or 4-speed with a Hurst shifter.

We expect that a lot of the competition are going to see the rear end of Mark Donohue's Javelin this season.

American Motors Javelin

From zero to Donohue in 3.1 years.

In 1967 we had nothing sporty to offer.

Then in 1968 we introduced the Javelin, our first sporty car.

Quicker than you can say "specially prepared and modified" we shipped the Javelin off to the races, where in Trans Am events it did itself, and us, proud.

1969 saw an expansion of our embryonic racing program when Jim Paschal drove a Javelin to victories in 5 NASCAR GT events and also won the Northern Tour Championship.

Now it's 1970, and our ambitions to win in Trans Am are stronger than ever.

We've signed Mark Donohue and Roger Penske, the top driver-manager team in road racing, to a three year contract.

Together they've won two consecutive Trans Am championships. And, of course, we're hoping they'll make it three straight.

At this point, Donohue's ready and his Javelin's ready. You'll notice, when you see it, something in the rear that wasn't there before: a spoiler specially designed by Donohue.

But you don't have to wait to see it on Donohue's Javelin, because you can see it on your own.

We're offering a limited number of Javelin SST's with the Donohue designed spoiler.

And we're offering a not-so-limited number of regular Javelins which also have a lot of interesting possibilities.

Javelins with optional 360 engines. Or 390's.

With standard vinyl upholstery trim for the high-back buckets. Or optional corduroy. Even leather.

A Ram-Air induction system. Mag style wheels.

Fat tires. Dual exhausts. Power front discs. Console shift automatic or a 4-speed with a Hurst shifter and a big tach to keep tabs.

And some other very intriguing optional etceteras.

The point is: if you're going to buy a sporty car, buy one that's going places.

American Motors Javelin

A Javelin for the track.

On this page you see a basic Javelin specially-prepared and modified for Trans-American Road Racing.

It's been clocked at 175 mph, goes from 0 to 60 in under 5 seconds, does the quarter-mile in under 11 seconds.

One of the country's top performance writers, Karl Ludvigsen, said in a recent article: "Hopefully, American Motors will see fit to sell an exact street equivalent of its Trans-Am Javelin, because it could be one of the nicest in a nice class of cars."

Which brings us to the Javelin on the opposite page.

This year, we're producing a limited number of Javelins in racing red-white-and-blue.

We couldn't make it an *exact* street equivalent. That's illegal.

We have, however, put in standard equipment that's optional in most other cars.

It has a 390 engine. Ram-air hood. Dual exhaust system. Heavy-duty engine cooling. Twin-grip differential.

A Javelin for the road.

4-speed close-ratio gear box with Hurst shifter. Power disc brakes in front. Heavy-duty springs and shocks. Front and rear spoilers. F70 x 14 tires with raised letters. 140 mph speedometer and tachometer.

Now, if the racer's a little too much for you, there's the Javelin that started our sports car craze in the first place.

We've put in standard highback bucket seats and redesigned the instrument panel.

We've also added a lot of new options.

Like corduroy upholstery trim in five colors, leather trim in three. Landau-style vinyl roof. New style rally and accent stripes.

And a lot of other things that can make the Javelin look and act just as racy as you want it to.

American Motors

Introducing a sensible alternative to the money-squeezing, insurance-strangling muscle cars of America. The Hornet SC/360.

The Hornet SC/360 lists for only $2,663¹. Which is surprising when you consider what the September issue of Motor Trend had to say about it:

The SC/360 is just a plain gas to drive. It has lightning quick performance…It handles like a dream, especially on the TransAm road course at Michigan International Speedway where we had an opportunity to test it.

A 360 CID V-8 engine with 245 horsepower is standard.

So is a 3-on-the-floor, all synchromesh transmission. A heavy-duty clutch. D70 x 14 Polyglas™ tires. 14 x 6 mag style wheels. Space saver spare. Rally stripe. And individual reclining seats.

To make it even gutsier, the SC/360 also comes with a long list of options.

Among which you'll find a 4-barrel 360 V-8 that develops 285 horsepower. An all synchro 4-on-the-floor with Hurst shifter. Ram air induction with hood scoop. 3.54 or 3.91 rear axle with Twin-Grip. Dual exhausts. White letter tires. Heavy-duty suspension. And a big tach.

But even with the added cost of these options, the SC/360 ends up with a lower list price than most of its bigger, muscle-bound competitors.

And because of its standard 12.5:1 weight-to-power ratio, insurance on the SC/360 ends up lower, too.

As a leading car magazine has said, "The day of the heavy 400-cube, 400-horsepower supercar may be just about over."

Manufacturer's suggested retail price. Federal taxes included. State and local taxes, if any, destination charges excluded.

If you had to compete with GM, Ford and Chrysler what would you do? ◢◼ American Motors

American Motors and Mark Donohue specially prepared and modified the new Javelin-AMX, so you don't have to.

Last season, in Trans-Am Road Racing, Mark Donohue was racing for us and winning.

Obviously, we were thrilled. We had never won in Trans-Am before. And that gave us an idea.

Why not ask Donohue to take some of his special preparations and modifications for the track, and incorporate them into a Javelin for the road.

And that's what he did.

The new Javelin-AMX is a completely redesigned performance car. From its fast, glacial slopes on the outside. To its cockpit console on the inside.

But first and foremost, as a true performance car, it is built around the principle that air pressure has to work for you. Not against you.

It has a body that is wider and lower on the outside. With a wider rear tread for better stability.

It has a front wire-mesh grille screen that is flush with the wind.

A rear spoiler specially designed by Donohue.

New intake manifolds for deeper breathing. New exhaust manifolds to reduce back pressure. A new

optional cowl-air induction system. And an optional front spoiler.

Of course, the new Javelin-AMX also has everything else you'd normally expect on a performance car.

A standard 360 CID V-8 engine that develops 245 horsepower. Or an optional 4 barrel carb for 285 horsepower.

A standard 3-speed all synchromesh floor shift transmission with an 11" heavy duty clutch. Or an optional 4-speed with a Hurst shifter.

An optional heavy duty suspension system, big tach, and gauges. Standard fat Polyglas™ tires, mag style wheels, and a couple of things you wouldn't expect.

New optional ventilated-rotor front disc brakes to fight brake fade. And a new optional 401 CID engine that generates 330 horsepower.

Mark Donohue will be driving the new Javelin-AMX in next season's Trans-Am.

You could be driving it right now.

If you had to compete with GM, Ford and Chrysler, what would you do? ◢◼ American Motors

LIME ROCK, CONN.
Javelin wins first event
of Trans-Am season by five laps.

EDMONTON, CANADA
Donohue drives Javelin
to second victory
over Mustang and Camaro.

DONNYBROOKE, MINN.
Javelin finishes first and second,
gains point lead for season.

ELKHART LAKE, WIS.
Leading all the way,
Javelin wins over Mustang
and Camaro at Road America.

ST. JOVITE, CANADA
Donohue and Javelin
take fourth consecutive
triumph at Le Circuit.

WATKINS GLEN, N.Y.
World-famous course
is scene of Javelin's
sixth Trans-Am win.

IRISH HILLS, MICH.
Javelin makes it six in a row,
seven out of nine to clinch championship
at Michigan International Speedway.

IF YOU'RE GOING TO BUY A SPORTY CAR, BUY ONE THAT'S BEEN PLACES.

American Motors

THE 1971 TRANS-AM CHAMPION.
Mark Donohue drove this specially modified Javelin-AMX
to the SCCA Trans-American Road Racing Series Championship.

THE 1972 JAVELIN-AMX.
One of two Javelin models you can test-drive right now
at your American Motors dealer.

It's nice to know you're driving the winner.

Last year a specially modified Javelin AMX beat every other car in its class in the Trans Am racing series. In the last race of the year at Riverside, we blew everybody off the track finishing one, two, three.

This year the AMX has blown up another storm by clinching its second Trans Am Championship in a row.

But when we call the AMX a winner, we're talking about more than racing, we're talking about the way the AMX looks inside and out.

We're talking about the room you have even in the back seats; the stability of the car at all speeds; the nice balance of performance and comfort.

And only American Motors makes this promise: The Buyer Protection Plan backs every '73 car we build and we'll see that our dealers back that promise.

Buckle up for safety.

AMERICAN MOTORS BUYER PROTECTION PLAN

1. A simple, strong guarantee, just 101 words! When you buy a new 1973 car from an American Motors dealer, American Motors Corporation guarantees to you that, except for tires, it will pay for the repair or replacement of any part it supplies that is defective in material or workmanship. This guarantee is good for 12 months from the date the car is first used or 12,000 miles, whichever comes first. All we require is that the car be properly maintained and cared for under normal use and service in the fifty United States or Canada, and that guaranteed repairs or replacement be made by an American Motors dealer.

2. A free loaner car from almost every one of our dealers if guaranteed repairs take overnight.

3. Special Trip Interruption Protection.

4. And a toll free hot line to AMC Headquarters.

AMC Javelin

We back them better because we build them better.

Chapter Two

Chrysler Corporation

Dodge Division

YOUNG-HO DODGE!

A torrid new chapter for our current best seller

Street, strip or showroom—Dodge is a winner. The stock-bodied Dodge Charger above is the latest example. It's the world's fastest full-bodied stocker, with 850-900 supercharged horses supplying the power.

Dodge celebrates its Golden Anniversary this year. (Sales are up almost 30% over last year's, making '64 the best selling year in our 50-year history.)

Yet Dodge is more youthful than ever. Always experimenting. Looking for the action. And finding it. From the Daytona tri-oval—where a Dodge Hemi-Charger powered to the fastest 100 miles ever driven, 170.77 mph—to Tucson Dragway—where a Dodge Charger set a new S/FX record of 135.33 mph in the quarter-mile.

That's the Dodge spirit . . . Young-Ho! It swings. Try it yourself.

DODGE DIVISION **CHRYSLER** MOTORS CORPORATION

This is a Top Stock Eliminator. What did he eliminate? And why.

Dave Strickler in his '64 Dodge Ramcharger. Top Stock Eliminator in the 1964 AHRA Phoenix Dragstrip Championships.

On a straightaway track, from a standing start, he beat another car to the finish line one quarter of a mile away. He continued to beat (and eliminate) one car after another in his class. Until only he was left.

Dragstrip racing—America's newest million-fan sport—operates under clearly defined, rigidly enforced rules. It is a supreme challenge in acceleration.

It was not surprising that a competition equipped Dodge won. It would be highly unusual if a Top Stock Eliminator was not a Dodge or Plymouth.

Dragstrip competition, stock car races, and road rallies continue to confirm the excellence of Chrysler Corporation engineering, developed through years of extensive research and testing in the laboratory and on the proving grounds.

Want to eliminate all other cars? Test drive a '64 from Chrysler Corporation.

Plymouth · Dodge · Chrysler · Imperial

 **CHRYSLER** CORPORATION

Visit Chrysler Corporation's "Autofare" at the N. Y. World's Fair

INTRODUCING THE DEPENDABLES FOR '64

We used to win automatically

Now you have a choice

Winning on the strip with Dodge has been as easy as pushing a button and putting your foot down. Thumb through the record book and you'll see what we mean. The Dodge Ramcharger (with three-speed automatic transmission) owns nearly every strip it's touched a slick to. And that's still the case.

But now we've got a hot new four-on-the-floor for you. It shifts smoothly, precisely. All forward gears on this do-it-yourself go-box are fully synchronized. This one is just itchin' to transmit all of that power up front to the pavement below.

And speaking about "up front," Dodge stables a wide choice of horsepower. Five V8's in all, ranging from a big 318 cubic inch standard V8 to a hot and hairy 426 cubic inch job. Automatic or do-it-yourself—if you go for action, get with the 1964 Dodge. The man to see is the man who's got it—your nearby Dodge Dealer.

Hot '64 Dodge

DODGE DIVISION ✦ CHRYSLER MOTORS CORPORATION

Our new 426 Coronet ought to have its head examined

You know what a Hemi is. It's that wailing stocker that's about a car length ahead at the end of the quarter. It's that bright red streak that's taking home the lap records on the big ovals. And ever since the day the unmistakable sound it makes was first heard on the tracks, competitors screamed unfair.

It is. It's got valves as big as stove lids. A plug jammed right in the middle of the combustion chamber. 426 cubes. And a thermal efficiency that is making a lot of people see red . . . taillights. If you insist on playing fair, forget it. But if you have just a trace of mean in your make-up . . . by all means, get one.

Why not drop a Hemi in the new Coronet 500. The hot new Dodge at a new lower price. Hardtop or convert, this one's got buckets, padded dash, console and an impatient attitude toward getting you away from it all. (Happy note: You'll find Coronet prices start a couple of bills less than you'd expect, if you care about that sort of thing. And there are 10 great models to choose from.) All in all, it makes quite a package.

Your Dodge Dealer is the man to see. See him soon.

'65 Dodge Coronet

DODGE DIVISION ✦ CHRYSLER MOTORS CORPORATION

DODGE DIVISION ✶ CHRYSLER MOTORS CORPORATION

Dodge cools off Winter Nationals competition . . . again

Cool gas means hot runs. So drag racers pack intake manifolds with ice, as the famed Dodge Ramchargers are doing above. This gives the densest possible mixture per cylinder.

But gas was the only cool thing about Dodge at the '65 American Hot Rod Association Winter Nationals at Bee Line Dragway, Arizona. New '65 Dodge Coronets, specially equipped for drag race competition, took Top Stock Eliminator—a class Dodge also topped in '64. They walked away with Mr. Stock Eliminator and turned low elapsed time and top speed among stock cars.

Mike Buckel won Top Stock Eliminator title in the Ramchargers' Dodge, blasting to a 10.73-second elapsed time and 132.15-mph top speed during eliminations. Bud Faubel and his "Hemi-Honker" roared through one of the fastest 16-car fields in stock car dragging history to become Mr. Stock Eliminator. Other competition-equipped Dodges took three of the four major stock class wins.

How's that for openers in a new season? Can't hardly beat it with a club. Like you can't hardly beat Dodge's great way of going . . . and going . . . and winning. Try it.

Hot '65 Dodge

Animal Tamer

(Bring on the Mustangs, Wildcats, Impalas . . . we'll even squash a few Spyders while we're at it.) Dodge has made it a little harder to survive in the asphalt jungle. They did it with Coronet: the newcomer that's a real goer.

Additup.

All new styling—and ten models to pick from. Build it and buy it. Your choice of engines: 225 cu. in. Six (1 bbl.) standard; 273 V8 (2 bbl.) opt.; 318 V8 (2 bbl.) opt.; 361 V8 (2 bbl.) opt.; 383 V8 (4 bbl.) opt.; and that wild wedge, the 426 V8 (4 bbl.) opt.

Your choice of sticks: 3-speed manual standard; 4-speed manual optional; and the optional TorqueFlite. Play with them on the column or on the floor. You'll find all these goodies at your Dodge dealer's. And at a very reasonable price. Stop. Pick what you want. Then go out and tame a few tigers.

'65 Dodge Coronet

DODGE DIVISION ✶ CHRYSLER MOTORS CORPORATION

MOTOR TREND: MAY '65 AND **HOT ROD:** JUNE '65. ICE ON THE MANIFOLD. WHAT A WILD TRICK OF THE MUSCLE CAR TRADE.

MOTOR TREND: APRIL '65

CHARGER

...new leader of the Dodge Rebellion.

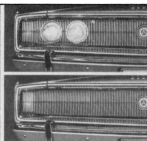

You never had it so luxurious, sports. Bucket seats, center console with padded armrest and full carpeting are just a few standard '66 Dodge Charger comfort features.

Dodge Charger's tach is no add-on afterthought. It's right up next to the speedometer, where it belongs. The swivel clock mounted on the console is optional.

Charger's "now-you-see-'em, now-you-don't" headlights look great no matter what position they are in, and move into place automatically.

This beautiful new bomb comes from the drawing board to your driveway with all the excitement left in. It's Dodge Charger, and it's loaded. With fresh ideas, eye-tempting styling, explosive performance. "What a handsome home for a Hemi!" you say? We thought you would—so a big, bad 426 Street Hemi is optional. In a package deal with a heavy-duty suspension— 0.92-inch torsion bars, link-type sway bar, high-rate rear springs and heavy-duty shocks—to keep you firmly in control. Plus 11-inch brakes and 4-ply nylon Blue Streak tires for extra safety. Add to the package with options like a heavy-duty TorqueFlite automatic transmission (set for full-throttle shifts at 5500 rpm) or a competition-type, 4-speed manual gearbox. Check out Charger, the hot new one from Dodge that proves sports cars can also be luxurious.

Cross a sporty-type car and a station wagon, and what happens? Dodge Charger! These handsome rear seats fold down to give you lots of extra luggage space—enough to handle a pair of skiis.

A winner, going away. That's Dodge Charger, the new smoothy. And just as it packs a big punch under the hood up front, you'll find you can pack a big load under that clean, crisply styled rear deck lid. Fold the rear seats down, and you've got about 7½ feet of completely carpeted cargo space.

* YOU HAVE A CHANCE OF WINNING A DODGE CHARGER—REGISTER AT YOUR DODGE DEALER'S.

Dodge Charger

DODGE DIVISION ✶ CHRYSLER MOTORS CORPORATION

The Hemi was never in better shape

Beauty and the beast. That's a sleek Dodge Charger with come-hither fastback styling and a deep-breathing 426 Street Hemi growling under the hood. Looks like a pampered thoroughbred, comes on like Genghis Khan. Got to be the toughest combination on the road. And good news: The optional Street Hemi comes in a package deal with heavy-duty suspension, 4-ply nylon Blue Streak tires, and big 11-inch brakes to put you safely and firmly in control. To keep an even tighter rein on Charger (or Coronet), new front disc brakes are now optional. If you're looking for a "charger" that looks great, with go and handling to match, look no further than Dodge Charger. See your nearest Dodge dealer; he'll introduce you to the hot new leader of the Dodge Rebellion.

Dodge Charger

DODGE DIVISION CHRYSLER MOTORS CORPORATION

Dodge Charger—named "Top Performance Car of the Year" by CARS magazine.

Dodge CHRYSLER MOTORS CORPORATION

GT+383=NEW DART GTS.

That's what we did. Took a well-tested 383-cubic-inch 4-bbl V8 and slipped it under the hood of Dart GT. The result: Dart GTS. A brand-new optional package of performance goodies featuring:
■ Dual exhausts. ■ Heavy-duty suspension. ■ Red Line wide-oval tires. ■ Disc brakes up front. ■ Either four-speed manual or three-speed automatic transmission. ■ And a low moan from the 383's low-restriction air cleaner that your mother-in-law won't understand and your wife will eventually get used to.

The GTS package is available on both Dart GT models, two-door hardtop and convertible. And with either GT, you start with such standard features as ■ All-vinyl upholstery. ■ Foam-padded seats. ■ Full carpeting.

GT + 383. The newest winning formula from Dodge. Check it out right now at your nearby Dodge Dealer's.

And for your free copy of Dodge Performance "Tune-up Tips," send your name and address to: P.O. Box 179 A, Dept. C, Detroit, Michigan 48232. Indicate your preference.
■ Engine basics.
■ Small engines.
■ "B" Series engines.
■ Hemi and race engines.

DODGE DIVISION | CHRYSLER MOTORS CORPORATION

ENTER THE BIG BORE HUNTER

Dodge Coronet R/T... with 440-Magnum

Drag fans, here's your car. Coronet R/T packs 440 cubic inches of go! The big-inch, deep-breathing 440-Magnum sports a special 4-barrel carburetor, larger exhaust valves, longer duration cam and low-restriction dual exhaust. Underneath there's a heavy-duty suspension with sway bar and special shock absorbers for better handling, high-performance nylon cord Red Streak tires, and big 3-inch-wide brakes—front and rear—for surer stops. Front disc brakes are optional. An extra leaf in the right rear spring copes with torque and helps prevent wheel hop. Coronet R/T comes on strong with sizzling style, too. Body side paint stripes, distinctive hood air-scoop design, bucket front seats, and special R/T insignia put it lengths ahead of the look-alike crowd. Hunting for trophy-winning performance that handles beautifully on the road? Check the odds. They're 440 to 1 in favor of Coronet R/T... a balanced automobile engineered for the enthusiast.

"Dodge Rebellion Operation '67 Wants You"

Dodge

road

runner

 the newest hot one from Dodge

It speaks softly, but carries a big kick. Dodge Coronet R/T. Just about the hottest thing going since the cast-iron stove. Witness these credentials: a rampaging *440-cubic-inch Magnum V8* that deals out **375 bhp** and *480 lbs.-ft. of torque.* 4-barrel carb . . . long duration cam . . . chrome engine dress-up . . . low-restriction dual exhaust . . . heavy-duty brakes and suspension . . . high-performance Red Streak tires . . . special air scoop design. With this standard getup, R/T is described by Super Stock magazine as "one of the best all-around performance packages being offered . . . as much or more performance per dollar than any other car currently available." If you wish, you can have the optional Hemi. And a tach. And mag-type wheel covers. And a lower-body paint stripe available through your Dealer. Check out R/T at your nearby Dodge Dealer's now.

Dodge CHRYSLER

The newest hot one from Dodge

You read it right. "R" means Road. And "T" means Track. And that means R/T from Dodge. Sweet as can be on the road. Hot as you want it on the track. With a *440-cubic-inch Magnum V8* under its bonnet, turning out *375 horsepower* and 480 lbs.-ft. of torque, through your choice of four-on-the-floor or three-speed automatic. With *heavy-duty brakes and suspension* underneath. And *high-performance Red Streak tires* to show their treads to the also-rans.

Dual exhausts. Bucket seats up front. Full-length paint stripes. And big, shiny R/T medallions front, rear and sides. All that comes standard. If you want your R/T packed, we can give you a 426-cubic-inch Hemi V8 at extra cost. One other choice. Two-door hardtop or convertible. How do you get into your own R/T? Easy. Just show the proper enthusiasm to your nearby Dodge Dealer, and you'll have it made.

RUMBLE BEE

Want to start something?
Try a hot-cammed 383-cube mill in a light coupe body.
Just for kicks, throw in the heavy-duty suspension,
oversized brakes, a brute of a hood, bumblebee stripes
—the works. It's tough. Check the price. Good news!
Dodge has started something all right. Super Bee.
Why sit there dreaming when you could be running? See
the man with the cars with the bumblebee stripes.
Your Dodge Dealer.

STANDARD SUPER BEE EQUIPMENT
● Special 4-bbl. 383-cid V8 (has the 440 Magnum V8 heads,
valve gear, hot cam, and manifolds), 335 hp at 5200 rpm
● Dual exhausts ● 4-on-the-floor manual with HD clutch
● HD suspension ● HD shocks ● HD brakes ● Dodge Charger
Rallye instrument panel ● F70 x 14 Wide-Treads.

OPTIONAL
The Hemi~425 hp.

Dodge Scat Pack ... the cars with the Bumblebee stripes

DRIVE SAFELY—
SPEED CONTESTS BELONG ON THE STRIP

Dodge CHRYSLER MOTORS CORPORATION

WAILER

CHARGER R/T

There you sit in silence. Cool. Unruffled. But
you're about to be discovered. George.
That gaping split grille. The
Charger R/T badge. The Hurst
competition-plus shifter. Twin 2½" pipes
and wide-treads to boot. Your secret's
out. That's no kiddy car . . . take it to the
strip where the men are. Class will tell.

STANDARD CHARGER R/T EQUIPMENT
● 440-cid Magnum (4-bbl.) V8, 375 hp
● Choice of 3-speed automatic or
Hurst 4-speed manual ● Dual exhausts
● HD suspension ● HD shocks
● HD brakes ● Dodge Charger
Rallye instrument panel
● F70x14 wide-treads

OPTIONAL
● 426 Hemi

SAFETY IS NO ACCIDENT. DRIVE WITH CARE.

Dodge CHRYSLER MOTORS CORPORATION *Dodge Scat Pack ... the cars with the Bumblebee stripes*

CAR CRAFT: JUNE '68

CAR CRAFT: OCTOBER '68. PLYMOUTH HAS ITS ROAD
RUNNER CHARACTER, DODGE LOVERS HAVE THEIR SUPER
BEE.

6,000 RPM
FOR LESS THAN $3,000
DART SWINGER 340

Play your cards right, and three G's can put you in a whole lot of car this year. Dart Swinger 340. Newest member of the Dodge Scat Pack. You don't make it on looks alone. 340 cubes of high-winding, 4-barrel V8. A 4-speed Hurst on the floor to keep things moving. All the other credentials are in order. Just check at right. Then check with your Dodge Dealer. Especially about the price.

STANDARD DART SWINGER 340 EQUIPMENT

- 340-cubic-inch 4-bbl. V8
- 4-speed full synchromesh with Hurst shifter
- Heavy-duty suspension
- Dual exhausts
- D70x14 wide-tread tires
- Dart Swinger bumblebee stripes
- Performance hood with die-cast louvers
- 3.23 axle ratio. 3.55 and 3.91 are optional ratios, with Sure Grip differential.

Dodge CHRYSLER MOTORS CORPORATION

Dodge Scat Pack ... the cars with the Bumblebee stripes

Mother warned me...

that there would be men like you driving cars like that. Do you really think you can get to me with that long, low, tough machine you just rolled up in? Ha! If you think a girl with real values is impressed by your air conditioning and stereo . . . a 440 Magnum, whatever that is . . . well—it takes more than cushy bucket seats to make me flip. Charger R/T SE. Sounds like alphabet soup. Frankly, I'm attracted to you because you have a very intelligent face. My name's Julia.

Join the fun . . . catch

DODGE *fever*

SEE OUR SENSATIONAL NEW OPENING NUMBER AT THE AUTO SHOW

'70 DODGE CHALLENGER

Don't miss this one. It's the star of the show. Dodge Challenger R/T. Only all-new sports compact for 1970. A car with engine choices that run from a thrifty Six right up to the optional 426 Hemi. (Applause.) Nine—count 'em—nine models in all, priced to compete with the pony cars. If you haven't caught Challenger's sun roof act at your Dodge Dealer's, be sure to look in at the auto show. But get there early. It could be Standing Room Only.

Dodge CHRYSLER MOTORS CORPORATION

OPTIONS TO MOVE YOU

Ramcharger Air Induction System

Hemi engine

Hurst 4-on-the-floor

Cast road wheels

1969 DODGE SPECIFICATIONS

		DART		CORONET		CHARGER
		SWINGER 340	GT SPORT	SUPER BEE	R/T	R/T
ENGINES—cu. in./hp	Std.	340/275	340/275	383/335	440/375	440/375
	Opt.	—	383/330	426/425	426/425	426/425
TRANSMISSIONS	Std.	4-Speed Manual	TorqueFlite	4-Speed Manual	TorqueFlite	TorqueFlite
	Opt.	TorqueFlite	4-Speed Manual	TorqueFlite	4-Speed Manual	4-Speed Manual
AXLE RATIOS	Std.	3.23	3.23	3.23	3.23	3.23
	Opt.*	3.55, 3.91	3.55	3.55, 3.91	3.55, 4.10	3.55, 4.10
TIRES—Std. wide-tread		D70 x 14	E70 x 14	F70 x 14	F70 x 14	F70 x 14

*Optional axle ratios shown are with standard engines and transmissions. All rear axle options are Sure Grip only. Optional axles for Coronet and Charger models are available as part of performance axle packages only.

1969 DODGE DART, CORONET, POLARA AND MONACO GENERAL SPECIFICATIONS*

EXTERIOR	WHEELBASE	OVERALL LENGTH	OVERALL WIDTH	OVERALL HEIGHT	TRACK FRONT	REAR
DART	111"	195.4"	69.6"	53.9"	57.4"	55.6"
CORONET	117"	206.6"	76.7"	54.5"	59.5"	59.2"
CHARGER	117"	208.0"	76.6"	53.2"	59.5"	59.2"
POLARA	122"	220.8"	79.3"	56.8"	62.1"	60.7"
MONACO	122"	220.8"	79.3"	56.8"	62.1"	60.7"

INTERIOR	HEADROOM FRONT	REAR	LEGROOM FRONT	REAR	HIPROOM FRONT	REAR	SHOULDER ROOM FRONT	REAR
DART	38.3"	37.3"	41.7"	35.2"	57.2"	57.2"	55.4"	55.4"
CORONET	38.6"	37.4"	41.9"	36.3"	60.4"	60.4"	58.1"	58.1"
CHARGER	37.4"	36.4"	41.4"	34.1"	60.6"	60.4"	58.0"	58.1"
POLARA	38.8"	38.4"	41.8"	39.7"	63.1"	63.4"	63.4"	62.8"
MONACO	38.8"	38.4"	41.8"	39.7"	63.1"	63.4"	63.4"	62.8"

*Dimensions are for V8 4-door-sedan models except for Charger.

Catalogs with complete specifications for all 1969 Dodges…Dart, Coronet, Charger, Polara and Monaco…are available at the Dodge display.

FOLLOW THE CROWD TO THE DODGE EXHIBIT.

Dodge CHRYSLER MOTORS CORPORATION

SHOW-OFF

DODGE CHARGER R/T

Meet the high-performance version of the Great Shape. 1969 Dodge Charger R/T. Muscled its way to the top of the Dodge Scat Pack with a 440 Magnum V8. Inside, you'll be surrounded with sports features . . . bucket seats, side pockets, Rallye instrumentation. And at the Dodge exhibit, you'll see the rest of the Scat Pack. Biggest pack in the performance field. Coronet R/T, Coronet Super Bee, Dart GTSport, and the newest member—Dart Swinger 340. Not a wishy-washy car in the bunch. All completely performance-equipped. See them while they're standing still. The 1969 Dodge Scat Pack—the supercars with the bumblebee stripes—at the Dodge exhibit.

OFFER GOOD IN U.S.A. ONLY.

JOIN THE DODGE SCAT PACK—GET YOUR DODGE SCAT PACK PACKET!

Fill in coupon—and send it with 50¢ (no stamps) to:

Dodge Scat Pack Headquarters
P.O. Box 5212, Seven Oaks Station
Detroit, Michigan 48235

HERE'S WHAT YOU GET: (1) Dodge Scat Pack Official Membership Card; (2) 4-inch Dodge Scat Pack Bee Full-Color Vinyl Decal; (3) 4-inch Super Bee Vinyl Decal; (4) Dodge Scat Bee Full-Color Bumper Sticker; (5) Dodge Scat Pack Bee Full-Color Iron-on Transfer; and (6) Super Bee Metal Badge . . . So "Bee" with it. Join the Dodge Scat Pack today!

NAME
ADDRESS
CITY   STATE   ZIP

Dodge introduces a new model Super Bee at a new lower price. $3,074.00.

Manufacturer's Suggested Retail Price for standard Super Bee two-door hardtop, including federal excise tax and suggested Dealer preparation charges. Price excludes destination charges, state and local taxes (if any), and optional equipment.

That's $64 less than last year's standard hot dog hardtop. A triumphantly backward idea since most performance car prices have gone up. What happened is Super Bee's new gear box. It's a fully synchronized, three-speed manual. Naturally, last year's four-speed job cost more. But don't think the whole idea of the new Super Bee is getting less.

We've added as standard equipment a couple of last year's popular options—like fiber-glass-belted, wide-tread tires. Then we put in what you couldn't get with last year's Super Bee: Lane-change signal • Key-left-in-ignition buzzer • Three-way ignition, steering and transmission lock. One thing is the same. You still get a hot 383 Magnum V8. And torsion-bar, heavy-duty suspension. New 1970 Dodge Super Bee for $64 less. We think you just might buy the idea.

... the cars with the Bumblebee stripes

Dodge CHRYSLER MOTORS CORPORATION

Our Plum Crazy Challenger R/T Is No Shrinking Violet.

No way is 1970's all-new, high-performance car going to go unnoticed. Not with a mean 383 Magnum V8. Nor with an optional choice of engines, all the way up to the "Haulin' Hemi." Nor with that super-purple paint job—one of the new high-impact colors* for the Dodge Scat Pack. Challenger R/T comes with all the other going goodies, too: 3-on-the-floor full-synchro manual transmission • Rallye Suspension (includes front torsion bars for extra-stable handling) • Rallye Instrument Cluster • HD drum-type brakes • Wide-tread tires • New longitudinal stripe or popular bumblebee stripe. 1970 Plum Crazy Challenger R/T. Be the first in your crowd to drive the Dodge Super Grape.   *Optional, at extra cost.

... the cars with the Bumblebee stripes

Bobby Isaacs tests Charger Daytona: He drives a winner.

"Well, there's one obvious thing about a Charger Daytona. Nobody, but nobody, walks by without breaking his neck to take a second look. This is the slightly civilized version of the shark-nose built specifically for the long NASCAR ovals. Old Slippery has a snout that strikes out a country mile in front, and an adjustable spoiler that looks two stories tall in the rear. Standard mill is the 440 Magnum but the one I tested packed the optional street

version of the 426 Hemi. Now the Hemi may idle like a coffee can full of rocks, and it may need a wrench applied a little more often than usual. On the other hand, as far as acceleration is concerned, the Hemi turns on where the others shut off. The heavy-duty Rallye Suspension is firm. The test car exhibited moderate understeer under hard driving . . . but there's plenty of torque to break the rear end loose if you have the foot for it.

"Inside, the NASCAR heritage is obvious only in the full-dash equipment. The buckets fit well. Visibility is excellent in the front, not so hot to the rear due to the rear quarter fairings. The standard and heavy-duty rear drums are solid and reliable. You can put down your non-performance friends by pointing out that you have carpeting, disappearing headlights, and a car that you'll never lose in a crowded parking lot."

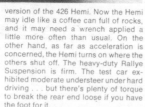

Dodge Charger Daytona
DIMENSIONS

WIDTH	
Track, front	59.7
Track, rear	59.2
Maximum overall car width	76.6
LENGTH	
Wheelbase	117
Overall car length	208.5
HEIGHT	
Overall height	53.0
FRONT COMPARTMENT	
Effective headroom	37.4
Maximum eff. legroom, accelerator	41.4
Shoulder room	58.1
Hiproom	60.6
REAR COMPARTMENT	
Effective headroom	36.4
Minimum eff. legroom	34.1
Rear comp. room	25.3
Shoulder room	58.1
Hiproom	60.4
CAPACITIES	
No. of passengers	5
Fuel tank, gal.	19
Crankcase, qt. . . 4 (5 when replacing oil filter)	
CHASSIS/SUSPENSION	
Body/frame type	unitized
Front suspension	torsion bars
Rear suspension . . . asymmetrical leaf springs	
Steering system . . . recirculation ball gear	
BRAKES—DRUM	
Heavy-duty brakes, standard, (automatic adjusting)	
Front	11 x 3
Rear	11 x 2½
WHEELS/TIRES	
Wheels	14 x 6.0JJ
Tires	F70 x 14 whitewall
ENGINE	
Type and no. of cyls.	V8
Bore and stroke	4.32 x 3.75
Displacement, cu.-in.	440
Compression ratio	9.7:1
Fuel req.	premium
Rated BHP @ RPM	375 @ 4600
Rated torque (lbs./ft. RPM).	480 @ 3200
Carburetion	Carter 4-BBL
Valve train	Hydraulic lifters, pushrods and overhead rocker arms
Cam timing	
Intake duration	268°
Exhaust duration	284°
Exhaust system	dual
DRIVE TRAIN	
Transmission type	3-speed TorqueFlite automatic
Gear ratios	1st 2.45:1
2nd	1.45:1
3rd	1.00:1
Rev.	2.20:1

The only additional item of optional equipment on the Charger Daytona tested by Bobby Isaacs was a set of road wheels.

Challenger. Watch it!

Dodge Challenger is the kind of sports compact you buy when you don't want one like everybody else's. When you'd like a little more living room in the back seat. When you'd appreciate a wider stance that carves curves with extra authority. When you want a look a little cleaner, a door a little thicker, and a choice of engines that starts with a new, livelier, thrifty Six and runs all the way up to the 426 Hemi. The new Dodge Challenger is the kind of sports compact you buy when you want a choice of standard hardtop,

formal hardtop, or convertible. When you want a model choice of the standard Challenger or the R/T. (The R/T offers a special hood and a Rallye Instrument Cluster with simulated walnut dash as standard equipment. Optional on the Challenger.) New Dodge Challenger is the car you buy when you decide you don't want to be like everyone else. There's a big difference between good and great. New Dodge Challenger has it all. And you'll find very little of it is reflected in the price.

If you have your own idea of what a car should be . . .

you could be
DODGE MATERIAL.

MOTOR TREND: OCTOBER '69. ONE PAGE FROM AN EIGHT-PAGE AD FOR THE 1970 SCAT PACK.

PLAYBOY: OCTOBER '69

DEMON 340
...the performance is a lot more than painted on.

Some people today seem to be building performance cars for your kid sister. They offer a brand-new stripe, but the same old Six.

Dodge kids you not. This may be our lowest priced performance car, but you'd never know it from the way it keeps up with the big boys.

This year, you get our high-revving small V8. With new frenched rear lights and a clean-looking grille. All this runs on heavy-duty torsion-bar-sprung Rallye Suspension; heavy-duty shocks; big brakes; and a slick, full-synchro floor-mounted box. Add a readable speedometer with resetable

trip indicator and a sanitary, roomy, all-vinyl interior, and you're ready to roll.

Demon 340. Compared to some of the other new ones you've seen, it's a nice honest car . . . with a nice honest price.

STANDARD EQUIPMENT
340-cu.-in. 4-bbl. V8 (premium fuel) □ Vinyl front bench seat—Blue, Tan or Black □ Body side tape stripe—Black or White only □ Ventless door glass □ Custom-contoured outside door handles □ 2-speed windshield wipers □ Dome lamp □ 150-mph

speedometer, with trip odometer □ Fuel, alternator, temperature, and oil pressure gauge □ Cigarette lighter □ Heater/windshield defroster with 2-speed fan □ Transistorized regulator □ 3-speed manual transmission, fully synchronized with floor-mounted shift lever □ Rallye Suspension Package (includes heavy-duty torsion bars, heavy-duty rear springs and sway bar with heavy-duty shock absorbers) □ Brakes: 10" x 2¼", front; 10" x 1¾", rear □ E70 x 14 wide-tread, bias-belted tires □ 14 x 5.5J wheels □ Dual exhausts □ 17-gallon fuel tank.

Hood pins

Rear spoiler

Dual scoop hood

"Tuff" steering wheel

CHALLENGER T/A
End of the road for the Do-It-Yourself Kit.

This is one car where the list of standard equipment is longer than the list of options. Hey, man, this isn't the beginning of something great, it's the driving end.

Big bias-belted skins in front, bigger ones in back. The good shift, Hurst style. Power discs up front; drums, heavy-duty, in the rear. Dual exhausts with low restriction mufflers, chrome side exit megaphones.

Challenger T/A. Just the way you'd do it yourself. If you had the time. And the money. Yeah, the money. Frankly, it would probably cost you more to do it yourself. So why bother

with do-it-yourself dreams? Check out this bargain for the man who'd rather be moving than building.

Check out the Standard Equipment List carefully. You'll find that everything is in order. From engine to drive train, Dodge puts it all together for you.

STANDARD EQUIPMENT
340 4-bbl. V8 □ TorqueFlite automatic transmission or 4-on-the-floor fully synchronized manual transmission □ Fiber-glass hood with Fresh Air Pack □ Hood pins □ Special Rallye Suspension (includes rear sway bar, larger front sway bar, heavy-duty shock ab-

sorbers, increased camber of rear springs) □ Rear duck tail □ Low-restriction dual side exit exhaust with megaphones □ Tires: E60x15, front; G60x15, rear; raised white letters □ 15x7.0JJ wheels □ Power front disc brakes with special semimetallic pads; 10" rear drums □ 3.55 axle ratio—8¾ ring gear □ Vinyl front bucket seats □ Deep-pile carpeting □ Simulated wood-grained door trim inserts □ Locking flip-top gas cap □ Flush outside door handles □ T/A body side tape stripes □ Grille and deck panel blackout.

1973 Dodge Charger Rallye. For the hard driving man.

If you're the kind of man that responds to the pulsating beat of a performance car, grab hold of Charger Rallye. Charger's got the low, lean look that tells you exactly what it is—a performance machine that enjoys being on the road. Go ahead, get in. Settle your frame into Charger's optional, soft bucket seats. Turn the switch on this beautiful baby. Charger's new Electronic Ignition System will give you surer starting because it delivers up to 35 percent more voltage to each spark plug. Then pop the clutch on Charger Rallye. That optional floor-mounted, four-speed Hurst shifter and 440 four barrel will let you put this Rallye through its paces. Charger's rugged Torsion-Quiet Ride and front and rear sway bars can take it. This go anywhere, do anything Charger Rallye can be an expression of whatever you want it to say. And those no-nonsense Rallye instrument gauges say a lot about the car and the man who uses them. When you take off with that power bulge hood and those raised white letter tires, there's one thing sure, you'll be remembered . . . as the hard driving man.

Extra care in engineering makes a difference in Dodge...depend on it.

Wanted: Men who can handle a real road machine. Dodge Challenger Rallye.

There are special men who develop an almost spiritual attachment to their cars. They want a no-nonsense road machine that grabs a rough, winding stretch of road and holds on. One that stays low and close to the road like a snake. For these men, Dodge builds Challenger Rallye. A trim, taut, tough car that hugs every inch of road it goes over. Why? Because of Challenger's torsion bar suspension. No mushy coil springs for this car—only responsive torsion bars and leaf springs will do. They combine to give you a firm, honest ride all the time.

These special men will also appreciate Challenger's Electronic Ignition System. Because there are no points and condenser, this system is virtually maintenance free and your tuneup costs will be reduced. Neither wet nor weather affect this special system. And each spark plug will get up to 35 percent more starting voltage every time.

Dodge Challenger Rallye. A special kind of road machine for a special breed of men. Test-drive one at your nearby Dodge Dealer's today.

Extra care in engineering makes a difference in Dodge...depend on it.

Plymouth Division

This car set 26 dragstrip records. What's a drag?

Visualize a quarter-mile strip of roped-off pavement. Bring 2 cars up to the starting line at one end. Start them off.

Then time how long it takes each to travel to the other end. Also record their speeds as they cross the finish line.

That's one of the elimination heats in dragstrip competition. A million-fan sport, sanctioned by national organizations, operating under clearly defined rules, scrupulously observed.

It calls for tremendous acceleration. It also calls for expert drivers.

Tom Grove of Oakland, California, for example.

In one season, his "Melrose Missile" (a Plymouth Super Stock with factory-option engine) broke 26 track records.

Cars from Chrysler Corporation have a fabulous record in dragstrip competition. It further confirms the excellence of Chrylser Corporation engineering, developed through years of research and testing. For example: The superiority of Chrysler Corporation automatic transmissions over others including stick shifts!

For personal confirmation of this excellence take a ride in one of our new '64's. Engineered for greater response, dependability, performance and safety for you.

Plymouth · Chrysler · Imperial · Dodge

CHRYSLER CORPORATION

SEE BOB HOPE AND THE CHRYSLER THEATRE, NBC-TV, FRIDAYS

Meet the "Orange Monster"

Plymouth's explosive Super Stock 426-III

"We proved to our own satisfaction that the Super Stock 426 Plymouth has to be just about the hottest stock car available!" said HOT ROD Magazine's technical editor, Ray Brock. But even while the 426-II was racking up records, the engineers were making improvements and now have come up with a new high-performance engine—the 426-III.

Improved specifications (see below) and more optional equipment, plus a whole raft of no-extra-cost standard equipment, make the car with the "orange monster" under the hood the one to beat on any track. Increased engine efficiency enables it to deliver maximum power over even wider engine speed ranges than the previous super stock engines. New manifolding, both intake and exhaust, is a big improvement for this power plant. New, larger, dual 4-barrel carburetors are there for top drag strip performance.

STANDARD EQUIPMENT on the 426-III includes, among other things, a 426-cu.-in., 8-cylinder engine, dual 4-barrel carbs, ram induction intake manifold, special heads, pistons, camshaft, valves and valve springs. Without extra charge, you also get such special items as the heavy-duty radiator, heavy-duty rear springs, and heavy-duty 3-speed manual transmission.

DUAL CARBS, 4-barrel, downdraft, with high-capacity un-silenced air cleaners are calibrated on the dynamometer for maximum power, with throttle blades set at precisely the proper angles.

NEW CAMSHAFT, designed to run at speeds up to 6500 r.p.m., with an increased lift for both intake and exhaust, provides the highest lift offered on any currently mass-produced passenger car engine.

SPECIFICATIONS

Displacement: 426 cu. in.; bore: 4¼ in.; stroke: 3¾ in.; standard rear axle ratio for 11:1 is 3.91; for 12.5:1, axle ratio is 4.56. Other ratios—dealer installed only—include: 4.10, 4.30, 4.56 and 4.89.

ENGINE OUTPUT

	STANDARD	OPTIONAL *
Compression ratio:	11:1	12.5:1
Horsepower:	415 @ 5600 r.p.m.	425 @ 5600 r.p.m.
Torque:	470 ft. lbs. @ 4400 r.p.m.	480 ft. lbs. @ 4400 r.p.m.

* Includes aluminum front sheet metal with hood scoop.

Plymouth Super Stocks hold seven of the National Hot Rod Association records set in 1963 for quarter-mile drag races. We know of 971 trophies won by Plymouths—this year alone—on the drag strips. As one 54-trophy-winning driver, John Abraitis, says, "It's the most fantastic stock car ever built by any manufacturer. What other car can you take as it comes off the assembly line and turn such times?"

Why not see your dealer for an order blank tomorrow? Then you can . . .

Get up and go Plymouth!

4-ON-THE-FLOOR Chrysler-designed 4-speed transmission with a Hurst shifter is one option on all 8-cylinder models. (Gear ratios: 2.66 in low, 1.91 in second, 1.39 in third and direct in high.) Another popular option is the 3-speed TorqueFlite automatic transmission, an outstanding performer with the 426 engines.

DESIGNED TO WIN, the Plymouth Super Stock 426-III is built for competition only. Preceded by the popular 413, 426, and 426-II, it already has gained the respect of the men who really know their engines —the racing men!

PLYMOUTH DIVISION  **CHRYSLER** MOTORS CORPORATION

You are about to witness Plymouth's famous vanishing act.

We don't know what you'd call vanished, but we think an 11.39 e.t. is pretty near flat-out gone.

Bill Jenkins, piloting the "Black Arrow," turned in that one February 7, at NHRA's Pomona Winternationals. Notables: Top speed 126.05, and an armload of trophies. Top Stock Eliminator. And SS/A Class Champion.

Plymouth's 426 Hemi is behind it all, of course. And in '65 it's behind it stronger than ever.

Tear down Plymouth's new Hemi and you'll run across improvements like: A magnesium intake manifold. Aluminum cylinder heads. More chrome on the valve stems. Longer duration camshaft. Aluminum oil pump. Valve relief in the pistons. And a roller type timing chain for increased durability.

Our Plymouth Super Commando 426 Hemi goes with twin four-barrel jugs, ram-tuned intake manifold, non-silenced air cleaners and equal length tubing exhaust headers. This engine is designed specifically for competitive events—and this is the engine to beat.

If you can't beat us, join us. It's an ancient tactic, but it sure wins trophies.

THE ROARING '65s
FURY
BELVEDERE
VALIANT
BARRACUDA

PLYMOUTH DIVISION ✸ CHRYSLER MOTORS CORPORATION

Plymouth

Announcing the Hemi 426 Plymouth Belvedere

Now what this country needs is a dragstrip with a couple of good hairpin curves.

The Hemi-powered Plymouth Belvedere: a high-performance 426-cubic-inch hemispherical-head V-8. Dual four-barrel carbs. Dual-breaker distributor. High-lift, high-overlap cam. Special plugs, pistons and double valve springs. Low back pressure dual exhaust system. Blue Streak Special tires. Wide-rim wheels. Oversize front torsion bars. Sway bar. Added-leaf, high-rate rear springs. Firm-Ride shocks.

And every Belvedere Satellite has: Front bucket seats. Center console with glove box. Deep-pile carpeting. Padded instrument panel. Safety-Rim wheels, 3-speed automatic or 4-on-the-floor stick, optional.

Like an iron fist in a velvet glove, the Hemi 426 Plymouth Belvedere.

PLYMOUTH DIVISION ✸ CHRYSLER MOTORS CORPORATION

Plymouth ...a great car by Chrysler Corporation.

The only chance you'll get to pass Richard Petty's Hemi!

Small wonder, what with its high-performance 426-cubic-inch hemispherical-head V-8. Plymouth Belvedere . . . a beautiful piece of hairy machinery! Everything about the Hemi package is designed to move you out, fast. Like four-barrel carbs. Dual-breaker distributor. High-lift, high-overlap cam. Special plugs, pistons and double valve springs. Low-back-pressure, dual-exhaust system. Special Blue Streak tires. Wide-base, Safety-Rim wheels. Oversize front torsion bars. Sway bar.

Added-leaf, high-rate rear springs. And heavy-duty shocks. For performance stops, optional front-wheel disc brakes. Now that we've told you what goes into making a Hemi-powered Plymouth such a great winner, we'll tell you what it takes to beat one. Another Hemi-powered Plymouth.

PLYMOUTH DIVISION ◆ CHRYSLER MOTORS CORPORATION

 . . .a great car by Chrysler Corporation.

Plymouth Barracuda

There are plenty of fish in the sea, but there's only one '66 Barracuda.

Watch it get away.

Take a standard 8-cylinder Barracuda and light a fire under it. Result: The Formula 'S' Barracuda. A fish of a wholly different color.

This is the Formula 'S' option: A high-performance 273-cu.-in. V-8 with a high-lift, long-duration cam, domed pistons, 4-barrel carburetor, dual-breaker distributor and a low-back-pressure exhaust system. Heavy-duty torsion bars, shocks and springs. Anti-roll bar. Simulated bolt-on wheel covers. Special Blue Streak tires on wide-rim wheels. Tachometer. Optional front-wheel disc brakes. Optional racing stripe.

What a wonderful way to go. So, go. Straight to your Plymouth Dealer's.

Charter Membership in Plymouth National Barracuda Club open to all owners.

PLYMOUTH DIVISION ◆ CHRYSLER MOTORS CORPORATION

Let yourself go... *Plymouth*

VIP FURY BELVEDERE VALIANT BARRACUDA

Formula 'S' Barracuda

Special Blue Streak tires, stiff suspension, a high-performance V-8, optional center console, bucket seats, optional front disc brakes, tachometer.

And a short fuse.

Specially equipped Formula 'S' Barracudas finished first and second in their class at the 1965 850-mile Canadian National Rally. And took the class win at the SCCA-sponsored 12-hour endurance race for compact sedans at Marlboro, Md., last August. Barracuda has also clinched the California State Rally Championship with five wins in six rallies.

That's the kind of car it is. But don't forget this in the rush: Barracuda's back seat folds down to make a 7-foot-long carpeted cargo space. That goes to make our hot car a very practical hot car.

Plymouth ...a great car by Chrysler Corporation.

Scott Harvey's family car.

Some family car! Scott's car, like most of those campaigned in serious sedan racing, has been specially modified to make it a little more race car and a little less street machine.

It's sort of interesting to note, though, that there are several things that didn't need changing to turn our Formula 'S' Barracuda into a SCCA National Champion. Like disc brakes. And the limited-slip differential. And the basics of our 273-cu.-in. V-8. And the fast-ratio steering gear . . . all of these standard or available on the production Formula 'S'.

And so are a few other items that make the 'S' a car that's perfect for the street, and that can still knock off an occasional rally or gymkhana. Front bucket seats, a rear seat that flips down into a seven-foot-long cargo space and slippery fastback styling.

Now with all of this, don't you think it might be more fun to win a rally with a family car? Talk to your Plymouth Dealer right away and see.

Plymouth ...a great car by Chrysler Corporation.

Banzaiiiii

Plymouth is out to win you over.

You've just heard the battle cry of the Belvedere GTX.
Hemi-powered, that is—426 cubes, 425 hp. and 490 lbs.-ft. of torque—as sung by a 4-speed transmission and a Sure-Grip differential. All optional, naturally. And what a commotion they make! Amplified by the Hemi's two big AFB 4-barrels.

But then, similar war-whoops can be heard from the regular GTX, which packs a 440 cu. in. wedge-head. 375 hp., 480 lbs.-ft. of torque—at a fraction of the Hemi's price. That, good buddy, is music to the ears, right?

'67 Belvedere GTX

PLYMOUTH DIVISION CHRYSLER MOTORS CORPORATION

They don't call it King Kong for nothing.

Not hardly. A car doesn't get a name like that on looks alone. Not when it walks off with Top Stock Eliminator at the '66 Springnationals, Winternationals, Summernationals and World Championship Finals. Not when it idles like this one does. Not when it turns 11-second ETs and makes the trip sounding like—well—just ask the guy up there holding his ears.

This, you see, is a Hemi-powered Belvedere. More specifically, a Belvedere GTX. The Hemi part costs extra, and the car itself is specially set up for drag racing. But impressive? Man, it's devastating!

Your next question should be: *Do we build a street ver-* *sion of the GTX? With maybe just a little less hair?*

Glad you asked. We do indeed, and it comes with our 440 cu. in. (375 hp.) wedge-head as standard equipment. It also comes with a special heavy-duty suspension, hood scoops, Red Streak tires, wide rims, bigger brakes, low-restriction exhausts and a heavy-duty TorqueFlite automatic—again, it's all standard.

And if you order it with the 4-speed, you get coarse-pitch "Hemi" gears, a heavy-duty rear axle, viscous-drive fan, unsilenced air cleaner and a dual-point distributor as part of the bargain. Sound King-Kongish, too? It is. Because Plymouth is out to win you over. '67 Belvedere GTX

Plymouth CHRYSLER MOTORS CORPORATION

Goldilocks and the two Bears.

The Bear on the right is a stock Belvedere GTX.

That is to say it carries the standard 440 cu. in. V-8, which, aside from being the biggest GT engine in the world, generates 375 hp. and 480 lbs.-ft. of torque through a fast-shifting TorqueFlite automatic and the recommended 3.23-to-1 rear axle.

Said Bear also carries a heavy-duty suspension—including beefed-up torsion bars, ball joints, front stabilizer bar, shocks and rear springs—along with bigger brakes, low-restriction exhausts, a pit-stop gas filler, chromed valve covers, Red Streak tires, wide rims, hood scoops and bucket seats. And this is the *standard* Bear, mind you.

The Bear on the left is also a stock GTX—with a heavy-duty 4-speed gearbox—*and* a few extra-cost options, including the famed Hemi, with 426 cu. in. and 490 lbs.-ft. of torque. It also has our super-duty Sure-Grip differential; not to mention racing stripes and front disc brakes.

So what's the moral? Simply that GTX is one very tempting bowl of porridge. In one form, even Goldilocks can drive it (although you'll recall Goldilocks was a highly adventuresome kind of female). In another form, it's strictly for the "Move over, honey, and let a man drive" set. You know the story: there's bound to be one that's just right. After all, we're out to win you over. **'67 Belvedere GTX.**

Plymouth CHRYSLER MOTORS CORPORATION

Built in Detroit. By Heretics.

Obviously Barracuda isn't the product of everyday thinking. It's a daring car, and it had to come from daring people—automotive heretics, if you will.

Who else would offer a car this wildly good-looking? With a pit-stop gas filler that opens to the touch? Or rallye lights that go on simultaneously with the head-lamps? Or a torsion-bar front suspension? Or full in-strumentation? Or an inclined, 12-port six-cylinder engine? Or a 7 ft. storage compartment behind the front seats? Heresy. Pure heresy is what it is.

And that's just the standard equipment.

As for options, who else would offer you a 383 cu. in. V-8 or two 273 cu. in. V-8s? Or fast-ratio steering? Or a Formula S package that makes this one of the best handling American cars ever built?

Who else? Who else, indeed, but the heretics at Plymouth. Surely you must know them. They're out to win you over this year. **'67 Barracuda**

The new Sports Barracuda. A Hardtop and Convertible are also available.

Plymouth CHRYSLER MOTORS CORPORATION

The new Sports Barracuda. Hardtop and Convertible models also available.

It bites when cornered.

It bites all right, but it doesn't fight back. And the reasons it doesn't are many.

One is Barracuda's uncanny torsion-bar suspension and front end geometry that helps keep the wheels at right angles to the road, where they have to be for maximum adhesion.

Another is a teethy bag of tricks called Formula S, an option package that brings added sophistication to an already excellent-handling machine. Wide Oval tires, for example, provide a bigger, more tenacious footprint for Barracuda to ride upon. At the same time, items like higher rate springs, firmer shocks and a big front stabilizer bar help

add lateral stability by limiting body lean and front end "plough." Extra-wide 5½ in. rims help out, too, as does a fast 16.0-1 steering option.

The remainder of Barracuda's cornering power is supplied by just that: power. The spice rack starts with a 225 cu. in. Six, which is standard, and runs all the way through two 273 cu. in. V-8s, up to our biggest option, a 383 cubic incher. In all instances, there's enough reserve punch on tap to cope with the side forces encountered in hard turns. Call it power steering, if you like. From Plymouth. The people who are going flat-out to win you over this year.

'67 Barracuda

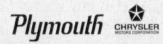

Plymouth CHRYSLER MOTORS CORPORATION

The new Sports Barracuda. Hardtop and Convertible models also available.

What happens when a ton and a half of Barracuda swallows a 383 cu. in. V-8?

Hoo-hah! Lights flash; heads turn; mouths gape; and when the smoke settles on the strip the guy at the helm is likely to walk off with the lion's share of the hardware.

The 383, you see, is Barracuda's new engine option. With a bore of 4.25 in. and a stroke of 3.38 in., it cranks out 280 hp and 400—yes, 400 —lbs.-ft. of torque. Intake is through an AFB 4-barrel and massive side-by-side ports, while exhaust exits through cast headers and low-restriction megaphones.

Sort of makes you want to turn trophy hunter yourself, doesn't it? In that case, you'll be glad to know the rear seat folds into a roomy 7-ft. utility compartment. When the smoke settles, maybe you'll need it for storage. Plymouth is out to win you over this year.

383 Cubes. And a trophy room in back.

'67 Plymouth Barracuda

PLYMOUTH DIVISION CHRYSLER MOTORS CORPORATION

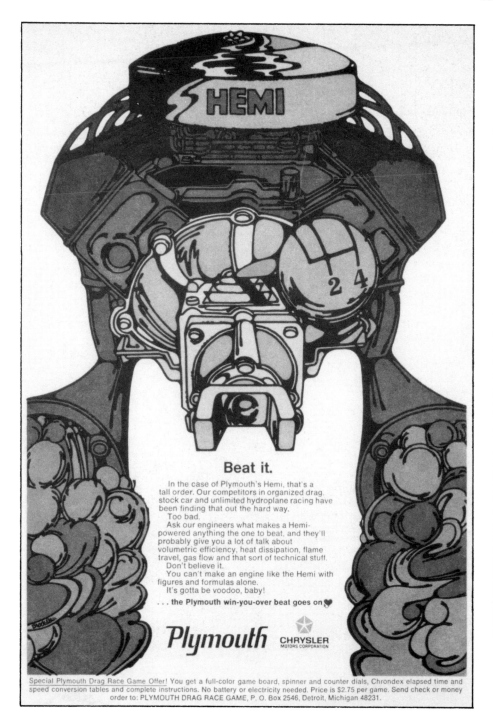

Beat it.

In the case of Plymouth's Hemi, that's a tall order. Our competitors in organized drag, stock car and unlimited hydroplane racing have been finding that out the hard way.

Too bad.

Ask our engineers what makes a Hemi-powered anything the one to beat, and they'll probably give you a lot of talk about volumetric efficiency, heat dissipation, flame travel, gas flow and that sort of technical stuff.

Don't believe it.

You can't make an engine like the Hemi with figures and formulas alone.

It's gotta be voodoo, baby!

. . . the Plymouth win-you-over beat goes on ♥

Plymouth   **CHRYSLER** MOTORS CORPORATION

Special Plymouth Drag Race Game Offer! You get a full-color game board, spinner and counter dials, Chrondex elapsed time and speed conversion tables and complete instructions. No battery or electricity needed. Price is $2.75 per game. Send check or money order to: PLYMOUTH DRAG RACE GAME, P. O. Box 2546, Detroit, Michigan 48231.

The 1968 GTX. The idle alone sounds like the William Tell Overture.

It goes "Rumpety-Rumpety-Rumpety-Rumpety-Rumpety-Rumpety-Rumpety . . ."

The reason for that is the high-lift, long-duration cam which nestles amid GTX's 440 cu. in., 375 hp V-8.

You turn it on. And it reciprocates. And the beat goes on. ♥

We figure a Supercar should look the part, too. *Form follows function,* and all that.

So this year we gave GTX a completely new body.

Note the new hood, grille, fenders, roofline, Wide Boots—everything. And the beat goes on. ♥

Inside, there's a new instrument panel and simulated wood accents everywhere you look.

If you order a tach, you'll find it mounted right near the speedometer.

And if you so specify, we'll connect it to our famed 426 Street Hemi.

It goes "Rumpety-Rump," also. And the beat goes on. ♥

Plymouth

CHRYSLER MOTORS CORPORATION

...the Plymouth win-you-over beat goes on

Acceleratii rapidus maximus. That's Latin for the fact Plymouth's Road Runner is some other kind of bird. Hang in here a moment, and we'll show you why.

Body: Road Runner, although it looks like a hardtop, is really a two-door coupe, which makes for extra rigidity. The entire structure is of unitized construction, and marked by an absence of exterior frills and ornamentation. Even the rear windows are simple swing-out units that offer additional savings in weight over roll-up types.

Engines: the standard Road Runner powerplant is an exclusive version of our 383 cu. in. V-8. Heads are borrowed from the big 440 cu. in. GTX engine because of massive intake and exhaust valves, 3.2 sq. in. ports and stiffer valve springs. The cam, intake manifold, valve train and exhaust headers are likewise GTX in origin. Resultant compression is 10.1 to 1; horsepower is 335 at 5200 rpm; torque is 425 lbs-ft. at 3400 rpm. Optional on all Road Runners is our 426 Street Hemi, which produces 425 hp at 5000 rpm and 490 lbs-ft. of torque at 4000 rpm.

Transmissions: standard on all Road Runners is a fully synchronized 4-speed. A manually shiftable, 3-speed TorqueFlite automatic is optional.

Rear axle: standard ring gear diameter on all 383 and Hemi automatic Road Runners is 8.75 in. 4-speed Hemis carry a 9.75 in. unit. Final drive ratio on all 383s is 3.23 standard. 3.55 optional. Hemi automatics also carry a 3.23 ratio as standard, with our 3.54 Sure-Grip differential available as an option. Hemi 4-speeds carry the 3.54 gear, standard.

Suspension: heavy-duty torsion bars, shock absorbers, rear springs, ball-joints, front stabilizer bar. Hemi-powered Birds use extra-heavy-duty rear springs with six leaves on the left, seven leaves on the right, for directional stability under acceleration.

Brakes: all Road Runners carry big 11x3 in. drums in front, 11x2½ in. drums in back. Front discs are optional.

Tires: F70 x 14 Wide Tread.

Horn: "Beep-Beep!"-type unit.

But before you take off on any coyote hunts, remember one thing. Hunt only at organized drag events.

Do that and Plymouth might even pay you money. Win Stock Eliminator at a NHRA National, and Plymouth will pay you $400.00; win Stock Eliminator at a Regional, and Plymouth pays $250.00. That way, coyote hunting's not only safer — it's downright profitable.

...the Plymouth win-you-over beat goes on. ♥

Road Runner.
(acceleratii rapidus maximus)

Plymouth

CHRYSLER
MOTORS CORPORATION

HOT ROD: DECEMBER '67 AND *CAR CRAFT:* APRIL '68

The 1968 Barracuda.
We gave it 4 new engines,
just for kicks.

We widened Barracuda's optional
Wide Oval tires.
And blended the taillights with the
rear deck.
And restyled the grille.
In short, we made it look a whole lot
cleaner and quicker.
And the beat goes on. ♥

We also gave Barracuda options
it never had before.
Like carpeting on the walls.
And map pouches on the doors.
Order a tach and you'll find the shift
points in the "12 o'clock" position.
They're easier to see that way.
And the beat goes on. ♥

Our new engines: 318, 340 and 383 cu. in.
V-8s and a 225 cu. in. Six.
Powering your choice of hardtop,
fastback or convertible body styles.
And the boat goes on. ♥

Plymouth

CHRYSLER
MOTORS CORPORATION

…the Plymouth win-you-over beat goes on

So you're coming up to the Christmas tree and the exhaust is going *bappetybappety-bappetybappety* and all those little internal bits are going *whumpawhumpawhumpa-whump* and you're out to grind the sound barrier into bite-sized equations with your howlin' Barracuda.

Say what? BARRACUDA? You're kidding! Nope. And this is why:

A new, lightweight, high-winding 340 cubic incher you can order. Its strength lies in things like intake valve diameters of 2.02 inches and exhaust diameters of 1.60 inches. Then there's the cam, which goes in 4-speed cars and is definitely of the "let's do it" variety: .445 inch lift on intake and .455 inch on exhaust, with 60 degrees of overlap. Intake duration is 284 degrees with 292 degrees on exhaust. The resultant idle is so wild an automatic box can't quite cope with it. Hence, the cam you get with TorqueFlite models is a bit less hairy. The score: 275 bhp @ 5,000 rpm.

As if that isn't enough, we have another engine option, this one with 383 cubic inches. For openers, the heads are new and have big 2.3 inch ports. The intake valves are 2.08 inches in diameter and the exhausts are 1.74. The cam provides a .425 inch lift on intake and .437 on exhaust.

Overlap is 40 degrees; duration is 264 degrees, intake, and 268 degrees, exhaust. For a total of 300 bhp @ 4,200 rpm. And *much* torque.

In either case, Barracuda is one running organization—a natural for sanctioned drag racing.

And just to show how we feel about sanctioned drags, we'll pay you to do your racing there. Any Plymouth that takes Stock Eliminator at a NHRA National or Regional gets a cash contingency award from us. You won't get rich from it, but it helps. Sort of makes safety pay.

…the Plymouth win-you-over beat goes on. ♥

Write for four 24 in. x 17 in. full-color cartoon posters of GTX, Road Runner and Barracuda (shown below). Send $1.00 to: Posters, P.O. Box 7749, Detroit, Mich. 48211.

Shortcut.

Plymouth CHRYSLER
MOTORS CORPORATION

SALT FLATS

383

©1967 Warner Bros.—Seven Arts. Inc.

"Beep-Beep!"

You say you want to know what our new bird, the Road Runner, is all about? Take a look at the standard equipment and you'll get the idea:

- Special 383 Wedge, exclusive to the Road Runner, turning out 335 bhp at 5200 rpm and 425 lbs.-ft. at 3400 rpm.

- A high-lift stick (.450 in. intake · and .465 in. exhaust) with 54 degrees of overlap and duration of 276 degrees (intake) and 292 degrees (exhaust).

- A tremendous brake/weight ratio, with 11 in. x 3 in. drums in front and 11 in. x 2½ in. at the rear, stopping a new two-door coupe configuration.

- F 70 x 14 Wide Boots.

- 4-speed fully synchronized gearbox.

- Heavy-duty torsion bars, springs, shock absorbers, ball joints and a .94 in. stabilizer bar.

- A special identity all its own, with Road Runner birds at the back, sides, and instrument panel, plus a horn that goes "Beep Beep!" Just like in the cartoons.

- A price way below what you would pay for a Supercar.

- A total lack of unnecessary doodads, gegaws, and falderal.

That's the standard stuff. Optional are things like a 426 Hemi. A special package including 3.55 rear end with Sure-Grip, viscous fan drive and heavy-duty shrouded radiator. And like that.

It's all put together for the guy who really digs cars, knows about tachs and staging lights and how to use 'em. Knows how to use his car in traffic, too, by following the rules and keeping his cool. Our kind of guy.

...the Plymouth win-you-over beat goes on♥

Plymouth   CHRYSLER MOTORS CORPORATION

HOT ROD: OCTOBER '67. ONE OF THE MOST FAMOUS CHARACTERS OF THE MUSCLE CAR ERA IS THE UNCATCHABLE "BEEP BEEP" ROAD RUNNER.

Engine: Standard is a 440 cu. in. V-8, with high-lift cam, Carter AVS 4-barrel, 2.08 in. intake valves, 3.2 sq. in. ports, cast-iron headers and stiffer valve springs. Compression is 10.1 to 1; horsepower is 375 at 4600 rpm; torque is 480 lbs-ft. at 3200 rpm. Optional is Chrysler's famed 426 cu. in. Hemi, which uses things like a nitride hardened crankshaft, two Carter AFB's, solid lifters, forged aluminum pistons and tulip-shaped intake and exhaust valves. Compression on the Hemi is 10.25 to 1; horsepower is 425 at 5000 rpm; torque is 490 lbs-ft. at 4000 rpm.

Transmission: Standard on all 440 cu. in. GTXs is a manually-shiftable, competition-type TorqueFlite automatic with an 11¾ in.

diameter torque converter. Special features include five front clutch discs instead of the usual four, a 2½ in. wide second gear band, an oil cooler and internal oil filter. Hemi-powered GTXs carry a similar unit, but with a 10¾ in. diameter converter. Optional to both is a heavy-duty 4-speed with coarse-pitch gears and ratios of 2.65, 1.93, 1.39 and 1.00.

Rear axle: Heavy-duty on all GTXs. Automatic-equipped cars carry an 8.75 in. diameter ring gear, while 4-speeds use a 9.75 in. unit. Final drive options range from 3.23 to 1 up to 3.54 to 1.

Suspension: Heavy-duty everything: including front torsion bars, ball-joints, stabilizer bar and front and rear shock absorbers. The rear springs are stiffer than normal, too, and the right spring carries

one more leaf than the left, to prevent torque steer under acceleration. Spring material is chrome steel with plastic innerliners.
Tires: F70X14 Wide Profile.
Brakes: Standard front drums measure 11 x 3 in.; rear drums measure 11 x 2½ in. Total swept area is 380.1 sq. in. Front disc brakes are optional.

As you can see, GTX is something of a departure in automobiles. A rapid departure. Hence, we recommend that it be driven very carefully on the street, and the full use of its potential restricted to organized drag events.

At the strip, however, it's a different story: when the light turns green, we urge you to politely bid competition "Adio-o-o-o-o-s-s-s!"

...the Plymouth win-you-over beat goes on. ♥

GTX. That's short for "Adios!"

Plymouth CHRYSLER MOTORS CORPORATION

Road Runner 2-Door Hardtop

Road Runner: Motor Trend's Car of the Year.
(Too bad only one of our cars can win at a time.)

If you want a high-performance car, Road Runner is one car to think about. Especially since Motor Trend named it Car of the Year. And MT had every car in the world to choose from. Surprising? Not when you consider this:

The Road Runner is a real performer. But not because it costs a lot of money. It doesn't.

It comes, nevertheless, with a standard 383 cubic inch V-8. A 4-barrel carburetor. An unsilenced air cleaner. And dual exhaust trumpets.

A 4-speed transmission with Hurst Linkage. A high lift cam. And Red Streak Wide Boots.

Options include a tachometer, and our new 160-position driver's adjustable bucket seat that does everything a power seat does. At roughly half the cost. Another new option: functional hood scoops, or "air grabbers."

There's also a large, full-color Bird on the deck lid, doors and instrument panel. Plus a new deluxe steering wheel—with the Bird perched right on the hub. "Beep-Beep!"

Road Runner comes in 21 exterior flavors, including red hot red, mint green and butterscotch. Chomp! With big stripes on the hood, optional. Pity the poor coyote.

If Road Runner doesn't baffle him with numbers, he surely will with plumage.

Catch the Car of the Year? It's easy when you know how. Just go where they show Plymouths. And while you're at it, look at the entire Plymouth line—Belvedere, Fury, Valiant and Barracuda. Be sure to get all the facts, because . . .

Plymouth tells it like it is.

Suggested for mature audiences.

Plymouth CHRYSLER MOTORS CORPORATION

1969 Plymouth GTX

Plymouth GTX. As a member of an elite group, you crave the finer things in life. You know, the beach in the spring. The Strip. Miniskirts. Neat cars. Blood rare steaks. Things like that.

Well, we have good news for you.

The Boss is back. Bossier than ever.

There's a new Air Grabber option that lets the engine breathe cool air through the hood scoops. Since cool air contains more oxygen, the engine runs stronger. (A shutoff control underneath the dash lets you stop the flow of outside air whenever you want to.)

There are a variety of new high-performance axle packages you can order. Ratios now extend from 3.54 to 4.10:1 for better acceleration in all gears.

We've also included goodies like a Hurst shifter (so you take less time going through the gears), a heavy-duty radiator with viscous-drive fan (more power ends up at the wheels), a dual-breaker distributor (better spark), and a Sure-Grip differential (maximum traction).

You still get our terrific 440 cubic inch Super Commando engine with 4-barrel carburetor, performance cam, extra large throttle bores, and oversize ports and valves.

One of the nicest things about the high-performance GTX is the luxury that comes along with it.

Deep foam buckets and deluxe all-vinyl interiors.

Maturity *does* have its benefits, doesn't it?

Watch AFL Football on NBC-TV.

Look what Plymouth's up to now.

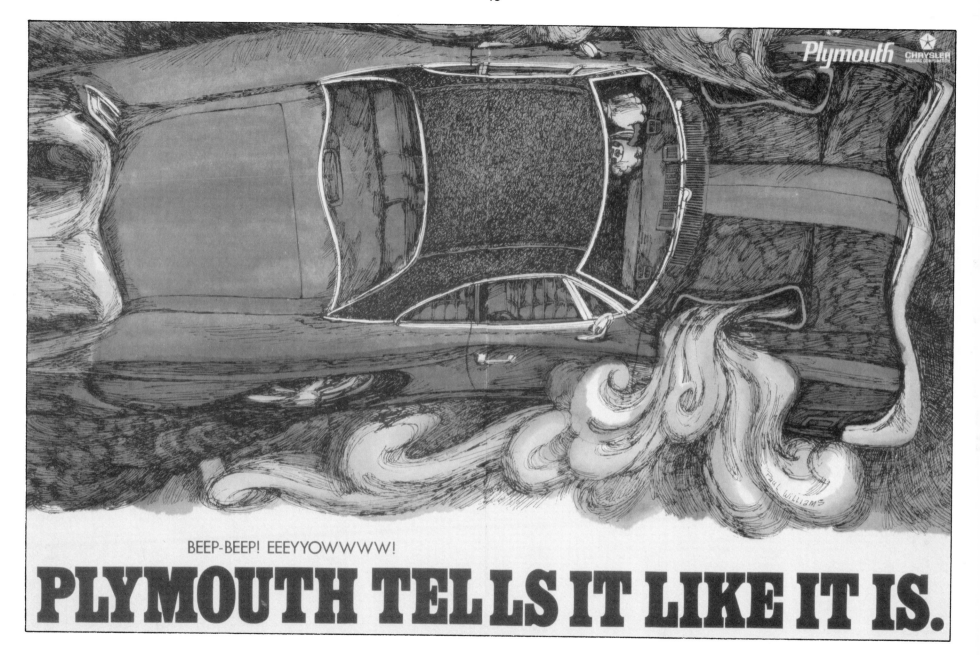

BEEP-BEEP! EEEYYOWWWW!

PLYMOUTH TELLS IT LIKE IT IS.

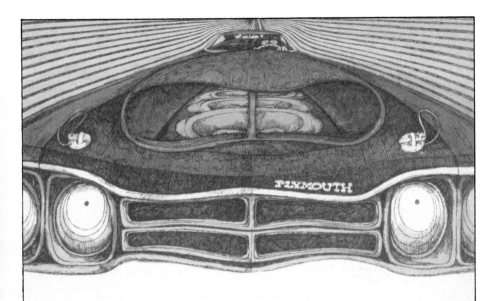

ET'S AND SPECS ON OUR NEWEST ROAD RUNNER:
440 CUBES, GLASS HOOD AND (HEH-HEH!) THREE HOLLEYS!

PLYMOUTH TELLS IT LIKE IT IS.

Special Features:

440 cu. in. V-8, standard.
Edelbrock "6-bbl." Hi-Rise intake manifold, standard.
Three Holley 2-bbl. carbs, standard.
Special low-taper 276°-292°-54° camshaft, standard.
Special hydraulic tappets, standard.
Chromed intake and exhaust valves, standard.
Hemi valve springs, standard.
Fiberglass hood with Super Stock air scoop, standard.
Four pin-type hood latches, standard.
Low-restriction "Air-Grabber"-type air cleaner, standard.
4.10:1 Sure-Grip rear axle, standard.
Dual-breaker distributor, standard.
Heavy-duty 26" radiator, standard.
Viscous-drive fan, standard.
4-speed with Hurst shifter or Torque-Flite automatic, standard.
Extra-heavy-duty "Hemi" suspension, standard.
Heavy-duty 11" drum brakes, standard.
Extra-wide 15 x 6" rims, standard.
Extra-fat G-70 x 15" Polyglas Red Streak tires, standard.

Drag Test:

Date: March 31, 1969
Location: Cecil County Dragoway
Test car: 440 6-bbl. Road Runner (4-speed)
Options on test car: power brakes, power steering, radio, heater, exterior decor package, lighting package.
Weight: 3,765 lbs.
Remarks: Test car in absolutely pure-stock condition—air cleaner and mufflers operating, street tires only; no special tuning.
Witnessed by: Jim McCraw and Roland McGonegal, Super Stock Magazine.

Professional Driver: Ronnie Sox

Run #	ET/Secs	Trap Speed/mph
1	13.21	110.02
2	13.24	110.42
3	13.24	110.29
4	13.22	109.89
5	13.12	110.83
6	13.02	111.52
7	13.14	110.70
8	13.22	111.11
9	13.00	111.52
10	13.00	110.15
Average:	13.14	110.65

Amateur Driver: Roland McGonegal

Run #	ET/Secs	Trap Speed/mph
1	13.95	107.27
2	13.32	109.89
3	13.42	109.22
4	13.48	109.75
5	13.33	110.42
Average:	13.50	109.31

Beep-Beep your *what?!?* To say our new 440 Six-Barrel is the Hot setup is the understatement of the year. Goes to show that nothing shrinks time and distance like cubic inches and a good induction system. Best of all, the whole rig costs a couple of hundred skins less than a Hemi! When you get yours and decide to see what she'll do, just follow our example and do it at a sanctioned strip. Saves wear and tear on the ol' driving record. Dig?

Plymouth

CHRYSLER
MOTORS CORPORATION

61

HEMI ROAD RUN

CAR

Hemi

Plymouth CHRYSLER

RR: 0-105 IN 13.5 SECS.! ONE OF THE REASONS MOTOR TREND NAMED IT...

OF THE YEAR

Look what Plymouth's up to now.

Well, there we were, all set to announce the results of our latest Road Runner acceleration tests, and—Zap!—*Motor Trend* up and names it Car of the Year. Needless to say, we were extremely pleased at the news. Not *surprised* particularly, but pleased. For some time now we've asserted that we, Plymouth, build the best high-performance cars in the industry. The Car of the Year award confirms the fact.

If anything, though, the *Motor Trend* award advances an even broader theory than our own—that, for the price, Road Runner is the most outstanding car in the industry, *period*. In that case, *Motor Trend* appears to be recommending it to vast legions of the Establishment—doctors, lawyers, bankers, Sunday school teachers, undertakers, librarians, bird watchers, dowager aunts. (Ah, we can just see good old Aunt Mildred now, suddenly the scourge of the sit-and-knit set, making the scene around town and putting it on all the young cats.) It staggers the imagination.

But then, why not? With the 383 engine and automatic, Road Runner's about as easy to drive as a golf cart. And what with the car's big 11" heavy-duty brakes, unpretentious exterior, tight construction and inherent good handling—well, maybe it is the right car for just about everyone. Maybe flabby cars went out with bolo ties and long hemlines. Maybe it's Aunt Mildred's cup of tea after all.

But enough about everybody's car. Above all, Road Runner is a car for purists. And our subject this month deals with the purest Road Runner of all—the *Hemi* Road Runner.

Hemi. No mistaking what that means: 426 cubic inches; two four-barrels; enormous black-crackle rocker covers; cavernous ports; tuliped valves; wild cam; solid lifters; nitride-hardened crankshaft; horsepower: 425 @ 5,000 rpm; torque: 490 lbs-ft. @ 4,000 rpm.

Hemi Test Car

Aside from the Hemi, however, our test car was notable for still another reason. It was a complete "sleeper." No racing stripes, no chrome to speak of, no mags—just a business coupe with little "taxi" hubcaps and bench seats. In fact, the only options on the whole car were the radio, heater and the Super Performance Axle Package, which is mandatory with the Hemi and includes such necessities as a 4.10:1 Dana Sure-Grip rear axle, a 26"-wide radiator and power disc brakes. Oh, and the tires were F-70 x 15" "Polyglas." The transmission was automatic—a high-upshift TorqueFlite with a high-stall-speed converter. It's a no-cost option with the Hemi.

And so, with a scant 322 miles on the odometer, we were off to nearby Irwindale Raceway. The plan, as before, was to run the car *pure stock*, with street tires, mufflers, suspension—stock *everything*. Ronnie Sox would make a series of runs first, then the amateurs would take over. NHRA would man the clocks and certify the results.

Pure Stock Times

This is what happened:

Driver: Ronnie Sox

Run #	ET/secs	Trap speed/mph
1.	13.44	106.25
2.	13.53	105.38
3.	13.69	104.28
4.	13.43	105.88
5.	13.50	105.50
6.	13.56	105.14
7.	13.35	107.39

Average: 13.50/105.68

Drivers: Dick Maxwell*, Jerry Gross*

Run #	ET/secs	Trap speed/mph
1.	13.55	105.75
2.	13.53	105.88
3.	13.57	105.14
4.	13.63	105.88
5.	13.63	105.75
6.	13.68	105.38

Average: 13.59/105.63
*denotes amateur

The figures were almost too good to believe; but there they were. Not bad for a "business coupe."

That night, the Road Runner received the usual "Nationals"-type teardown under the watchful eye of NHRA Technical Director "Farmer" Dismuke, just to make sure it was completely stock. It was. As a matter of fact, the weigh-in showed the car to be more than 200 pounds overweight.

Modified Hemi

Inspection completed, we decided to modify the Hemi a bit. Not that much that can be done to improve the Hemi, but a few well-chosen bolt-ons *do* help. The first step was the installation of a set of Hooker under-the-car headers; next came a Racer Brown SSH-25 hydraulic cam and lifter set and, finally, a set of Iskenderian outer valve springs. But otherwise, nothing else was changed. The next day, we drove our "package stock" back to Irwindale. There, the headers were uncorked; and with Ronnie shifting the TorqueFlite at 6,000 rpm, the following runs were recorded:

Run #	ET/secs	Trap speed/mph
1.	12.85	110.97
2.	12.98	110.70
3.	12.88	110.83
4.	12.93	110.02
5.	12.93	110.15
6.	12.83	110.50
7.	12.83	110.35
8.	12.79	110.52

Average: 12.87/110.50

Wild, huh? But then again, the 383 Road Runner is no slouch either. In an earlier test, it averaged 14.01/101.26, pure stock and 13.64/105.32, modified stock. (See Hot Rod, Dec. '68.)

Well, which Bird'll it be—383 or Hemi? The decision is up to you. But in either case, you'll be glad to know that complete tuning information on both engines is available free of charge from Chrysler. The same goes for price info' on many of the bolt-ons we've mentioned in our ads. Write Performance Parts Service, Chrysler Corp., P.O. Box 1919, Detroit, Michigan 48231.

Performance Catalogs

In addition, there's a brand-new "Motion by Plymouth" high-performance car catalog available—24 pages of facts, figures and illustrations on Road Runner, GTX and 'Cuda. It's *must* reading. Just send 50¢ to Supercars, P.O. Box 7749, Dept. B, Detroit, Michigan 48207. We'll throw in a copy of our Road Runner "Goodies" catalog at no extra cost.

Above all, remember that the only way to measure a car's acceleration is at a sanctioned dragstrip. We hope we've demonstrated that with our manner of testing. It's the only accurate way, the only safe way.

See you at the strip.

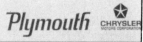 Plymouth CHRYSLER MOTORS CORPORATION

HOT ROD: FEBRUARY '69. THROUGH IMAGINATIVE ART-WORK, PLYMOUTH DID A SERIES OF ADS, SOME SHOWN HERE, THAT TOTALLY CAPTURED THE TRUE SPIRIT OF THE MUSCLE CAR.

CUDA 340 STORMS THE QUARTER RIGHT IN FRONT OF NHRA AND EVERYBODY

PLYMOUTH TEL LS IT LIKE IT IS.

For a copy of Plymouth's wild new high-performance car catalog, send 50¢ to Supercars, P.O. Box 7749, Dept. R, Detroit, Michigan 48207.

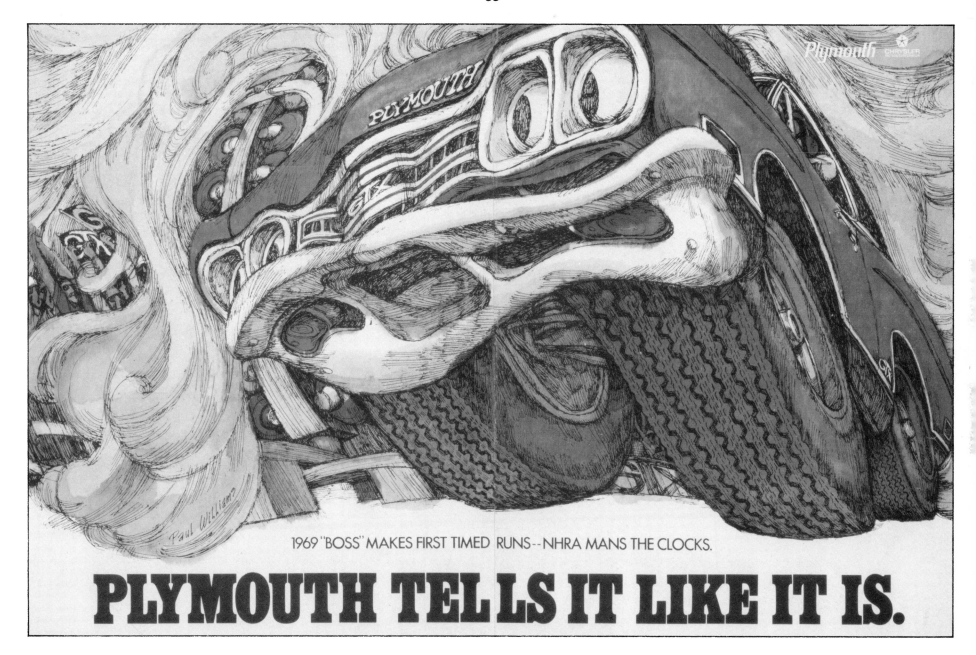

1969 "BOSS" MAKES FIRST TIMED RUNS -- NHRA MANS THE CLOCKS.

PLYMOUTH TELLS IT LIKE IT IS.

The Rapid Transit Authority.

It's Hemi-'Cuda. Our angriest, slipperiest-looking body shell, wrapped around ol' King Kong hisself.

Ah yes, and we've perched the entire setup atop the ruggedest ponycar suspension in the industry. The front suspension is the same extra-heavy-duty combination used on Hemi Road Runners and GTXs—the same torsion bars, shock absorbers, anti-sway bar, spindles, ball joints, etc. Ditto the rear suspension, which carries two extra half-leaves in the right rear spring, to prevent torque steer off the line.

As for the brakes, they're giant 11-inch diameter drum-type units.

The standard transmission is (1.) a heavy-duty 4-speed with Hurst linkage and our new "Pistol Grip" shift handle, or (2.) Chrysler's famed TorqueFlite 'auto' with our new "Slap-Stik" shifter.

Tires? Fiberglass-belted F60 X 15s.

Air induction? That's courtesy of Air Grabber, which sticks right up through the hood. Aside from the fact that it looks tough and the girls dig it, it's good for .15 to .20 of a second in the quarter. And the Hemi it connects to now has hydraulic lifters, so it stays in tune longer.

Availability? Why, at your Plymouth dealer's Rapid Transit Center, of course. There you'll find 'Cudas of all denominations—340s, 383s, 440s, and 440 Six-Barrels.

Giving people what they want is easy. When you have a System.

Plymouth · CHRYSLER

Everybody offers a car.
Only Plymouth offers a system.

Heck, anybody can build cars with big engines. Plymouth's Rapid Transit System is a lot more than that.

As the name implies, it's a system; a total concept in transportation that goes far beyond eight pistons and a steering wheel.

The Rapid Transit System is racing—at Daytona, Riverside, Cecil County—and the race cars themselves—Dragsters, Super Stocks, Oval Stockers—the essence of high-performance machinery.

The Rapid Transit System is information—the straight scoop from Plymouth to you—tips on how to tune your car, modify it, which equipment to use, and how to set the whole thing up for racing. For a free brochure on all that's available, just write Rapid Transit System—Dept. A, P.O. Box 7749, Detroit, Mich. 48231.

The System is person-to-person contact —us and you—at Supercar Clinics conducted throughout the country by our own racers.

The System is high-performance parts— now conveniently packaged and available through your Plymouth dealer.

Above all, the R.T.S. is the product— everything from a Valiant Duster 340, all the way to a Hemi-'Cuda with a quivering Air Grabber. Each car in the System is a complete high-performance car, with suspension, brakes, driveline and tires to match.

Compare Plymouth's Rapid Transit System with mere cars.

And if you can't beat it—join it.

Plymouth CHRYSLER MOTORS CORPORATION

The obvious reason Richard Petty came back.

SuperBird, the ultimate Road Runner.

It's not the only reason Richard returned to Plymouth, but you can put it at the top of the list. (We're building a limited number of completely *streetable* SuperBirds. Check your Plymouth Dealer.)

Another reason came from Richard himself: "The Pettys and Plymouth are like, well, like family." During an 11-year association with Plymouth, Richard won (among other things) two national championships, most total money and a legion of loyal fans. Richard's also won a record 101 victories, 92 of them in Plymouths.

Now the family's back together again. And we're glad.

The Pettys will prepare a couple of SuperBirds for the superspeedways and run the smaller Road Runners on the short tracks.

So we're officially back in NASCAR Grand National racing. With the most successful stock car driver in history.

Which is the sort of thing you could expect from Plymouth.

Because we have the most comprehensive high-performance program in the industry.

It's called the Rapid Transit System. And it offers everything from the cars themselves (Road Runner, GTX, 'Cuda, Duster 340 and Sport Fury GT), to factory tuning manuals and high-performance parts, all the way to TransAm racers, Super Stockers and AA/Fuel dragsters.

If you're a car enthusiast of one kind or another, you'll feel at home in the System. Because there's something for every kind of enthusiast.

It's sort of a family affair. In more ways than one.

The Rapid Transit System
Plymouth makes it.

Road Runner Character © Warner Bros.—Seven Arts, Inc.

MOTOR TREND: MARCH '70 AND *CAR CRAFT:* APRIL '70. A RARE AD FOR LEGENDARY SUPERBIRD.

The Rapid Transit System Announced

'Cuda

- Special high-performance 383 cu. in. 335 hp Wedge V-8, standard. ("Economy" versions not available.)
- 340 cu. in. 4-bbl., 440 cu. in. 4-bbl. 440 cu. in. 6-bbl. or 426 Hemi V-8 optional.
- High-performance camshaft, standard.
- High-performance Holley 4-bbl. carburetor, standard.
- High-flow cylinder heads and intake manifold, standard.
- Oil pan windage tray, standard.
- Heavy-duty 3-speed manual transmission, standard.
- 4-speed or high-upshift TorqueFlite automatic, optional.
- Floor-mounted shifter, standard.
- Heavy-duty suspension, standard.
- Heavy-duty 0.90" diameter front torsion bars, standard.
- Heavy-duty 4½-leaf rear springs, standard.
- Heavy-duty shock absorbers, standard.
- Heavy-duty 0.94" diameter front anti-sway bar, standard.
- Heavy-duty 0.75" diameter rear anti-sway bar, standard.
- Heavy-duty driveshaft and U-joints, standard.
- Heavy-duty 11" drum brakes, standard.
- Heavy-duty rear axle, standard.
- High-performance exhaust system with 2¼ in. exhaust pipes, twin mufflers, 2¼ in. tail pipes, standard.
- Heavy-duty, 59 amp/hr. battery, standard.
- Fiberglass-belted F70 x 14" tires, standard.
- E60, F60 x 15" tires, optional.
- Extra-wide 6 in. wheels, standard.

GTX

- High-performance 440 cu. in. 375 hp Wedge V-8, standard. ("Economy" versions not available.)
- 440 cu. in. 6-bbl. or 426 Hemi V-8, optional.
- High-performance camshaft, standard.
- High-performance Carter AVS 4-bbl. carburetor, standard.
- High-flow cylinder heads and intake manifold, standard.
- Oil pan windage tray, standard.
- Dual breaker distributor and viscous-drive fan, standard with 4-speed.
- High-upshift, competition-type TorqueFlite automatic or heavy-duty 4-speed (with mandatory extra-cost axle package), standard.
- Hurst Competition-Plus floor shift with "Pistol Grip" shift handle, standard with 4-speed.
- Extra-heavy-duty suspension, standard.
- Heavy-duty 0.92" dia. torsion bars, std.
- Heavy-duty shock absorbers, standard.
- Heavy-duty 0.94" dia. anti-sway bar, std.
- Heavy-duty 6-leaf left rear spring, std.
- Special right rear spring, 5 leaves, plus 2 half-leaves, standard.
- Heavy-duty 11 in. drum brakes, standard.
- High-performance dual exhaust system with 2½ in. exhaust pipes, twin mufflers, 2¼ in. tail pipes, standard.
- Heavy-duty driveshaft and U-joints, std.
- Heavy-duty rear axle, standard.
- Heavy-duty battery, 70 amp/hr., std.
- Extra-wide 6 in. wheels, standard.
- Fiberglass-belted F70 x 14" tires, std.
- F60 x 15" tires, optional.
- Bucket seats, standard.

Sport Fury GT

- High-performance 440 cu. in. 350 hp Wedge V-8, standard. ("Economy" versions not available.)
- 440 cu. in. 6-bbl. V-8, optional.
- High-performance Carter AVS 4-bbl. carburetor, standard.
- High-flow cylinder heads and intake manifold, standard.
- High-upshift, competition-type TorqueFlite automatic, standard.
- Heavy-duty suspension, standard.
- Heavy-duty 0.98" dia. torsion bars, standard.
- Heavy-duty shock absorbers, standard.
- Heavy-duty 0.98" dia. anti-sway bar, standard.
- Heavy-duty 6-leaf rear springs, standard.
- Heavy-duty 11 in. drum brakes, standard.
- High-performance dual exhaust system with 2½ in. exhaust pipes, twin mufflers, 2¼ in. tail pipes, standard.
- Heavy-duty driveshaft and U-joints, standard.
- Heavy-duty rear axle, standard.
- Heavy-duty battery, 70 amp/hr., standard.
- Extra-wide 6 in. road wheels, standard.
- Fiberglass-belted H70 x 15" tires, standard.

Road Runner

- Special high-performance 383 cu. in. 335 hp Wedge V-8, standard. ("Economy" versions not available.)
- 440 cu. in. 6-bbl. or 426 Hemi V-8, optional.
- High-performance camshaft, standard.
- High-performance Holley 4-bbl. carburetor, standard.
- High-flow cylinder heads and intake manifold, standard.
- Oil pan windage tray, standard.
- Heavy-duty 3-speed manual transmission, standard.
- 4-speed or high-upshift TorqueFlite automatic, optional.
- Floor-mounted shifter, standard.
- Heavy-duty suspension, standard.
- Heavy-duty 0.90" diameter front torsion bars, standard.
- Heavy-duty 4½-leaf rear springs, std.
- Heavy-duty shock absorbers, standard.
- Heavy-duty 0.94" diameter front anti-sway bar, standard.
- Heavy-duty driveshaft and U-joints, standard.
- Heavy-duty 11" drum brakes, standard.
- Heavy-duty rear axle, standard.
- High-performance exhaust system with 2¼ in. exhaust pipes, twin mufflers, 2 in. tail pipes, standard.
- Heavy-duty, 59 amp/hr. battery, standard.
- Fiberglass-belted F70 x 14" tires, standard.
- F60 x 15" tires, optional.
- Extra-wide 6 in. wheels, standard.
- Bench seats, standard.
- Beep-Beep horn, standard.

Valiant Duster 340

- High-performance 340 cu. in. 275 hp Wedge V-8, standard.
- High-performance camshaft, standard.
- High-flow cylinder heads and intake manifold, standard.
- High-performance Carter AVS 4-bbl. carburetor, standard.
- High-flow air cleaner, standard.
- Oil pan windage tray, standard.
- Heavy-duty 3-speed manual transmission, standard.
- 4-speed or high-upshift TorqueFlite automatic, optional.
- Floor-mounted shifter, standard.
- Heavy-duty suspension, standard.
- Heavy-duty 0.87" diameter front torsion bars, standard.
- Heavy-duty 6-leaf rear springs, standard.
- Heavy-duty shock absorbers, standard.
- Heavy-duty 0.88" diameter front anti-sway bar, standard.
- Front disc brakes, standard.
- 10-inch rear drum brakes, standard.
- High-performance dual exhaust system with 2¼ in. exhaust pipes, twin mufflers and 2¼ in. tail pipes, standard.
- Heavy-duty driveshaft and U-joints, standard.
- Heavy-duty rear axle, standard.
- Fiberglass-belted E70 x 14" tires, standard.
- Extra-wide 5.5 in. wheels, standard.
- Full instrumentation, standard.

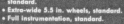

There are two kinds of Those that do
Barracudas in this world. ...and those that really do.

On the left you see one of Plymouth's super-tough 1971 'Cudas. A 340 cubic incher.

We recommend the 'Cuda 340 for those of you who tend to prefer the merits of a lightweight, high-winding engine . . . for those of you who are well aware that Swede Savage is not a Swede . . . and for those of you who just simply won't be happy with anything less than a for-real sporty car.

Like all 'Cudas, the 'Cuda 340 possesses an incredibly well engineered underside. ('Cudas carry virtually the same brawny chassis setup as our intermediate-size Supercars.)

Heavy-duty torsion bars, rear shock absorbers, rear springs, ball joints, front and rear anti-sway bars and brakes all come standard.

Now then, for you hard core straight-liners out there, there's the car on the right, and its legendary engine to consider—the Hemi-'Cuda.

Hemi-'Cudas come with *extra-heavy-duty* (what else) torsion bars, shock absorbers, rear springs and rear axle. As do our 440 6-barrel 'Cudas.

There is, of course, another way to go.

You can order a 1971 Barracuda and the good stuff (like fat tires, trick wheels and heavy-duty suspension) with a 225 cubic inch Six! Or 318 V-8. Or the 383 2-barrel V-8 engine.

So, in other words, you can order a 'Cuda from the Rapid Transit System—or its first cousin from our stable of Barracudas.

For some time now, Plymouth has offered the car enthusiasts of this country the most comprehensive selection of high-performance cars available.

And we still do.

The Rapid Transit System. Coming through.

Plymouth
CHRYSLER
MOTORS CORPORATION

It still goes beep-beep.

And it still has fat tires, high-flow cylinder heads, 4-barrel carburetion and heavy-duty brakes and suspension.

And it still *doesn't* have a lot of chrome or frilly adornments.

And it still *does* handle. (We've given it yet a wider rear track—by 3.2 inches—and a shorter wheelbase.)

And it's still, well . . . still everything you've come to know and love it for. In other words, a low-priced honest-to-goodness high-performance car with the right equipment built right in.

But, as you can see, it has one heck of a slick, altogether new body.

It's the 1971 Road Runner.

You'll find it and all the other 1971 Plymouths in the Rapid Transit System ('Cuda, Duster 340, GTX and Sport Fury GT) at any Plymouth Dealer.

Beep-Beep.

The Rapid Transit System. Coming through.

1971

383

Plymouth CHRYSLER MOTORS CORPORATION

Try to find a performance car that comes with heavy-duty torsion bars, heavy-duty rear springs, a front sway bar, high-control shocks, a dual exhaust system, 3:21 ratio rear axle, unibody construction and an engine equal to our 340 cubic inch Wedge.

Try to find a car like that for around $2,800. Just try.

Our '73 Duster 340 is that car.

And, like ads say, there's more.

You get our unique Electronic Ignition System. It gives up to 35% higher starting voltage than conventional ignition systems.

You can order a 4-speed with a Hurst shifter. Or a heavy-duty TorqueFlite automatic. A 3:55 ratio Sure-Grip differential. 14 x 5" Rallye Road Wheels and E70 x 14" raised white-letter tires like the ones below. Bucket seats. Dual racing mirrors. An inside hood release.

So if money and cars are coincidentally important in your life, you should probably go see the Duster 340. If exactly what (and how much) the money buys is even more important, there's no question about it.

Plymouth Duster 340
Extra care in engineering...it makes a difference.

CHRYSLER
Plymouth

One for the money.

Chapter Three
Ford Motor Company

Ford
Division

Those Super Torque **FORD** engines
climb hills like a homesick Swiss yodeler.
One is available with 425 horsepower
(a few more than the average private plane).
They're still talking about it at Daytona!
Try <u>total</u> <u>performance</u> on your local Matterhorn.
Just ask your nearest Ford dealer.

TRY TOTAL PERFORMANCE
FOR A CHANGE!

FORD

Falcon · Fairlane · Ford · Thunderbird

NEW FORD GT–Ford Motor Company's high-performance lab on wheels!

Wouldn't you think we'd show it hurtling through the straight at Sebring, or winging out of a hairpin turn at Watkins Glen?

Could be. But this 200-mph projectile wasn't built just to win more racing laurels—or for speed alone. Call it a research tool—blueprint to new and exciting machinery for you and your neighbors to drive.

The GT coupe, only 40 inches high, explores a bundle of way-out ideas. The build is semi-monocoque, letting the body share stresses with the chassis. A V-8 engine, displacing 256 cubic inches, is mounted midship between driver's seat and rear axle to put the pounds in the right places. For greater safety, fuel is fed from flexible plastic cells located in car side-members. Ducted ventilation, forced air cooling of seats, unit seat-and-body construction, rear axle-mounted 4-speed manual transmission, disc brakes, low-rate independent springing of all four wheels—all shed new light on car design, on sharper handling and safer driving.

Wheeled laboratories like the GT give us answers *right now* we otherwise might not get for years. What we learn today—about cams and carburetors, comfort and control, suspensions and stressed metals—pays off today, in cars better built because they are Ford-built.

FORD-BUILT MEANS BETTER BUILT MUSTANG · FALCON · FAIRLANE · FORD · THUNDERBIRD
COMET · MERCURY · LINCOLN CONTINENTAL

MOTOR COMPANY

Ride Walt Disney's Magic Skyway at the Ford Motor Company Wonder Rotunda, New York World's Fair

13

'64 Fairlane Sports Coupe; it can wear a Cobra kit, too!

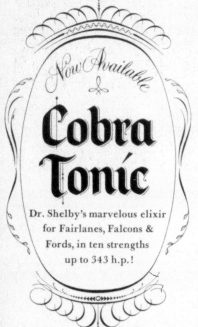

Now Available

Cobra Tonic

Dr. Shelby's marvelous elixir for Fairlanes, Falcons & Fords, in ten strengths up to 343 h.p.!

If you've ever yearned for a Secret Ingredient that would turn your chug into a real stormer—yearn no more. Crafty ol' Carroll Shelby and his Ford friends have been running back and forth to the toolroom and here they come with a mess of Ford-built Cobra kits that will really grow massive biceps on that modest little V-8.

This is bolt-on horsepower, dealer-installed, and the posted prices, in the glorious Ford tradition, are r-e-a-s-o-n-a-b-l-e! There were ten of these kits at last count, with something for everyone, whether he has the 221 cubic-incher, the 260 or the 289. There's not enough space here to run down the list but it ranges from a modest little single four-barrel job that pumps 23 more real horses into the 221 to a Thing with four two-barrel *Webers* that produces 343 h.p. Your Ford dealer has the details; you can spend many a happy hour there planning just how muscular you want your little jewel to get.

TRY **TOTAL** PERFORMANCE FOR A CHANGE!

FORD

Falcon · Fairlane · Ford · Thunderbird
WINNER OF MOTOR TREND'S CAR-OF-THE-YEAR AWARD

More good news for the strong-little-engine addicts

This Fairlane V-8 is beginning to look like the greatest thing since sliced bread — and, just to help matters along, we're adding some Good Things for '64.

The revised V-8 list reads like this: (1) The basic V-8; 260 cubic inches, two-barrel carburetor, 164 h.p., very smooth, a sipper of regular gas. (2) The new choice: 289 cubes, two-barrel carb, 195 h.p. This burns regular, has hydraulic lifters, runs like ball bearings on ice—but it is strong all day long and bridges the gap between the basic V-8 and (3) the Cobra's cousin. Also 289 cubes…but with four barrels, solid lifters, RPM's like an electric fan, 271 muscular horses and a violent urge to show up larger powerplants.

Take your pick, from mild to wild. They all come wrapped in Fairlane's neat no-fat body, with handling to match and one of the quietest, sturdiest chassis you've ever sampled. If you're in a real expense-no-object mood, add $13.30* and get heavy-duty springs and shocks (in any event you'll get 14-inch wheels) and the two top V-8's can be had with four-on-the-floor (except wagons). So O.K.; get in and show 'em displacement isn't everything!

*Manufacturer's suggested retail delivered price.

TRY **TOTAL** PERFORMANCE FOR A CHANGE!

FORD

Falcon · Fairlane · Ford · Thunderbird

Ford Mustang Convertible

the unexpected...

Mustang hits the starting line full bore!

Here's Ford's new kind of car . . . and no car ever hit the road quite so ready for action. Mustang has a long, long list of goodies *now*, not six months or a year after introduction. Let's check down the list:

1. Three V-8's, from the supersmooth 164-hp version with hydraulic lifters through a strong 210-hp two-barrel, right up to the solid lifter-header exhaust high-performance 271-hp stormer. And that's not the end: the whole Cobra kit bolt-on array is available. (You want the four-Weber 343-horse wild one? Just let us know.)

2. Transmissions? The V-8 choice starts with the all-synchro 3-speed manual. Or four-on-the-floor. Or Cruise-O-Matic Drive. All with floor shifts.

3. What else? A special handling package (included with high-performance V-8's) that makes the Mustang solid as a Pullman car on the corners. A Rally Pac that combines tach and clock with sweep-second hand. And, just to show we're versatile, air conditioning, a six-cylinder saver, power steering and all the other *dolce vita* items.

We hope we're not immodest, but the Mustang four-seater starts life with the kind of equipment and options most cars take years to come by. And the toughness and durability it takes to build a going competition machine.

Come down to your Ford Dealer's and take a long, careful look. If we've skipped anything that would make your heart glad we'd like to hear about it—but what could it be?

For a precisely detailed, authentic scale model of the new Ford Mustang, send $1.00 to Ford Offer, Department CB-1, P.O. Box 35, Troy, Michigan. (Offer ends July 31, 1964.)

TRY TOTAL PERFORMANCE FOR A CHANGE!

FORD

Mustang · Falcon · Fairlane · Ford · Thunderbird

VERSATILE!

The COBRA glides along in 15 mile per hour traffic in fourth gear as effortlessly as it tows a ski boat at 70. (Try that with your present sports car!) We really hesitate to brag for fear the so called "purists" will condemn us but... this remarkable high gear flexibility displayed by the COBRA is almost like having an automatic transmission! And...with Ford's revolutionary 289 cubic inch V-8 under the hood the COBRA will run comfortably with any company you wish to keep...or leave! COBRA's versatility is truly TOTAL PERFORMANCE, try it!

COBRA
POWERED BY FORD

SHELBY AMERICAN, INC. 1042 PRINCETON DRIVE, VENICE, CALIFORNIA

G.T. 350

Precise control takes on a new meaning behind the wheel of Shelby American's new Mustang GT-350! The complete suspension system has been re-designed to comply with a computer plotted geometry that allows the GT-350 to stick like nothing you've ever driven. Reflex quick steering, Koni shocks, and Goodyear 130 mph "Blue Dots" let you pick your exact line... and stick to it! No use mentioning the GT-350's 306 hp Cobra hi-riser 289 or the competition proven disc brakes until you've actually sampled a few corners at speed. The most complex blind apex closing radius bend becomes the expert driver's challenge instead of an exercise in frustration. When you go down to test the GT-350, ask the salesman to bring your present car along for comparison...you won't believe it! Suggested list price $4547.00

MOTOR TREND: NOVEMBER '63. AS RARE AS A REAL SHELBY COBRA—AN AD EXCLUSIVELY ABOUT THAT CAR.

HOT ROD: JUNE '65

The Total Performance Fairlane 500 Sports Coupe

Now Fairlane bolts 271 solid-lifter horsepower to a high-shift *automatic!*

The next time somebody quotes that old bit about "Well you can't please everybody!"—just point a stubby finger at Fairlane. In particular, point at Fairlane's marriage of the 289-cu.-in. High Performance V-8 to a special version of Ford's three-speed automatic.

Everybody knows about *this* 289 by now: 271 horsepower, beautiful balance and breathing and revs that just never quit, a solid little classic of a V-8. But mostly you think of it with four-on-the-floor and some big muscular chap (you?) throwing power shifts.

Scratch that: you can now think of your wife or Good Friend opening the gate on all those shaggy little horses while a beefy Cruise-O-Matic sits on the lid up to 5000 r.p.m.!

How's that for an option? It's certainly a big step in the something-for-everyone direction. How can she complain about shifting when you've provided an automatic—it just happens to be tied to the saltiest little V-8 in the business. She sure won't complain if the whole package comes in a Fairlane Sports Coupe—with Fairlane's big-car

ride and room, its easy-to-park size, its modest appetite for gas, its 14-inch wheels and low-silhouette tires, its very unobtrusive price and . . .

Come to think of it, we hope we're able to make enough of these.

Best year yet to go Ford
Test Drive Total Performance '65

FORD

A PRODUCT OF *Ford* MOTOR COMPANY

The Total Performance 1965 Ford Galaxie 500/XL 2-Door Hardtop

The velvet brute

Ford's still hanging tough on one rule: If you get a Big Ford with 425 horsepower you get it with heavy-duty suspension. Period.

For '65 we haven't changed the rule. Just the suspension. *And* any ideas you've had about how a firm-handling car couldn't be plushy.

This one is a paradox. Up front there's big muscle—427 cubic inches, two four-barrels, cross-bolted mains, 6000 rpm and 11.1-to-1 compression—the portrait of Brute Force. And when you get it rolling, don't look for

a Brute Force ride. It's firm—but it's velvety firm. Controlled but supple.

It got that way because we started with Ford's new four-coil springing, locator-linkage rear suspension and "recessive" front wheels—the best expression yet of the soft-but-stable idea. All we had to do was pump in enough shock-dampening and spring-stiffness to match the 427's extra potential. Most of the velvet remained.

It sounds pretty simple but the *result* is pretty sophisticated. Matter of fact, there just isn't anything else

like this Velvet Brute around. Try it—and if you still feel a red-hot performance car ought to ride like a dragster, even that needn't keep you out of an XL. Just run the tires up to 70 pounds and hang on.

Best year yet to go Ford!
Test Drive Total Performance '65

FORD

A PRODUCT OF *Ford* MOTOR COMPANY

RIDE WALT DISNEY'S MAGIC SKYWAY AT THE FORD MOTOR COMPANY PAVILION, NEW YORK WORLD'S FAIR

The Ultimate Total Performance car   —Ford GT

The car it inspired   —new MUSTANG GT

Here's Mustang's brilliant new package for the driver who knows what Total Performance really ought to mean. Who else delivers exhilaration like this: a 225-horsepower V-8, fueled through a four-barrel carburetor. A 3-speed all-synchronized floor shift.

A straight-through dual exhaust system with chrome "trumpet" extensions. Front disc brakes. Built-in fog lamps. The cornering power of Mustang's Special Handling Package. A GT insignia on the front fenders and the new symbol of Total Performance—the

GT stripe—above the rocker panels. And inside, a custom GT five-dial instrument cluster including ammeter and oil pressure gauge.

That's the basic GT package. It will light up most drivers' veins like neon tubing. But for even lustier appetites, there's a super-

option—Mustang's 271-horse-power solid-lifter V-8 and the 4-speed manual shift. Both packages are available on Hardtop, Convertible or 2+2.

Happy news—and it's all spelled out at your Ford Dealer's. Take a taste. Soon!

MUSTANG
Unique Ford GT stripe—badge of America's greatest Total Performance cars!

A PRODUCT OF **Ford** MOTOR COMPANY

Dress your Mustang from top to bottom with Ford Total Performance Kits

Whether you want to add some personal style touches to your Mustang or put more power under the hood, your Ford Dealer—"Your Total Performance Headquarters"—is the place to shop. The items shown here are just a sample of the accessories and performance kits he has for you.

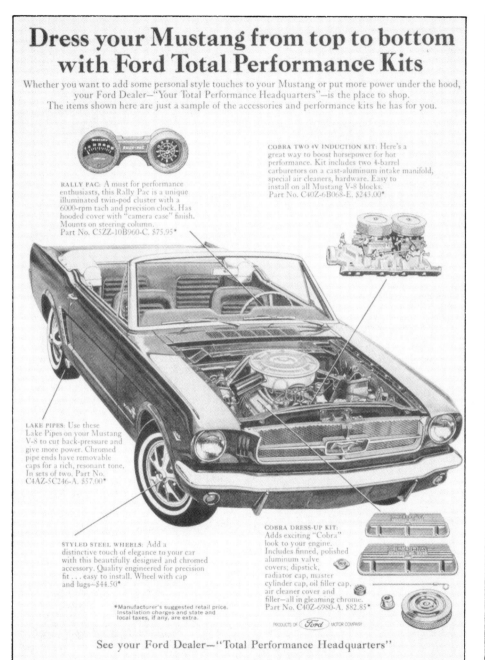

RALLY PAC: A must for performance enthusiasts, this Rally Pac is a unique illuminated twin-pod cluster with a 6000-rpm tach and precision clock. Has hooded cover with "camera case" finish. Mounts on steering column. Part No. C5ZZ-10B960-C. $75.95*

COBRA TWO 4V INDUCTION KIT: Here's a great way to boost horsepower for hot performance. Kit includes two 4-barrel carburetors on a cast-aluminum intake manifold, special air cleaners, hardware. Easy to install on all Mustang V-8 blocks. Part No. C4OZ-6B068-E. $243.00*

LAKE PIPES: Use these Lake Pipes on your Mustang V-8 to cut back-pressure and give more power. Chromed pipe ends have removable caps for a rich, resonant tone. In sets of two. Part No. C4AZ-5C246-A. $57.00*

STYLED STEEL WHEELS: Add a distinctive touch of elegance to your car with this beautifully designed and chromed accessory. Quality engineered for precision fit . . . easy to install. Wheel with cap and lugs—$44.50*

COBRA DRESS-UP KIT: Adds exciting "Cobra" look to your engine. Includes finned, polished aluminum valve covers; dipstick, radiator cap, master cylinder cap, oil filler cap, air cleaner cover and filler—all in gleaming chrome. Part No. C4OZ-6980-A. $82.85*

*Manufacturer's suggested retail price. Installation charges and state and local taxes, if any, are extra.

PRODUCTS OF Ford MOTOR COMPANY

See your Ford Dealer—"Total Performance Headquarters"

1966 Mustang Hardtop

Okay, you can stop asking, "Why doesn't Mustang bolt Cruise-O-Matic behind the 271 solid-lifter V-8"?

Now Mustang stampedes onto the scene with Cruise-O-Matic teamed up with the 271 horsepower solid-lifter V-8 as a new option for '66.

Here, at last, is a memorable high-performance machine that you're not afraid to let your wife drive to the supermarket!

Ford's 289-cubic inch V-8 in Cobra trim was already something of a liv-ing, fire-breathing legend. The hard part was finding an automatic strong and flexible enough to handle it.

Enter Ford's lightweight 3-speed Cruise-O-Matic. Note that *3-speed.* You can match gear ratios to road conditions almost like a manual shift. Or sit back and let things shift for themselves. Cruise-O-Matic makes swift, crisp shifts you'd be glad to call your own: a slushbox it's not.

Mustang's been reaping praise since the day it came out. With this new option, it becomes automatic.

America's Favorite Fun Car

MUSTANG
MUSTANG
MUSTANG

Left Ad

It's been a long time since bib overalls.

That farm boy outfit and the big black hat cropped up everywhere from Le Mans to Riverside. On tortuous racing circuits around the world, Carroll Shelby learned what a car should be...power when you need it, handling when you need it. And he proceeded to build America's first true sports car...the 289 Cobra. Laurels are not for resting on. Now, here are the new ones...the sensational 427 Cobra and the road hungry G.T. 350 from Shelby-American.

The Shelby G.T. 350 starts with a Mustang Fastback and there the similarity ends. The high performance Ford 289 has been reworked with an aluminum high rise manifold, four barrel carburetion and tuned exhaust headers. The result? 306 horses. Completely new front suspension geometry, torque controlled rear axle, the close-ratio Borg Warner gear box (high performance automatic optional) front discs and sintered metallic rear linings deliver superlative handling characteristics. Then add the rear quarter panel windows, functional hood and rear brake air scoops, tach, competition seat belts and optional fold-down rear seats. You don't have to go from zero to sixty in 5.7 seconds, but it's nice to know you can.

The Cobra is the perfect sports car. Those are strong words but they can be proven. The 7-litre Ford 427 is fitted out with two four-barrel carbs and delivers 425 horsepower. That's right. 425. The result is an acceleration curve that's as close to vertical as you can get. For instance, Ken Miles did zero to a hundred to zero in 13.8 seconds *with street tires*. The all-new computer-designed frame with independent coil sprung suspension is one of the most sophisticated designs on the road today. Anti-dive and anti-squat characteristics are excellent. And as far as braking is concerned...well, those massive Girling discs will really haul her down from top speeds. If you need roll up windows for perfection, then forget it.

SHELBY G.T. 350 COBRA

SHELBY-AMERICAN, INC., 6501 W. Imperial Hwy., Los Angeles, Calif. 90045

Right Ad

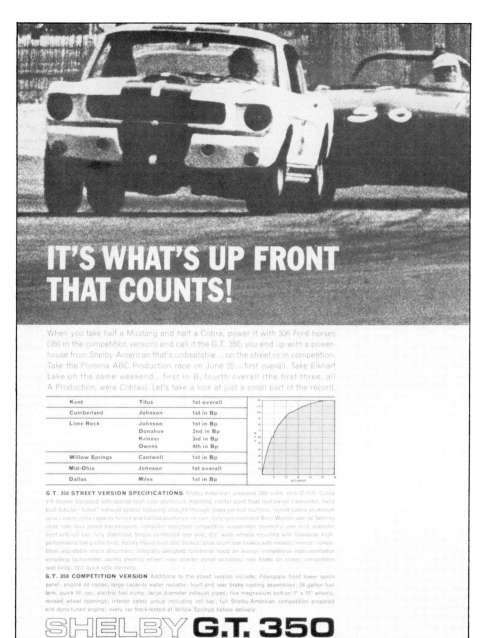

IT'S WHAT'S UP FRONT THAT COUNTS!

When you take half a Mustang and half a Cobra, power it with 306 Ford horses (350 in the competition version) and call it the G.T. 350, you end up with a powerhouse from Shelby-American that's unbeatable...on the street or in competition. Take the Pomona ABC Production race on June 20...first overall. Take Elkhart Lake on the same weekend...first in B, fourth overall (the first three, all A Production, were Cobras). Let's take a look at just a small part of the record.

Kent	Titus	1st overall
Cumberland	Johnson	1st in Bp
Lime Rock	Johnson	1st in Bp
	Donahue	2nd in Bp
	Krinner	3rd in Bp
	Owens	4th in Bp
Willow Springs	Cantwell	1st in Bp
Mid-Ohio	Johnson	1st overall
Dallas	Miles	1st in Bp

G.T. 350 STREET VERSION SPECIFICATIONS Shelby-American prepared 289 cubic inch O.H.V. Cobra V-8 engine equipped with special high-rise aluminum manifold, center pivot float four barrel carburetor; hand built tubular "tuned" exhaust system featuring straight through glass-packed mufflers; finned Cobra aluminum valve covers; extra capacity finned and baffled aluminum oil pan; fully synchronized Borg Warner special Sebring close ratio four speed transmission; computer designed competition suspension geometry; one inch diameter front anti-roll bar; fully stabilized, torque controlled rear axle; 6½" wide wheels mounted with Goodyear high performance low profile tires; Kelsey Hayes front disc brakes; wide drum rear brakes with metallic linings; competition adjustable shock absorbers; integrally designed functional hood air scoop; competition instrumentation including tachometer; racing steering wheel; rear quarter panel windows; rear brake air scoop; competition seat belts; 19:1 quick ratio steering.

G.T. 350 COMPETITION VERSION Additions to the street version include: Fiberglass front lower apron panel; engine oil cooler; large capacity water radiator; front and rear brake cooling assemblies; 34 gallon fuel tank, quick fill cap; electric fuel pump; large diameter exhaust pipes; five magnesium bolt-on 7" x 15" wheels; revised wheel openings; interior safety group including roll bar; full Shelby-American competition prepared and dyno-tuned engine; every car track-tested at Willow Springs before delivery.

SHELBY G.T. 350

One for the money

two for the show

Cobra 2-4V Induction Kit:
Great way to boost engine power with minimal effort. Includes two 4-barrel carbs, two air cleaners, special aluminum intake manifold. Bolts on Ford 260 and 289 engines. $240.15*

three to get ready

Cobra Three 2-V Induction Kit:
Here's three 2-barrel carbs on a cast aluminum intake manifold with a full-breathing air cleaner. Mechanical linkage lets you "run on one" for economy, cut in the other two for maximum "go." For 260 and 289 engines. $219.50*

and Ford to go!

Cobra Four 2-V Induction Kit:
The ultimate in carburetion for 260 and 289 engines. Ready to bolt on. Includes four Weber 2-barrel beauties, intake manifold, all necessary hardware. Get it now. $695.00*

*Manufacturer's suggested retail price. Installation charges, state or local taxes are extra.

go-go to your Ford Dealer...

He has a full range of performance and dress-up kits, accessories and car-care items waiting for you.

Add a dash of excitement to your next business trip. Get behind the wheel of a Shelby G.T.350-H. Only from Hertz.

Have one waiting for you at the airport on your next business trip.

Cobra engine. Disc brakes. High speed wheels and tires. Stick shift or automatic. Rally stripes. High performance shocks. Torque controlled rear axle.

Everything you need to look and feel like a new man on your next business trip or vacation. (Including room enough to seat four.)

Two stipulations. You have to be at least 25 years old. And you have to hurry. (It's all on a first-come-first-serve basis).

So make your reservation today. One local phone call reserves a G.T.350-H just about anywhere in the country.

Just call the only rent-a-car company that offers you a car that adds a dash of excitement to a business trip. Hertz.

Let Hertz put you in the driver's seat. (Isn't that where you belong?)

For the smoothest brute on wheels, add one cubic inch to 427

Everybody knows our 427-solid lifters, headers, double four-barrels and all. That's a *strong* engine and it comes on like Saturday night in Stanleyville.

Well, we've got a bigger one here—one cube bigger which works out to 428 cubic inches or 7-Litres, which is its name. But there's a silk shirt over all these muscles. Hydraulic lifters. Single four-barrel. 10.5 compression. An exhaust that doesn't play "The Ride of the Valkyries." And a lot of civilized joy like front power disc brakes, standard. Bucket seats. Console shift. Choice of four-on-the-floor or Cruise-O-Matic. Really rich carpeting, vinyl interiors, special striping. In two flavors: Convertible or 2-Door Hardtop.

So now we've got a new kind of car: a brute —but a very, very smooth brute. A 97-pound girl can herd this 7-Litre and never know it has 345 horses and 462 pounds-feet of torque—unless she gets mad and stamps her foot. *Then* she'll know!

AMERICA'S
TOTAL PERFORMANCE CARS

FORD

MUSTANG · FALCON · FAIRLANE
FORD · THUNDERBIRD

1966 Ford 7-Litre Convertible

Ford 7-Litre...either the quickest quiet car or the quietest quick car

Well, once again we've invented a new kind of car. It's not a competition car (that's why the overbore to 7 litres/428 cubic inches.) But it turns on like a competition car (after all, 462 pounds/feet of torque!) What it is is lightning without thunder. It *moves*—but it moves like mist over a millpond, smoothly, quietly, effortlessly!

It *stops*, too! Power disc brakes up front are standard. So are bucket seats. The V-8 comes in just one size, with a 4-barrel carburetor and the beefy bottom end that is the heritage of Ford's tremendous competition program. But the lifters are hydraulic for silence' sake and even the dual exhausts are very discreet. You get your choice of convertible or two-door hardtop, four-on-the-floor or Cruise-O-Matic . . . and just about any other added pleasure Ford makes, including air conditioning.

You'll have to decide whether it's a cool hot car or a hot cool car. But one thing you're bound to decide—there just isn't anything else like it!

AMERICA'S
TOTAL PERFORMANCE CARS

FORD

MUSTANG · FALCON · FAIRLANE
FORD · THUNDERBIRD

HOW TO COOK A TIGER

Take one part 335 HP V-8. Chrome plate the rocker covers, oil filler
cap, radiator cap, air cleaner cover and dip stick.

Blend high lift cam; bigger carburetor.

Mix in the new 2-way, 3-speed GTA Sport Shift that you can use either
manually or let shift itself.

Place the new shift selector between great bucket seats.

Now put on competition type springs and shocks.

Add a heavy-duty stabilizer bar.

Place over low profile 7.75 nylon whitewalls.

Touch off with distinctive GTA medallion and
contrasting racing stripe.

Cover with hardtop or 5-ply vinyl convertible top with glass
rear window. Serve in any of 15 colors.

This is the new Fairlane GTA. An original Ford recipe that may
be tasted at your Ford Dealers . . . Remember--it's a very hot dish!

FAIRLANE

GTA

A PRODUCT OF *Ford*

✓	427 V8
✓	Tachometer
✓	Front power disc brakes
✓	Handling package
✓	Super wide oval tires
✓	Styled steel wheels
✓	SelectShift
✓	Dual exhausts
✓	Bucket seats
✓	Shoulder harness
✓	Racing stripe
✓	*Ford*

O.K., now it's your move!

Fairlane GT/A Hardtop

427 V-8 not intended for highway or general passenger car use.

We really had the computer working over-time on the options for the Fairlane. Match-ing our handling package to the potential of those new super wide oval shoes. Mak-ing sure the front disc brakes have enough "feel" for real accurate road work. Tuning a sweet-sounding set of duals. Pin-point-ing shift points on the torque curve of that big V-8 so the SelectShift gearbox won't disgrace itself when you let it shift. Yes, we've given this new Fairlane GT/A the full treatment . . . now it's your turn!

You're way ahead
in a Ford

'67 FAIRLANE

MOTOR TREND AND *HOT ROD:* MARCH '66. "HOW TO COOK A TIGER." WAS THIS FORD'S WAY OF TELLING THE PONTIAC GTO'S THAT FORD WAS AFTER THEIR BUTTS?

CAR CRAFT: DECEMBER '66. LOOK CLOSELY AT THE FINE PRINT UNDER THIS FAIRLANE. CAN YOU BELIEVE THAT FORD ACTUALLY TOLD US THEIR 427 ENGINE IS NOT FOR HIGHWAY OR GENERAL PASSENGER USE?

The 427 Fairlane...

is also available
without numbers.

More and more people who take their driving seriously are turning to the 427 Fairlane. Some of them, like Parnelli Jones and Mario Andretti, go to the trouble of adding personalized touches — such as numbers 18 inches tall!

That's Mr. Jones' 427 Fairlane above, after a Sunday drive that began and ended at

Riverside, California recently. Mr. Andretti likes to go Fairlaning near Daytona, Florida.

Before you go to the line next Sunday take a good look at your equipment. If you're serious about your driving, try a real serious car...the 427 cubic inch Fairlane.

This machine produces a no-nonsense 425 horsepower, and a sincere 480 foot-pounds

of torque at 3700 revolutions per minute.

If you want to add numbers...go ahead. But, remember, you'll have to give every kid on the block from 8 to 80 a ride!

FORD

Mustang · Bronco · Falcon
Fairlane · Ford · Thunderbird · Cortina

Carroll Shelby Presents The Road Cars...
G.T. 350 and G.T. 500 for 1967

Do you agree with Carroll Shelby that good driving is a fine art? Then these all new 1967 Shelby GT cars are custom-crafted for you. By incorporating his competition-proved design and engineering features in the Mustang, Carroll Shelby has created two unique road performers that carry the *lowest* price tags of *any* true GT cars.

The GT 500 features a brand-new Cobra LeMans dual 4-barrel engine, developed from the V-8 that powered the 1966 LeMans winners. GT 350 power comes from the high performance Cobra 289 with free-breathing Shelby induction and exhaust. All-synchro four-speed box

or heavy-duty Cruise-O-Matic are optional on both cars.

These goodies make your Shelby GT one of the *safest* cars you can drive. Massive disc front and air-cooled drum rear brakes. Shelby-modified suspension for 30% less cornering roll. Crisp 16-to-1 power steering*. LeMans-proved wide tread nylon super-safety tires. Integral roll bar*, double shoulder harness*, quick-release seat belts and eye level brake and turn indicator lights.

Naturally, you'll find true GT features. Unique Shelby styling. Luxury interior with bucket seats, complete instrumentation, wood-rim steering wheel, folding rear seat*. You should expect a lot from a

car built by America's first F.I.A. World's Champion. You'll get all you expect when you drive a Shelby GT 350 or GT 500. One is waiting at your Shelby dealer's now.

SHELBY G.T.
350 and 500
The Road Cars
Powered by Ford

Shelby American, Inc., 6501 West Imperial Highway, Los Angeles, Calif. 90009. Builders of the Cobra, Manufacturers of Cobra high performance parts and kits.

*optional at extra cost

IS <u>THIS</u> ANY WAY TO SELL AN AUTOMOBILE?

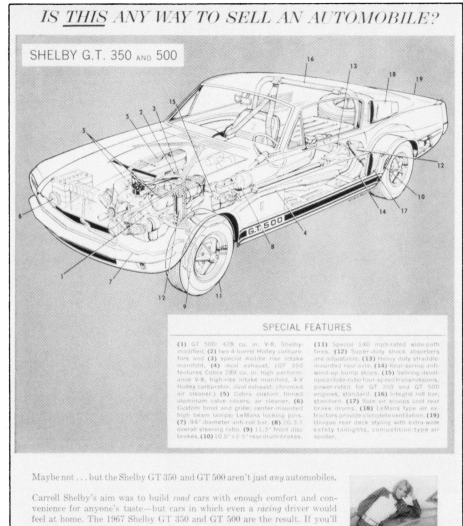

SHELBY G.T. 350 AND 500

SPECIAL FEATURES

(1) GT 500: 428 cu. in. V-8, Shelby-modified. (2) two 4-barrel Holley carburetors and (3) special middle rise intake manifold. (4) dual exhaust. (GT 350 features Cobra 289 cu. in. high performance V-8, high-rise intake manifold, 4-V Holley carburetor, dual exhaust, chromed air cleaner.) (5) Cobra custom finned aluminum valve covers, air cleaner. (6) Custom hood and grille; center-mounted high beam lamps; LeMans locking pins. (7) .94" diameter anti-roll bar. (8) 20.3:1 overall steering ratio. (9) 11.3" front disc brakes. (10) 10.0" x 2.5" rear drum brakes.

(11) Special 140 mph-rated wide-path tires. (12) Super-duty shock absorbers are adjustable. (13) Heavy duty straddle-mounted rear axle. (14) Rear spring anti-wind-up bump stops. (15) Sebring developed close-ratio four-speed transmissions, power-rated for GT 350 and GT 500 engines, standard. (16) Integral roll bar, standard. (17) Side air scoops cool rear brake drums. (18) LeMans type air extractors provide complete ventilation. (19) Unique rear deck styling with extra-wide safety taillights, competition-type air spoiler.

Maybe not . . . but the Shelby GT 350 and GT 500 aren't just *any* automobiles.

Carroll Shelby's aim was to build *road* cars with enough comfort and convenience for anyone's taste—but cars in which even a *racing* driver would feel at home. The 1967 Shelby GT 350 and GT 500 are the result. If you'll read the features listed above, you'll see why these cars are unique.

They're all yours for just $3995 (GT 350) or $4195 (GT 500).*

Did you read every word? Then you deserve a touch of *traditional* auto advertising. So there!

SHELBY G.T. *350 and 500* **The Road Cars** Powered by *Ford*

Shelby American, Inc., 6501 W. Imperial Highway, Los Angeles 90009

*Manufacturer's suggested retail prices. Options, accessories, delivery, dealer preparation, state and local taxes additional.

***MOTOR TREND:** JUNE '67*

Summer Place

What better way to get there—or anywhere—than a Shelby GT? Pleasure begins the second you turn the key and bring alive America's answer to Europe's finest GT cars.

Let your Shelby dealer deliver the goods . . . and save enough to rent a summer place, buy a boat— or just chuckle all the way to the bank.*

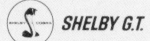

SHELBY G.T. *350 and 500* **The Road Cars** Powered by *Ford*

Shelby American, Inc., 6501 W. Imperial Highway, Los Angeles 90009

*GT 350: $3995 Manufacturer's suggested retail price. Includes Cobra 289 CID 306 h.p. V-8, dual exhaust, competition-based front and rear suspensions, 4 speed transmission, h.d. rear, full instrumentation, safety bar, exclusive GT styling. GT 500 with dual quad Cobra 428 CID V-8, just $200 more. Options, accessories, delivery, dealer preparation, state and local taxes, additional.

***MOTOR TREND:** AUGUST '67. THIS IS ONE OF THE MORE BIZARRE ADS I'VE ENCOUNTERED. FROM THE LOOK OF IT, THE SHELBY GT IS SPEEDING AWAY, THE BOY WITH THE GUN IS RUNNING RIGHT IN ITS PATH AND THE GIRL IN THE DOORWAY FRANTICALLY LOOKS ON.*

Mustang 2+2 with Cobra Jet 428-cubic-inch V-8 during Hot Rod Magazine performance tests

"Hot Rod" Sees the Light

"The Cobra Jet will be the utter delight of every Ford lover and the bane of all the rest because, quite frankly, it is the fastest running Pure Stock in the history of man."

HOT ROD MAGAZINE
March, 1968

Ford introduces the 428-cu.in. Cobra Jet V-8

With some 36 years of experience behind them in making strong, relatively lightweight big bore blocks, Ford's performance-minded engineers set out to build the Cobra Jet. They took the bottom end and beefed it up with the 428-cubic-inch Police Interceptor V-8, high pressure oil pump and large diameter con-rod bolts.

On the top end they dipped into the barrel of Ford race-track goodies. Cylinder heads are straight from the trophy-winning 427 Series 1 engine. Compression ratio was pegged at 10.7 to 1 and quiet hydraulic lifters open the oversize valves.

With a bore and stroke of 4.13 by 3.98 inches, the Cobra Jet develops 335 hp at 5400 and produces 440 lbs-ft of wall-climbing torque. The carburetor is a special new 2-float, 4-barrel Holley and exhaust headers are of special low-restriction design.

That's it. Cobra Jet 428. What it does for Mustang GT's in the 0-60 mph run will make your eyeballs click! It's on the production line right now. The performance option for all Fairlanes, Torinos, and Mustang GT's. Immediate delivery. All you do is order it . . . and GO!

See the light—the switch is on to Ford!

RESULTS OF HOT ROD MAGAZINE TESTS	
Vehicle: Mustang Cobra Jet	
Performance	
0-30	3.0 seconds
0-40	3.4 seconds
0-50	5.0 seconds
0-60	5.9 seconds
Standing quarter-mile . . . . . 106.64 mph in 13.56 seconds	

FORD ...has a better idea.

Carroll Shelby has gone and done it!

Convertible types, rejoice! He's built Shelby COBRA GT performance, handling, style and safety into a Mustang *convertible* complete with the best-looking roll bar in the business. If you don't flip your lid over this, you just don't flip (unless his Mustang-based Cobra GT 2 + 2 fastback gets to you). ☐ Both styles are available in GT 350 or GT 500 versions. The GT 350 boasts 302 cubic inches of Ford V-8 performance with an optional Cobra supercharger for added zip. The GT 500 really delivers with your choice of two great V-8's . . . 428 cubic inches are standard. A new 427 engine is the ultimate performance option. ☐ All the Le Mans-winning handling and safety features are better than ever for 1968. They're wrapped up in a fresh new luxury package. And the Mustang base means an exciting price. ☐ Any questions? Your Shelby Cobra dealer has some great answers!

S. Shelby COBRA GT 350/500
POWERED BY Ford

HOT ROD AND *CAR CRAFT:* MAY '68

SPORTS ILLUSTRATED: OCTOBER '67 AND *MOTOR TREND:* NOVEMBER '67

Ford Torino.
It came up the hard way, easy.

A pack of rough, tough supercars
is hard to beat. Specially
modified Torinos make it
look easy. Won all 3 U.S.
stock-car championships:
NASCAR, ARCA, USAC.
22 major trophies so far.

Easy to get excited about,
another nonstop winner:
Torino GT SportsRoof.
With new 428 Cobra Jet V-8
option. See Torino '69.
Moving out fast.

On tracks.
On highways.
Off showroom floors.

Cobra Jet 428

FORD
It's the going thing!

For more information on 1969 Torino GT SportsRoof, write:
Torino Catalog, Dept. 50, P. O. Box 1000, Dearborn, Mich. 48121.

TORINO Ford

Richard Petty's Cobra—Winner of Riverside 500

Bargain day at the muscle works.

1969—Year of the Snake. Torino Cobras started it. Driven by racing's top pros, these specially modified SportsRoofs punched the ticket 1, 2, 3 in the Riverside 500. After that the wins came fast: the ARCA 300, the fabulous NASCAR win at the Daytona 500 and the Carolina 500 at Rockingham. And that's only the beginning! Torino was the big crunch last year too, winning the championship in all three major racing circuits: NASCAR, USAC and ARCA. That oughta tell you something about the automobile!

For those of you who'd rather drive performance cars than eat . . . we've built Cobra. It's the street version of the racing Torino Cobra. And because we know that the good guys aren't always rich guys, we make it all basic muscle. Dig the standard specs: the Big Vee Cube—428 CID 4-barrel, 335-horsepower; fully

synchronized 4-on-the-floor, competition suspension with staggered rear shocks; 6-inch rims, belted wide F70 x 14s, hood lock pins and more. For a few dollars extra, go full house—option the 4V Cobra Jet Ram-Air V-8 and bring home *all* the trophies! Catch the hissin' honker soon in your Ford Dealer's Performance Corner. Cobra—the Bargain Bomb!

See your Ford Dealer for your free copy of Ford's 1969 Performance Buyer's Digest, or write: Performance Digest, Department MT, P.O. Box 1000, Dearborn, Mich. 48121

For full color Cobra decal, send 25¢ in coin to: COBRA, P.O. Box 1000, Dearborn, Mich. 48121

COBRA *Ford*

Cobra: brought up in a tough neighborhood

(Daytona, Darlington, Riverside)

1969 COBRA HARDTOP WITH OPTIONAL 428 CID COBRA JET RAM-AIR

1969 COBRA SPORTSROOF

COBRA

The 1969 Boss Snake is blood brother to the specially modified Torinos that let it all hang out on this year's NASCAR circuit. Here's what we deal out as a stock machine: 428 4-barrel V-8, all-out competition type suspension, 4 on the floor box, 6-inch-wide wheel rims, belted wide-oval tires, staggered rear shock absorbers, and external hood lock pins.

If you want to make your Cobra even tougher you can add a locker rear axle. It's our new King Kong rear end—you won't lose it and they can't beat it.

The optional Cobra Jet V-8 with through-the-hood Ram-Air induction kicks in a huge gulp of cold, outside air for max power. This Cobra Jet belts out enough torque to leave two black lines right out to the horizon.

There are a lot of other things like: quick and slick SelectShift automatic, six grand tach and power front disc brakes, to mention a few.

You can put all of these goodies under one of two different rooflines . . . hardtop or SportsRoof—pick the one you think looks faster. That's our twosome for 1969! No doubt about it . . . kustom kar drivers are going to get badly Cobra bit this year!

FORD (Ford)

CAR AND DRIVER: OCTOBER '68 AND *HOT ROD:* OCTOBER '68. TWO PAGES FROM A MULTIPAGE AD FOR FORD PERFORMANCE CARS.

Carroll Shelby's COBRA GT ...for the man who wants everything in <u>one car</u>

Distinctive styling, superb performance, reassuring safety—you can have all these at an attractively low price. ☐ Both the custom-styled Cobra GT convertible and the 2+2 fastback are strictly limited editions designed by Carroll Shelby (no meeting yourself around every corner). ☐ Exterior styling features are distinctive *and* functional — hood scoops for carburetor air, fastback louvers as air extractors. Even sequential tail lights. ☐ Interiors are luxurious. They gleam with unique simulated wood grain on instrument panel, steering wheel and door trim. There's a richly fitted console. ☐ These *road* car features were designed by *racing* car builders for you: new 302 Ford V-8 (GT 350) or 428 Ford V-8 (GT 500); disc front brakes; competition-based suspension; heavy-duty driveline and rear axle; custom hi-performance 130 MPH rated nylon tires; wide-rim wheels; full instrumentation with an 8,000 RPM tachometer; 4-speed transmission (a close-coupled automatic is a low-cost option). ☐ Cobra's safety features are built-in. These include front seat shoulder harnesses, high intensity fog lights and other safety items. Integral overhead bar is standard in both models. ☐ Carroll Shelby engineered all these features into the Mustang, winner of two Trans-Am road racing championships. ☐ Result: '68 Cobras that rival Europe's finest limited production cars— but sell for thousands of dollars less. ☐ Try "everything" at your Shelby Cobra dealer.

Shelby COBRA GT 350/500   POWER BY *Ford*

People will talk...

You better believe they'll talk if you show up one day in a Shelby GT. After all, this is a car with a reputation. And the wherewithal to back it up. Your choice of 351 or 428 Ram-Air V-8 heads the list, followed swiftly by front disc brakes, built in roll bar, air-ducts for brake cooling, a suspension that's the toughest set-up this side of Daytona, and your choice of a 4-speed manual or 3-speed automatic transmission . . . even 5 racy "Grabber" exterior colors . . . the whole shot. In short, the sort of thing people want in a car that looks that mean.

But, somehow you don't expect to find *luxury* with this kind of performance machine. But with Shelby the luxury is all there. Plush high back bucket seats, wall to wall carpeting, padded vinyl-covered steering wheel, tasteful touches of simulated teakwood trim, door mounted courtesy lights, bright trimmed pedal pads and sequential turn signals. True elegance and luxury!

So go ahead! Open the doors, invite the folks in and really give them something to talk about.

Shelby GT 350/500

Shelby GT for 1969

POWER BY *Ford*

Ford-Powered Double A Fuel Dragster.

Here's what happens when you put a 10.5:1 cr, 429 cid, V-8 in a Mustang...

Boss 429!

The cars in Ford's Performance Corner have to be winners. So we called all our competition engineers together and built a new road car—Boss 429.

We start with the same 429 block casting the NASCAR boys get. We four-bolt the mains, put in a forged steel crank, forged rods with ⅜ inch bolts, and forged pop-up pistons. She redlines at six and a half grand.

On top we went a little ape. Aluminum heads mated to the deck, huge canted valves that open way up on hydraulic lifters and forged rocker arms that just don't bend. Ports are oversized, chambers are crescent shaped. Manually controlled Ram-Air induction comes on strong via a 735 cfm 4-barrel Holley and aluminum high riser manifold. It all adds up to 375 horsepower, and that's understating it considerably.

We put the power on the ground through a 4-speed, heavy-duty box and a 3.9-to-1 Daytona type locker axle driving 7-inch chrome-styled-steel wheels carrying F60 x 15 Polyglas belted wide ones. The car stays where you point it with high-rate springs and shocks, plus heavy-duty roll bars fore and aft. Staggered shocks handle the torque problem. Power front discs do the stopping; power steering directs all the action.

What's the model? Thought you'd never ask! Mustang SportsRoof with dual racing mirrors, bright exhaust extensions, tach, front spoiler and full instrumentation. Another Going Thing. You'll find it at your Ford Dealer's Performance Corner. Or at the strip.

For your free copy of Ford's 1969 Performance Buyer's Digest, write: Performance Digest, Department MT. P.O. Box 1000, Dearborn, Michigan 48121

MUSTANG Ford

1969 Trans-Am Boss 302 Mustang

Nearest thing to a Trans-Am Mustang that you can bolt a license plate onto.

Boss 302

Our objective was to build a reasonably quick machine with a tight power to weight ratio. Power starts with a lightweight, precision-cast short-stroke 302 C.I.D. block. Top it with 10.5:1 heads with inclined 2.23" intake and 1.71" exhaust valves under aluminum rocker covers. Bolt on an aluminum high-riser manifold and a 780 CFM 4-barrel Holley carb. Add low-restriction headers and large-diameter dual exhausts. Fire it with dual-point ignition. You get 290 hp at 6000 easy revs. And it can be tuned for more.

Power gets to the road via a high-capacity 10.4" clutch and a trigger-quick 4-speed box. There's a "Daytona" axle with a standard 3.50 ratio. You can order it with a 3.50, 3.91 or 4.30 locker axle if you're that kind of guy. Wheels are styled-steel 7" rims with F60 x 15 fiber-glass belted tires. (These smokers are 2 inches wider than F70's. We had to flair the wheel wells a bit to get them on.) Quick-ratio steering, floating-caliper front disc power brakes, competition-handling springs, shocks, front stabilizer bar and front spoiler are standard. Comes with a collapsible spare tire in case you're wondering about trunk space. One body only—'69 Mustang SportsRoof.

Options include rear spoiler, backlight louvers, power steering and chrome plated (15 x 7) styled steel wheels.

Objective accomplished. You're invited to inspect one at your Ford Dealer's Performance Corner. Also on display at various Trans-Am events coming up soon.

For your free copy of Ford's 1969 Performance Buyer's Digest, write: Performance Digest, Department HR, P. O. Box 1000, Dearborn, Michigan 48121.

MUSTANG **Ford**

1969 Mustang Mach I with 428 CID 4V Cobra Jet Ram-Air V-8

Ford's Exclusive "Shaker" scoop actually protrudes through the hood—rams air directly into the carburetor under full throttle.

Mustang Mach I—Holder of 295 land speed records.

This is the one that Mickey Thompson started with. From its wide-tread, belted radials to its wind tunnel designed SportsRoof, the word is go. There's just one body — the same wind-splitting sheetmetal as the specially modified Mach I that screamed around Bonneville, clocking over 155, hour after hour, to break some 295 USAC speed and endurance records. Underneath that sleek, new shape is more Mustang than ever before. Standard are a new lightweight, free-breathing 2V 351 CID V-8, rated at 250 hp; competition handling suspension, hood scoop, exposed lock pins and matte black hood, chrome styled steel wheels, and white sidewall belted tires. In the high back, bucket seat you sit behind a three-spoke sports steering wheel with integral horn rim switch, and look in dual, color-keyed racing mirrors. Check the complete instrument cluster mounted in the simulated teakwood-grained panel. Shift the fully synchronized manual transmission from the center console. Then and only then, you'll begin to realize what kind of great machine you got for $3122. 1969 Mustang Mach I with 428 CID 4V Cobra Jet Ram-Air V-8, F70 x 14 wide-oval belted tires and 4-speed manual transmission, tach and trip odometer (as illustrated)—$3746.43.*

Mustang GT—Stack extra performance on the Mustang you fancy.

Mustang's all-new GT's come in three sporty shapes—hardtop, convertible and SportsRoof. And all of them have a big slice of the all-out performance that has made our specially prepared Mustangs the big Trans Am gun over many a rough road course. The GT Equipment Group includes styled steel wheels, wide-tread belted white sidewall tires, hood scoop and locking pins, special handling package, racing stripes, and more. Performance comes on strong with the new, lightweight 351 CID 2V 250-hp V-8. And price comes on cool at only $2928.05 Hardtop or SportsRoof GT. (Convertible GT—$214 additional.)*

1969 Mustang GT Hardtop

Mach I Specifications—*Standard engine:* 351 CID 2V V-8. Bore and stroke, 4.00 x 3.50 in. 9.5:1 compression, regular fuel. 250 hp at 4600 rpm. Torque 355 lbs-ft at 2600 rpm. *Optional engines:* 351 CID 4V V-8, compression 10.7:1, premium fuel, 290 hp at 4800 rpm. Torque 385 lb. at 3200 rpm. 390 CID 4V V-8 (see page P6). 428 CID 4V V-8 (see page P6). 428 CID 4V V-8, 335 hp (see page P2). All 4V engines have dual exhausts. *Transmissions:* Std. 3-speed fully synchronized floor shift, ratios 2.42:1, 1.61:1, 1.00:1. Optional 4-speed floor shift, ratios 2.78:1, 1.93:1, 1.36:1, 1.00:1. Select-Shift, ratios 2.46:1, 1.46:1, 1.00:1. *Brakes:* 10.0 in. drums, lining area 173.3 sq. in. *Wheelbase:* 108.0". Overall length 187.4". Weight 3244 lb. *Wheels:* Styled steel, 14 x 6 with wide-oval belted white sidewall tires. Optional FR70 radial ply. *Suspension:* GT handling with 351 & 390 CID V-8's; competition HD with 428 CID V-8. **Mustang GT Specifications**—*Standard engine:* 351 2V V-8 (see Mach I specifications). *Optional engines:* 351 4V V-8, 290 hp, 390 CID 4V V-8, 320 hp (see page P6), 428 CID 4V V-8, 335 hp (see page P2), 428 CID Cobra Jet Ram-Air 4V V-8, 335 hp with through-the-hood functional air scoop (see page P2). All 4V engines have dual exhausts. *Transmissions:* Standard 3-speed fully synchronized floor shift. Ratios 2.42:1, 1.61:1,

1.00:1. Optional 4-speed floor shift, ratios 2.78:1, 1.93:1, 1.36:1, 1.00:1. SelectShift, ratio 2.46:1, 1.46:1, 1.00:1. *Brakes:* 10.0 in. drums, lining area 173.3 sq. in. *Wheelbase:* 108.0". Overall length 187.4". *Weights:* Hardtop—3210 lb., SportsRoof—3244 lb., Convertible—3330 lb. *Wheels:* Styled steel, 14 x 6 with wide-tread belted tires. Optional FR70 radial ply. *Suspension:* GT handling with 351 & 390 CID V-8's, competition HD with 428 CID V-8. **Mach I and Mustang GT Options:** Extra charge over 351 CID V-8: 351 CID 4V V-8 (290 hp)—$25.91; 390 CID 4V V-8 (320 hp)—$99.74; 428 CID 4V V-8 (335 hp)—$224.12 (390 and 428 CID require Cruise-O-Matic or 4-speed manual transmission at extra cost); 428 CID 4V Cobra Jet Ram-Air V-8 (335 hp) —$357.46 (requires Cruise-O-Matic or close ratio 4-speed manual transmission and F70x14 wide-oval belted tires at extra cost) • SelectShift Cruise-O-Matic – 351 2V or 4V V-8 – $200.85 • 390 4V, 428 4V or 428 Cobra Jet V-8—$222.08 • Four-Speed Manual—351 2V or 4V V-8—$204.64—390, 428 and 428 CID Cobra Jet V-8's (includes tach & trip odometer)—$253.92 • Power Steering—$94.95 • Traction-Lok Differential—$63.51 • Power Front Disc Brakes—$64.77 • F70x14 Wide-Oval Belted Black Sidewall Tires with raised white letters—$27.27 •

P5

CAR CRAFT AND *HOT ROD*: JANUARY '69. TWO PAGES FROM AN EIGHT-PAGE AD FOR THE 1969 FORD MUSCLE CARS.

Ford wins Virginia 500!

Torino Talladegas finish 1-2

The 1969 winning streak rolls on. The Ford victory at Martinsville makes it six big wins for Torino over all the other specially modified stock cars.

DATE	EVENT	DRIVER
February 1	Riverside 500	Richard Petty
February 16	ARCA 300	Benny Parsons
February 23	Daytona 500	Lee Roy Yarbrough
March 9	Carolina 500	David Pearson
April 13	Richmond 250	David Pearson
April 27	Virginia 500	Richard Petty

With a roaring start like this the Torinos are well on their way to a repeat of last season's Grand Slam when Torino took the NASCAR, USAC and ARCA championships.

1969 Torino GT SportsRoof

TORINO GT corners performance for you!

Torino GT SportsRoof, Hardtop and Convertible have the same kind of muscle car personality as the roaring Talladegas. The difference is we've cooled them down just a bit and added enough style and comfort to make them America's plushest performance cars. You get a lively 302 CID V-8,

GT handling suspension, belted wide-tread tires, hood scoop and more—all standard. Want more? Then option the mighty 428 4V Cobra Jet, 335 hp with Ram-Air, 4-speed fully synchronized floor shift, Ford pioneered front power disc brakes, buckets, Traction-Lok differential, and 6,000 rpm ta-

chometer. Join Ford's winning streak yourself: check out one of these new Torino GT's. You'll find them in your Ford Dealer's Performance Corner.

TORINO

FORD XL

1969 Ford XL GT SportsRoof

Ford XL GT—
the Michigan Strong Boy.

It's the big one. Sleek, solid, and silent—until you crack the throttle on 360 horses in that new 4V Thunder Jet 429 CID V-8. With 480 pounds of torque this optional muscle machine could move a mountain . . . what it does for these sport luxury XL GT's is completely up to your imagination. (If your performance requirements are a shade less than all-out, order your XL GT with the 2V 390 CID V-8 of 265 hp, or the 2V 429 CID V-8 of 320 hp.) With any of these three great engines you get the glued-to-the-ground roadability of Ford's low, wide-tread all-coil spring chassis. And every XL GT, whether SportsRoof or Convertible, carries power front discs, heavy-duty shocks, mag-type wheel covers, extra heavy-duty coil springs front and rear, high-rate front stabilizer bar, H70-15 belted wide-tread white stripe boots, GT stripe and ornamentation. Only Ford could give you this much moving luxury for $3474.43 — 2-Door SportsRoof. (XL GT Convertible—$228 additional.)*

Ford XL GT Specifications—*Required engine:* 390 CID 2V V-8, bore and stroke 4.05 x 3.78 in., compression ratio 9.5:1, regular fuel, 265 horsepower at 4400 rpm, 390 lbs-ft torque at 2600 rpm. Single exhaust. *Optional engines:* 429 CID 2V Thunder Jet V-8. Bore and stroke 4.36 x 3.59 in. 10.5:1 compression ratio, premium fuel. 320 hp at 4400 rpm. Torque 460 lbs-ft at 2200 rpm. Single exhaust. 429 CID Thunder Jet V-8, 4V carburetor. Bore and stroke 4.36 x 3.59 in. 10.5:1 compression ratio, premium fuel. 360 hp at 4600 rpm. Torque 480 lbs-ft at 2800 rpm. Dual exhausts. *Transmission:* 3-speed manual fully synchronized, ratios 2.42:1, 1.61:1, 1.00:1. Optional SelectShift Cruise-O-Matic, ratios 2.46:1, 1.46:1, 1.00:1. "U" handle selector on optional center console with SelectShift. Rear axle ratio 3.25:1. *Brakes:* Power front disc, swept area 217.3 sq. in. *Wheelbase:* 121", overall length 216". *Weights:* SportsRoof—4135 lb. Convertible—4285 lb. *Suspension:* Maximum handling package. **XL GT options:** Extra charge over 390 CID V-8: 429 CID 2V Thunder Jet V-8 (320 hp) (requires Cruise-O-Matic transmission at extra cost)—$163.24; 429 CID 4V Thunder Jet V-8 (360 hp) (requires Cruise-O-Matic or 4-speed manual transmission at extra cost)—$237.07 • SelectShift Cruise-O-Matic with 390 2V V-8 — $200.85; with 429 2V or 4V V-8 —$220.08 • 4-Speed Manual Transmission—$194.31 • Power Steering — $100.26 • Limited-Slip Differential—$41.60 • Bucket Seats and Console—$168.62.*

IMPORTANT NOTICE—All prices shown are manufacturer's suggested retail prices, F.O.B. Detroit. Optional equipment prices are based on factory installation. Transportation charges, gasoline, license and title fees, and state and local taxes are not included. At the time of printing this guide (10/14/68), prices, product information, and specifications were in effect and correct. Ford Division of Ford Motor Company reserves the right to change prices, product specifications and designs at any time, without notice and without incurring obligation.

Products used in Racing Competition are specifically excluded from any Warranty or Guarantee, expressed or implied. Products utilized for Racing Competition shall be deemed "subjected to abnormal use" and do not qualify for Warranty protection.

See your Ford Dealer for a complete list of options and prices.

P6

CAR CRAFT AND *HOT ROD:* JANUARY '69. ONE PAGE FROM AN EIGHT-PAGE AD FOR THE 1969 FORD MUSCLE CARS.

New shape of muscle for '70.

Striking Power!
Cobra-429 Drag Pack

Cobra's the one. A 429 CID V-8's the standard engine; 360 is the standard horsepower. Ford's great, butter-smooth 4-speed box with Hurst Shifter® is standard too. And for serious drag people, we've got the real earth shaker. Cobra Jet 429 Ram-Air V-8 with Drag Pack. It's got 11.0:1 compression, heavy-duty con rods and mains, a high riser intake manifold and header type exhausts. The 700 cfm 4-barrel carb breathes in from a through-the-hood shaker scoop. Then comes the drag pack: Traction-Lok Differential with 3.91 or 4.30:1 ratio, engine oil

cooler, forged aluminum pistons and 4-bolt center main bearings. All this lean muscle is controlled by Cobra's competition suspension. It's nailed to the pavement with 7" rim wheels and F70 x 14 wide-tread glass belts. So get yourself a Big Snake and strike.

P.S.: If you've already got a Ford Stocker and you want to turn it into a real screamer, do your own thing with Ford MUSCLE PARTS. You'll find 'em in your Ford Dealer's Performance Corner. **Ford Power turns it on!**

For the full story on all the performance Fords for 1970, visit your Ford Dealer and get our big 16-page 1970 Performance Digest. Or write to:

FORD PERFORMANCE DIGEST, Dept. CC-10, P.O. Box 747, Dearborn, Michigan 48121.

COBRA

Meet the Winners

David Pearson
1969 NASCAR driver Champion

Lee Roy Yarbrough
First NASCAR driver to pull off a grand slam victory at all 5 major Southern tracks in a single season!

and the 429 C.I.D. FORD V-8!

This is the team that has dominated NASCAR for two years in a row. Ford Power and the top drivers, David Pearson and Lee Roy Yarbrough. Winning here is the most winning you can do. The banks are steeper, the speeds are higher, the competition is tougher—you go flat out all the way to win.

And we wouldn't have it any other way. When these boys put our specially modified Torino Cobras in the winner's circle, we know we've built the best there is. And in race after race, Ford engineers can't help coming away with

better ideas on brakes, handling and engine performance that make the Ford you buy a better car.

So, go to your Ford Dealer's Performance Corner and see if we haven't earned our leadership. Let Ford Performance turn you on!

For the full story on all the performance Fords for 1970, visit your Ford Dealer and get our big 16-page 1970 Performance Digest. Or write to:

FORD PERFORMANCE DIGEST, Dept. MT-17, P.O. Box 747, Dearborn, Michigan 48121.

FORD

Torino: Winner of Motor Trend's "Car of the Year" Competition

Torino's at home on the high bank at Daytona, too. And winning the 1969 NASCAR championship proves it.

Torino — a great race car makes a beautiful pace car.

TORINO GT–The Luxury/Mover For 1970

A beautiful blend of glamour and go. No wonder Motor Trend named Torino "Car of the Year." Torino won out over a pack of the newest and best the competition had to offer.

Why? Because Torinos have more of everything. Start with styling. That sleek SportsRoof silhouette could be an Italian coachbuilder's dream car.

Glamour is standard on any Torino GT, too, with hidden tail lamps, deep carpeting, and special wheel trim. And that's only the beginning, you can option much more: hidden headlamps, dazzling side stripes and chrome-plated Magnum 500 wheels.

But Torino GT's performance (with the optional 351 4V) impressed Motor Trend's panel of experts as much as its luxury and looks. "An especially desirable combination of power and weight" which added up to "good marks in handling in the mountains."

For the experts, Torino's "broad range of choice was the deciding factor." You almost need a computer to check out the possible combinations of power and plush, sport and style that you get in Torino GT.

Your choice of six great V-8's, from a lively 302 all the way up to the powerful 429 Cobra Jet Ram-Air V-8.

Torino GT can be as sporty as you like, with buttersmooth 4-speed and knife-quick Hurst Shifter®. Or, you take your choice of automatic or manual action with Ford's great SelectShift transmission. Competition suspension is standard with any of the three 429 CID V-8's and you get wide-oval belted white sidewall tires on every model.

Add more luxury if you want, with high-back vinyl bucket seats, blazer stripe upholstery, power steering, and air conditioning.

Torino GT—you'll find it in your Ford Dealer's Performance Corner. One of the "Car of the Year" Torinos!

For the full story on all the performance Fords for 1970, visit your Ford Dealer and get our big 16-page 1970 Performance Digest. Or write to:

FORD PERFORMANCE DIGEST, Dept. MT-20
P.O. Box 747, Dearborn, Michigan 48121.

TORINO Ford

When Mach I is set up to win 8000 miles of rallying in stock trim, its got to be a great car to get across town in.

Mach 1–pronounced Mach Won!

Winning is a habit with Mach 1. The latest triumph is the top rally award a car can win on this continent—the SCCA Manufacturer's Rally Championship for 1969. To win it you've got to run over 8,000 miles of rallies on all kinds of roads in all kinds of weather and finish every stage with split-second precision. That means sprinting acceleration; hanging tight when you corner, brakes that won't quit and power to ram your way through snow-clogged mountain passes. Mach 1 wins rally after rally because Mach 1's got what it takes: a balanced wide-tread chassis and sports-car design suspension, with front and rear stabilizer bars, extra-heavy-duty springs, shocks, and wide-rim wheels.

Power is what you get with any of Mach 1's great V-8's—a 351 2V is standard. Your first option is the brand-new free-breathing 351 4V Cleveland engine with canted valve heads and 300 horsepower that turns on

right now. From there on you option the 428 Cobra V-8 and its partner in power, the Cobra Jet Ram-Air. That's the one with the functional "Shaker" that pops up through the hood to ram cool air.

For '70 the Mach 1 looks as good as it goes. There's a unique black grille with special sports lamps, matte black hood, aluminum rocker panels, high-back buckets, full instrumentation, woodtoned panel and console, electric clock, and more. Get yourself a Mach 1 and really "shake up" the troops.

See your Ford Dealer for a free copy of the 1970 Performance Buyer's Digest or write to:

FORD PERFORMANCE DIGEST, Dept. HR-22, Box 747, Dearborn, Michigan 48121.

MUSTANG

After 8000 miles of gruelling competition the Mustang team wrapped up the Manufacturers Rally Championship for 1969.

Ford's new street numbers for '70

Engine	Availability	Carb.	Bore and Stroke	Cyl. Head Type	Comp. Ratio	Valves and Camshaft	Horse-power RPM	Torque	Transmission Availability
302 4V "Boss" V-8	Mustang Boss 302 SportsRoof	4-Barrel 780 CFM	4.00 x 3.00	Polyangle Wedge Canted Valves	10.6:1	Solid Lifters	290 @ 5800	290 @ 4300	4-speed Manual
351 4V V-8	Torino GT, Mustang Mach I	Ford 4-Barrel Air Valve 600 CFM	4.00 x 3.50	Polyangle Wedge Canted Valves	11.0:1	Hydraulic Lifters	300 @ 5400	380 @ 3400	3-speed Manual 4-speed Manual SelectShift Cruise-O-Matic
429 4V Cobra Jet Ram-Air V-8	Cobra, Torino GT	4-Barrel 700 CFM Ram Intake	4.36 x 3.59	Wedge Canted Valves	11.3:1	Hydraulic Lifters	370 @ 5400	450 @ 3400	4-speed Manual SelectShift Cruise-O-Matic
429 4V "Boss" V-8	Mustang	4-Barrel 735 CFM Ram Intake	4.36 x 3.60	Aluminum Crescent	10.5:1	Solid Lifters	375 @ 5200	450 @ 3400	4-speed Manual

Ford's got hot new numbers for '70. And we mean new. Not just a different manifold heat valve or distributor advance curve. But new blocks, new heads, new cranks, new valves. That kind of new.

Start with BOSS 302. A breathing screamer of a light V-8. Fire it up and you've got Trans-Am action going for you.

Take the 351 4V in Torino GT or Mach I. A real easy rider of an engine. Lightweight but loaded with zap. Take it to the strip and lay rubber all afternoon.

Our Big Gun comes in three packages: 429 Cobra 4V, 429 Cobra Jet Ram-Air and BOSS 429. The BOSS comes on strong with crescent aluminum heads, valves like manhole covers, forged crank and ram-air. Mickey

Thompson's specially modified Mustangs blew the records right out of the book at Bonneville. We call it "The Salt Shaker."

Try one of our winning numbers. Visit your Ford Dealer's Performance Corner. He's got the cars to match the engines. **Ford Power Turns it on!**

For the full story on all the performance Fords for 1970, visit your Ford Dealer, and get our big 16-page '70 Performance Digest. Or write to:

FORD PERFORMANCE DIGEST, Dept. SS-9, P.O. Box 747, Dearborn, Michigan 48121.

FORD

'70 Mach 1—quickest pony of them all!

Mach I. Just one model—the fastback with built-in spoiler. You don't need any more, and neither did Mickey Thompson when he boomed the prototype across the endless Bonneville Salt Flats to shatter an armload of Class B and C records.

Obviously the big hit with the Mustang Mach I has always been the great choice of power, and that's just the way we're going to keep things. To start off, there's the standard 351 2V job . . . and for street work it's a bushy-tailed mill indeed. Then come the options. Exhibit A: one brand-new 351 4V V-8. This is the all-new Cleveland engine. It has huge (2.19" intakes, 1.71" exhausts), canted valves and a walloping 11.0:1 compression ratio. Power? Three hundred big, strong, born-and-bred-in-America horses.

Not bad for the first option . . . right? Next is the 428 4V Cobra. This puts 440 foot-pounds of torque where it will do the most good. If you really want to shake up the troops you can have your Mach I with a 428 Cobra Jet. This giant jewel of an engine features the functional "Shaker" hood scoop. It shakes and so does the competition. Nice thing about the people who build the Mach I . . . they don't do half the job and then lay down their tools. No matter which engine you pick—and we know it's a tough decision—you get the competition suspension. This includes extra heavy-duty front and rear springs, extra heavy-duty shock absorbers, and front and rear stabilizer bars. Also you get fiberglass belted wide-tread tires. All the power you need, plus a suspension that lets you get it to the road. That's what makes the Mach I a complete package. And for '70, the Mach I looks as good as it goes. There's a unique black grille with driving lamps, black or white hood paint, wide aluminum rocker panel trim, high-back buckets in knitted vinyl, full instrumentation, wood-toned applique on panel and console, sweep-hand electric clock, and more. Get yourself a Mach I 428 and really "shake up" the troops.

From its Cobra Jet 428 Shaker scoop to lowered Sport Slats option and supertires, Mach I is Number One.

Put one of these under your local Christmas Tree. Specially prepared Mach I drags in Super Stock . . . wins in Super Stock.

These two pages tell you all about the 1970 Mach I. They are part of Ford's 16-page '70 Performance Buyer's Digest. It includes detailed specifications and options on all the great 1970 performance Fords . . . Cobra, Torino GT, Boss 302, and Mach I. There are also sections on Ford performance fun vehicles and Ford Muscle Parts. The Digest wraps it all up for you. For a copy just write to:

FORD PERFORMANCE DIGEST, Dept. MT-3
Box 747, Dearborn, Michigan 48121

MUSTANG Ford

Boss 429. An earth-shaking combination of big-bore engine and Trans-Am Body. Limited production, coax your dealer.

Two Trans-Am Championships for Mustang taught us how to set up Boss 302.

MUSTANG **Ford**

These two pages tell you all about the 1970 Boss 302. They are part of Ford's 16-page '70 Performance Buyer's Digest. It includes detailed specifications and options on all the great 1970 performance Fords . . . Cobra, Torino GT, Boss 302, and Mach I. There are also sections on Ford performance fun vehicles and Ford Muscle Parts. The Digest wraps it all up for you. For a copy see your Ford Dealer or write to.

FORD PERFORMANCE DIGEST, Dept. MT-2
Box 747, Dearborn, Michigan 48121

'70 Boss 302–Son of Trans-Am.

The Mustang Boss 302 is what comes from winning those Trans-Am championships. From its 5-litre, F.I.A. sanctioned V-8 to its 16-to-1 steering, the Boss is designed to go quick and hang tight. The standard specs sound like a $9,000 European sports job instead of a reasonably priced, reliable American pony car. Boss 302 comes in just one body style—the wind-splitting Sports-Roof shape. The engine is Ford's high output 302 CID 4V V-8, with new cylinder heads to permit canting the valves for better gas flow and larger diameter—2.18" intake, 1.71" exhaust. That's what gives you a big 290 horsepower from a small, lightweight 302 CID engine.

Choose either close or wide ratios on Boss 302's buttersmooth, fully synchronized 4-speed. We've made it an even quicker box by adding a T-Handle Hurst Shifter.® Brakes are power boosted, ventilated floating-caliper front discs. When we tell you the suspension is competition type with staggered rear shocks to combat rear wheel hop on takeoff, don't take our word for it, give it a try. We glue the Boss to the road on 15-inch wheels with hub cap trim rings, shod with F60x15 superwide fiberglass belted bias-ply tires. All this standard equipment leaves you little to option but the fun things—like Magnum 500 chrome wheels, and those great Sport Slats for the tinted back-lite. That's Boss 302. Your only problem . . . deciding whether to drive it or "Trans-Am" it.

Car and Driver Magazine says: "The Boss 302 ... may just be the new standard by which everything from Detroit must be judged."

Paint a number on your Boss 302, put a big gas tank in it, and call yourself Parnelli Jones.

Mercury Division

COMET: BOSS DRAGSTER

On the strips, the clock decides who's boss. And the clocks keep saying "Comet." Like at Emporia, Va., January 5: 11.30 seconds elapsed, topping out at 123.11 mph—a pair of new track records. And at Long Beach, Cal., February 9: 11.33 sec., to a 121.62 top mph. And at Fontana, Cal., 11.72 sec. (another track record) and 123 mph. Watch for these specially modified Comet Dragsters at A/FX class events at the tracks. They're the cars with the bulge in the hood to make room for that big 427 cu. in. mill. And twin air scoops where the inboard lights used to be. If you can't identify them by that, just look up front and see who's leading the pack. Chances are it's a Comet—the World's Durability Champion. Or see Comet at your Mercury dealer's.

LINCOLN-MERCURY DIVISION (Ford) MOTOR COMPANY

Comet wails...

climb aboard!

The way competition-modified Comet FXers are coming out of chutes around the country has started a band wagon rolling. And this is one you'll enjoy joining.

The place to climb aboard is at your Mercury Comet dealer's.

Eyeball the whole beautiful Comet lineup. There are eleven models for you to choose from. When you see the one you like, take it out for a solo.

Back at the dealer's, ask about the great Comet list of options. It will make your eyes pop.

Engines range up to a Comet Cyclone Super 289 V-8. Wild. And down to a hefty 200 cu. in. Comet "6"—which is pretty "up" for a "6." Buckets? Tach? Four-on-the-floor? Three-speed Multi-drive Merc-O-Matic? You name it, Comet's got it.

Some things just are not optional in a Comet, of course. Good looks, for example. A sporty flair. Solid heft. Big comfort. Authority on any kind of road.

So move down to your Comet dealer's. Drive the model of your choice. See why every '65 Comet's a winner. And discover how easy it is to climb aboard this band wagon.

Mercury Comet

the world's 100,000-mile durability champion

RIDE WALT DISNEY'S MAGIC SKYWAY AT THE FORD MOTOR COMPANY PAVILION, NEW YORK WORLD'S FAIR

A PRODUCT OF Ford MOTOR COMPANY · LINCOLN-MERCURY DIVISION

A PRODUCT OF Ford MOTOR COMPANY · LINCOLN-MERCURY DIVISION

This one will drive you out of your ever-loving mind | '65 Comet Cyclone

What's with this special new edition of the World's 100,000-Mile Durability Champion? Front buckets with catch-all console between...special wheel covers with bright lugs showing...special Cyclone grille...cowl-mounted tach...225 hp, 289 cu.-in. V-8 mill with 4V snorkel—Daytona-bred and chrome-dressed for a party. (271 hp, 289 cu.-in. on special order!) For special occasions, add these options...vacuum gauge and elapsed-time clock...four-on-the-floor or Multi-Drive Merc-O-Matic ...a performance-handling package including "quick answer" steering (16:1 ratio), with heavy duty front suspension, plus higher rate springs all around to give you an honest seat-of-the-pants feel for the road. Is Cyclone the boss? Track this 2-door hardtop. See for yourself. The place: your Mercury Comet dealer's.

Mercury Comet

the world's 100,000-mile durability champion

HOT ROD: JULY '65 AND *CAR CRAFT:* AUGUST '65. MANY PEOPLE DO NOT REALIZE THAT MILD-MANNERED MERCURY HAD A BRIEF HISTORY WITH MUSCLE CARS IN THEIR COMET CYCLONES.

HOT ROD: DECEMBER '64

"Indy" 500 discovers Mercury Cyclone GT!

"Performance Car of the Year" Named Pace Car For Memorial Day 500

"Performance Car of the Year"

Mercury COMET

Indianapolis officials do not select their Pace Car lightly. They look to a leader like Mercury Comet, the one that's repeatedly proved leadership. This, Comet has in spades and cubes and records—a heritage of

more world's records, in fact, than any other U.S. make. Also worth noting is everything up front in our Cyclone GT. The swift, 390 4-bbl. V-8. Its heavy-duty performance handling package. Also, options like Sport

Shift Merc-O-Matic (the automatic that lets you shift manually, too), or 4-on-the-floor. Want to try this big, exciting driving machine? This year "Indy" is as near as your nearby Mercury dealers.

Have you driven a Mercury Comet lately? Take a discovery ride!

Ford LINCOLN-MERCURY DIVISION

"Super Stock" discovers Mercury Comet!

Car enthusiasts' magazine applauds Comet as the "Performance Car of the Year."

Why did Comet earn Super Stock & Drag Illustrated's first annual performance award? Because of Comet's heritage as a "can-do" car. Daytona, 1963: 100,000 miles at over 108 mph in specially equipped Comets for more world's records than any other U.S. make. Then: Cape Horn to Fairbanks, Alaska, in a never-before 40 days. Now the awarding editors say: "The 1966 Comet is one of the best all-around packages of performance anywhere." Give this big, new-generation driving machine a whirl and discover what performance is all about!

Here are things you, too, can discover...
• Discover Mercury Cyclone GT excitement! For 1966, a wider tread. Longer wheelbase. Twin scoop GT hood. Convertible. Hardtop. Bucket seats. Chrome engine dress-up kit. All standard!
• Discover Mercury Cyclone GT zip! 390 CID 4-bbl. 335 HP V-8. 7.75 x 14" nylon whitewalls. 5½" rims. Power booster fan!
• Discover Mercury Cyclone GT handling! Heavy-duty high-rate springs and shocks! Heavied-up stabilizer bar! All standard!

"Performance Car of the Year"

Mercury COMET

Have you driven a Mercury Comet lately? Take a discovery ride!

Ford LINCOLN-MERCURY DIVISION

COMET CYCLONE HARDTOP WITH OPTIONAL TWIN SCOOP GT HOOD.

Driving machine of the year: lively, big, new-generation Comet.

This Comet looks the way it goes. Beautiful. And there are 13 Comets like it. Sleeker. Roomier. Up to 8 inches longer. Sedans, convertibles, wagons, hardtops... from rakish 202's to hot new Cyclone GT's. All with a very special kind of luxury.

Plus the features and options you want most. Built-in air conditioning. Bucket seats. Vinyl roof. Four-speed floor shift. Or three-speed automatic. Or three-speed manual, fully synchronized in all gears. Power steering,

power brakes, power windows, power everything. Including a new 390 4-barrel V-8 in the new Cyclone GT. Look into it. Closely. At your Mercury dealer's.

Mercury COMET

Ford LINCOLN-MERCURY DIVISION

the big, beautiful performance champion

Name: Mercury.

Anatomy: glass-wrap over a rail.

Drag Racing Magazine recently named this one "Performance Car of the Year."

Don Nicholson drove it to 135 victories in 10 months for a 90.6 winning percentage.

Jack Chrisman cranked it up to a strip-gobbling 184.42 mph at Riverside.

However you slice it, Mercury is the boss on the drag strips.

We thank Drag Racing Mag for the recognition.

And we invite you to make your Mercury dealer your headquarters for high performance parts and equipment.

See your Mercury Man. Let him shape up a hauler for you.

Meet the top hauler.

Mercury believes a man's car should be a going machine.
Wait till you take the wraps off the 14 goodies in this Cyclone GT.

Mercury thinks good looks aren't enough in a man's car. He wants *action*.

He gets it in the new Cyclone GT. A 390 cu. in. 4-barrel V-8 is standard. So are dual exhausts. A power booster fan. And you can add "in" extras like a tach mounted in the dash (right). Or a 4-speed stick, instead of the standard 3.

There's not an ounce of bluff in Cyclone GT. From the twin-scoop hood through higher-rate springs, heavy-duty shocks, big-diameter stabilizer bar, it's all man's car.

See your Mercury Man.

GT stripes and emblem, front power disc brakes, Wide Oval tires on wider rims—they're all standard.

Mercury

Marquis • Brougham • Park Lane
Montclair • Monterey • Cyclone • Caliente
Capri • Comet 202 • Cool new Cougar

Mercury, the Man's Car.

LINCOLN-MERCURY DIVISION Ford

Mercury Cyclone GT.
Fast-backed. 4-stacked. Radial-tracked.

The golden girl in our picture ordered her Cyclone GT with a 4-stack Marauder 390 GT V-8. And with optional wide-tread whitewall radials.

Which is a pretty neat way to get around the wild West. Or South. Or East.

You may like something tamer in engines. A 390 2-barrel V-8. Or our basic 302. But in any case you'll still get our special GT performance package. Extra-stiff springs, fore and aft. Heavy-duty shocks. A big D

sway bar. And wide wheel rims for the wide oval tires.

Our GT double side striping is unique. So are the turbine-type wheel covers. And the racer-oriented black-out job in the grille area.

Inside, the Fine Car Touch of our Lincoln Continental designers has worked tailored wonders.

In the clean, elegant, functional lines of the dash. In bucket seat richness, without a bit of fussiness.

Give yourself a whirl in a Mercury Cyclone GT.

The Fine Car Touch inspired by the Continental.

LINCOLN-MERCURY DIVISION Ford

Cougar with CJ 428 Ram

Lincoln·Mercury's zip code: CJ 428

CJ 428 is guaranteed to move the U.S. male. Advertised horsepower 335 @ 5200 rpm; torque 440 @ 3400. Huge 735 cfm 4-barrel carburetor. 10.6:1 compression. Performance-tailored camshaft, free-flow breathing, and low restriction dual exhausts and air cleaner. 3.50:1 rear axle. Competition handling package. Fiberglass-belted wide tires. Everything it takes for special delivery! CJ 428 is optional with all Cougars, Montego MX, Montego, Comet Sports Coupe, and Cyclone. It's standard with Cyclone CJ. "More" you ask? "CJ 428 Ram" we answer! Deep-breathing Ram air induction with functional hood scoop is optional for the 1969 Cougars, Cyclone, and Cyclone CJ. Also optional: hood locking pins.

CJ 428 may be our hottest news, but it's not the only news. We also have two completely new 351 cu. in. engines and an improved 390. Lincoln-Mercury engines swing through the performance range from spirited, regular-fuel 351-2V to aggressively competitive CJ 428. Tag one yours and we'll wrap it to go in one of four sports-sized Cougars or eleven intermediate-sized Montegos.

Decisions, decisions. You choose the right engine and body style, and then start on the options. Tires, tachs, and tinted glass. Traction-Lok differential. Racing mirrors. Select-Shift, or 4-speed manual with wide or close ratios. Heavy-duty batteries. Power steering and front disc brakes. Optional axle ratios. Buckets. Vinyl roof. Styled steel wheels, or deluxe wheel covers. AM/FM stereo radio. Et cetera. You don't have to read between the lines to see that we can give you anything you want in high performance.

Cyclone CJ with CJ 428 Ram

ENGINE:	351-2V	351-4V	390-4V	CJ 428
C.I.D.	351	351	390	428
Adv. H.P. @ RPM	250 @ 4600	290 @ 4800	320 @ 4600	335 @ 5200
Adv. Torque Lb.-Ft. @ RPM	355 @ 2600	385 @ 3200	427 @ 3200	440 @ 3400
Compression Ratio	9.5:1	10.7:1	10.5:1	10.6:1
Carburetor	2-Barrel	4-Barrel	4-Barrel	4-Barrel
Exhaust	Single	Dual	Dual	Dual
Availability:				
Cougar	Std.	Opt.	Opt.	Opt.
Cougar XR-7	Std.	Opt.	Opt.	Opt.
Cyclone CJ	N.A.	N.A.	N.A.	Std.
Cyclone	Opt.	Opt.	Opt.	Opt.
Comet Sports Coupe	Opt.	Opt.	Opt.	Opt.
Montego	Opt.	Opt.	Opt.	Opt.
Montego MX	Opt.	Opt.	Opt.	Opt.
Montego MX Brougham	Opt.	Opt.	Opt.	N.A.

Engines, cars and options. Sort them into the right combination and visit your Mercury dealer for details and a price. Remember . . .

Lincoln-Mercury leads the way

LINCOLN·MERCURY

Cyclone Spoiler. Password for action in the 70's. Better bring along a drag chute.

Here's the muscle machine that puts wind to work for you. Tested out at 100 mph, front spoiler drops lift from 186 to 120.5 pounds. Rear spoiler cuts it down from 67.5 to a 5.8. This Cyclone comes equipped with all basic competition hardware. CJ 429 V-8 (370 hp) force-fed by ram-air induction. Four-speed Hurst Shifter®. The works. Get on top of the action with Cyclone Spoiler from Mercury, password for action.

'70 Mercury Cyclone Spoiler

MERCURY CYCLONE   Ford

New Mercury Cyclone. Password for action.
We made it hot [429 V-8]. You can make it scream.

New, do-it-yourself Cyclone. Mercury's going street machine for driving men looking at performance, looks, and price. 429 V-8 with 360 hp. Four-speed Hurst Shifter®. Competition Handling Package. G70 x 14 WSW belted tires. All standard.

After that? Super CJ 429 V-8 with 375 hp. Ram Air. 4.30:1 axle. Detroit locker. Build a Cyclone for sanctioned competition. Make it scream. There's a book full of things you can do. Get a copy of our high-performance catalog at your Lincoln-Mercury dealer.

'70 Mercury Cyclone

MERCURY CYCLONE · Ford

Cougar Eliminator. Password for action in the 70's.
Spoilers hold it down. Nothing holds it back.

You're looking at raw muscle. Muscle straining for the kind of action you want. The Eliminator sports aerodynamic spoilers front and rear. A standard 351-4V kicks up 300 horsepower. Optional powerplants include a high-output "Boss" 302-4V with mechanical lifters and the CJ 428-4V. Standard features include: high-performance axle ratios, hood scoop, rally clock, tach, black-out grille. Optional 4-speed Hurst Shifter.* Everything you need to take on the competition. Cougar Eliminator from Mercury, password for action in the 70's.

'70 Mercury Cougar Eliminator

MERCURY COUGAR

Cyclone GT. Password for action in the 70's
The streeter that looks like a racing car.

New, sophisticated Cyclone GT. The street machine for men on both sides of 30. Scooped hood. Concealed headlights. Hi-back buckets. Competition Handling Package. F70 x 14 belted tires. 351 V-8. All standard. This side of 30? Heavy it up with a Super CJ 429 V-8 (375 hp) and 4-speed Hurst Shifter*. That side of 30? Do the same. Want more? Ask your Lincoln-Mercury dealer for a copy of our high-performance catalog.

'70 Mercury Cyclone GT

MERCURY CYCLONE Ford

Cyclone CJ is the new name to reckon with in the performance world. Supermuscle in a Mercury fastback. 428 cubic inches of bold. And you can have 428 straight (CJ 428), or with optional deep-breathing Ram air induction (CJ 428 Ram) which includes functional hood scoop. Also optional: hood locking pins. Either way, your bonnet shades a complete performance package. Standard Cyclone CJ equipment gives you CJ 428 engine with 335 hp and 440 lb.-ft. of torque. 4-speed manual. 3.50:1 rear axle. Low-restriction dual exhausts. Fiberglass-belted tires. Competition handling package, and more. Options, too! Tach. Traction-Lok differential. Optional axle ratios. Select-Shift. Styled steel wheels. Anything you want. And available now at your Lincoln-Mercury dealer, who reminds you that in performance Lincoln-Mercury leads the way.

**Cyclone CJ wears two bonnets...
one with Ram air induction.**

LINCOLN · MERCURY *Ford*

CAR AND DRIVER: DECEMBER '68 AND *MOTOR TREND:*
MARCH '69

Chapter Four
General Motors

GM
Corporate

Just building them better isn't good enough.

For instance, when we first bolted a big-bore V-8 onto a small, well mannered chassis, we didn't sit around on our trophies.

The SS 396 now has "Porcupine" heads with individually ported intake and exhaust valves.

GTO's new Ram Air package lets the engine breathe cool outside air instead of heated inside air.

The thermostatically controlled air intake on the 4-4-2 eliminates cold engine starts.

And the GS 400 has a totally new engine; lighter, yet stronger than the old one.

These and other advances aren't accidents. They come from things like 30,000,000 miles of test driving each year. Plus a lot of other testing that would probably bore you.

Until you get behind the wheel.

Look to the General Motors mark of excellence

CHEVROLET · PONTIAC · OLDSMOBILE · BUICK · CADILLAC

Left to right: The GS 400, GTO, 4-4-2, and SS 396

Dream sequence— 1968 edition.

We can't think of four better ways to take that new-car gleam out of your eye and put it in your driveway instead. That's if you're the kind who thinks an automobile is something other than a set of wheels.

And if the looks aren't enough to turn a young man's fancy, think about the total combination of engineering you've got going for you.

Just for starters, you've got a parcel of V-8's . . . each one a super sophisticate with tachs available to keep you aware of the numbers. For transmissions, take your pick of automatics like Turbo Hydra-Matic, Super Turbine and Powerglide (if you're a clutchless fan); or a choice of all-

synch 3- and 4-speed manuals, if you're the kind of guy who wants to do it yourself. Match these to a raft of axle-ratio options and you've got a power train ready to do just about any job you want it to do.

Then consider suspensions. We've paid plenty of attention to these. And the result is that the road testers call this troupe the best handling in GM's history. And don't forget brakes. We've got hefty drums standard all around —with power discs available.

Still trying to make up your mind? Why not get down to earth with the man who sells your favorite.

The more you look, the more our mark of excellence means.

CHEVROLET • PONTIAC • OLDSMOBILE • BUICK • CADILLAC

Our dream stable: Pontiac's GTO, Chevelle SS 396 from Chevrolet, GS 400 by Buick and Oldsmobile's 4-4-2.

MOTOR TREND: FEBRUARY '68 AND CAR AND DRIVER: MARCH '68. WHAT A DREAM AD. IMAGINE FOUR BRAND NEW MUSCLE CARS SITTING IN YOUR DRIVEWAY.

Camaro SS
with choice of 350 or 396 V-8

Engine	The "350"	The "396"
Horsepower	295 @ 4800	325 @ 4800
Torque	380 @ 3200	410 @ 3200
Type	V-8	V-8
Bore and Stroke	4.0 x 3.48	4.094 x 3.76
Displacement	350	396
Compression Ratio	10.25:1	10.25:1
Carburetion	4-BBL	4-BBL

Capacities. The fuel tank holds 18 gallons. Oil capacity is 4 quarts, 5 with filter.

Transmissions
350. Fully synchronized 3-speed column shift with 2.54, 1.50, 1.00 ratios.
396. Fully synchronized special 3-speed on the floor with 2.41, 1.59, 1.00 ratios.

Also available. Fully synchronized 4-speed on the floor with 2.52, 1.88, 1.46 and 1.00 ratios. Special 3-speed on the floor (for 350) with 2.41, 1.59 and 1.00 ratios. Powerglide (for 350). Maximum torque multiplication ratios are 3.70 to 1 range in "Drive," 3.70 to 1.76 range in "Low." Turbo Hydra-Matic (for 396). Maximum torque multiplication ratios are 5.06 to 1 range in "Drive," 5.06 to 1.48 range in "Low 2," 5.06 to 2.48 in "Low 1." Selector positions are P-R-3-2-1 with console.

Axle Ratios

Engine	Transmission	Standard	Also Available	
295 hp	3-speed, Special 3- or 4-speed	3.31	3.07	3.55
	Powerglide	3.07	2.73	3.31
325 hp	Special 3- or 4-speed	3.07	2.73	3.31
	Turbo Hydra-Matic	2.73*	2.56	3.07

*3.07 with Rally Sport Option.

Steering. Manual with recirculating ball gear. Standard overall ratio is 28.3:1. Power steering is 17:1. Fast ratio available—15.6:1 with power.

Suspension. Special front coil springs and multiple-leaf rear springs. Bias-mounted rear shock absorbers for improved suspension control.

Brakes. Self-adjusting with finned front drums. Front discs available with power assist.

Features. New Astro Ventilation system with full door-glass styling. Special hood with simulated louvers. Front accent band. Red stripe wide-oval tires. All-vinyl bucket seats. Bright-finished engine accents. Concealed headlights, special exterior and interior appointments, console, special instrumentation and new houndstooth pattern cloth trim (for Sport Coupe) also available.

Firebird 400

Engines	Standard	Also Available	
Horsepower	330 @ 4800	335 @ 5000	335 @ 5300
Torque	430 @ 3300	430 @ 3400	430 @ 3600
Type	V-8	V-8	V-8
Bore and Stroke	4.12 x 3.75	4.12 x 3.75	4.12 x 3.75
Displacement	400	400	400
Compression Ratio	10.75:1	10.75:1	10.75:1
Carburetion	4-BBL	4-BBL	4-BBL

Capacities. 18.5 gallons in the gas tank, 17.8 quarts in the radiator. Oil capacity is 5 quarts, 6 with filter.

Transmissions
Standard. Fully synchronized heavy-duty 3-speed with Hurst floor shifter. Ratios are: 2.42, 1.61, 1.00.

Also available. Fully synchronized 4-speed with Hurst in two versions: Wide-ratio—2.52, 1.88, 1.46, 1.00. Close-ratio (available only with 3.90 and 4.33 axle ratios)—2.20, 1.64, 1.28, 1.00.

Turbo Hydra-Matic. Ratios are 2.48, 1.48 and 1.00 with a total torque multiplication at the start of 5.70. Governor is set for a maximum automatic upshift of 5000 rpm.

Axle Ratios

Engine	Transmission	Standard	Also Available
330 hp	3- or 4-speed	3.36	3.55
	Turbo Hydra-Matic	3.08	3.23
335 hp (H.O.)	3- or 4-speed	3.36	3.55
	Turbo Hydra-Matic	3.08	3.55
335 hp (Ram Air)	4-speed	3.90	
	Turbo Hydra-Matic	3.90	

3.90 and 4.33 ratios are available on all 3 engines on special order. Be sure to order the close-ratio 4-speed with these axles. Special 4.11 ratio is available dealer installed.

Steering. Manual with recirculating ball gear. Standard ratio is 24:1. The power unit is 17.5:1.

Suspension. Heavy-duty, multiple-leaf springs in the rear, heavy-duty coil springs in front, heavy-duty shocks all around. All standard.

Brakes. Self-adjusting drums. Power front discs available.

Features. All-new suspension with asymmetrically mounted multiple rear leafs smooth out the ride. Wide-oval redlines or whitelines are standard fittings, as is a Hurst shifter and heavy-duty suspension. Among other things, you can order our hood-mounted tach and exclusive new knitted-vinyl upholstery. Don't look for vent windows—a new upper-level ventilation system has made a beautiful disappearing act possible.

Chevelle SS 396

Engines	Standard	Also Available
Horsepower	325 @ 4800	350 @ 5200
Torque	410 @ 3200	415 @ 3400
Type	V-8	V-8
Bore and Stroke	4.094 x 3.76	4.094 x 3.76
Displacement	396	396
Compression Ratio	10.25:1	10.25:1
Carburetion	4-BBL	4-BBL

Capacities. The fuel tank holds 20 gallons. Oil capacity is 4 quarts, 5 with filter.

Transmissions
Standard. Fully synchronized floor-mounted special 3-speed with 2.41, 1.59 and 1.00 ratios.

Also available. Choice of two fully synchronized 4-speeds. Ratios are: 2.52, 1.88, 1.46, 1.00; 2.20, 1.64, 1.27, 1.00.

Powerglide automatic. Ratios are 3.70 to 1.00 range in "Drive," 3.70 to 1.76 range in "Low."

Turbo Hydra-Matic. Maximum torque multiplication ratios are: 5.06 to 1 range in "Drive," 5.06 to 1.48 range in "Low 2," 5.06 to 2.48 range in "Low 1." Selector positions are P-R-3-2-1 with console.

Axle Ratios

Engine	Transmission	Standard	Also Available				
325 hp	Special 3- or 4-speed	3.31*	3.07	3.55	3.73	4.10	
	Powerglide	3.07	2.73	3.31	3.55	3.73	4.10
	Turbo Hydra-Matic	2.73*	2.56	3.07	3.31		
350 hp	Special 3- or 4-speed	3.55*	3.31	3.73	4.10**		
	Powerglide	3.31*	3.07	3.55	3.73	4.10	
	Turbo Hydra-Matic	3.07	2.73	3.31			

*3.07 with air conditioning
**3.07, 4.56, and 4.88 ratios also available with 2.20 4-speed.

Steering. Manual with recirculating ball gear. Standard ratio is 28:1. Power steering is 20.4:1.

Suspension. Special front and rear coil springs and shock absorbers. Special front stabilizer bar. Built-in control of acceleration and braking forces.

Brakes. Self-adjusting, with special linings and finned front drums. Power front discs available.

Features: Special twin-domed hood, body striping, Hide-A-Way wipers, bright engine accents and black accents on grille, lower body and rear panel are standard. Bucket seats, console, special instrumentation and wide accent striping available.

GTO

Engines	Standard	Also Available	
		H.O.	Ram Air
Horsepower	350 @ 5000	360 @ 5100	360 @ 5400
Torque	445 @ 3000	445 @ 3600	445 @ 3800
Type	V-8	V-8	V-8
Bore and Stroke	4.12 x 3.75	4.12 x 3.75	4.12 x 3.75
Displacement	400	400	400
Compression Ratio	10.75:1	10.75:1	10.75:1
Carburetion	4-BBL	4-BBL	4-BBL

Capacities. The gas tank holds 21.5 gallons. The radiator holds 17.8 quarts. Oil capacity is 5 quarts, 6 with filter.

Transmissions
Standard. Fully synchronized heavy-duty 3-speed with Hurst floor shifter. Ratios are: 2.42, 1.61, 1.00.

Also available. Fully synchronized 4-speed with Hurst in two versions: Wide-ratio—2.52, 1.88, 1.46, 1.00. Close-ratio (available only with 3.90 and 4.33 axle ratios)—2.20, 1.64, 1.28, 1.00.

Turbo Hydra-Matic. Ratios are 2.48, 1.48 and 1.00 with a total torque multiplication at the start of 5.70. Governor is set for a maximum automatic upshift of 5000 rpm.

Axle Ratios

Engine	Transmission	Standard	Also Available				
350 hp	3- or 4-spd.	3.55	3.08	3.23**	3.36*	3.90*	4.33*
	Turbo H-M	3.36	2.93**	3.23**	3.55*	3.90*	4.33*
360 hp (H.O.)	3- or 4 spd.	3.55	3.08	3.23**	3.36*	3.90*	4.33*
	Turbo H-M	3.55		3.23**	3.36*	3.90*	4.33*
360 hp (Ram Air)	4 spd	4.33*					
	Turbo H-M	4.33*					

*Air conditioning not available. **Standard ratio with air conditioning. Special 4.11 axle ratio is available, dealer-installed, when car is ordered with heavy-duty 3-speed or close-ratio 4-speed and 3.90 axle ratio.*

Steering. Manual with recirculating ball gear. Standard ratio is 24:1. The power unit is 17.5:1.

Suspension. Heavy-duty coil springs and stabilizer bar are standard. Stiffer shocks available.

Brakes. Self-adjusting finned drums. Power front discs are available.

Features. Fastrak redlines and whitelines are standard, with Wide-oval redlines available. Standard also are the new and freer breathing combustion chambers, big exhaust and intake valves and the exclusive bumper that's the same color as the car, but won't chip, peel or fade. Hood-mounted tach and the Ram Air engine with functional scoops are options worth looking into. Hideaway headlights are extra cost, but the disappearing wipers aren't. Wheelbase is a shortened 112", overall length 200.7".

4-4-2

Engines	Standard	Also Available	
		Force-Air	Turnpike Cruising
Horsepower	350* @ 4800	360 @ 5400	290 @ 4600
Torque	440 @ 3200	440 @ 3600	440 @ 2400
Type	V-8	V-8	V-8
Bore and Stroke	3.87 x 4.25	3.87 x 4.25	3.87 x 4.25
Displacement	400	400	400
Compression Ratio	10.5:1	10.5:1	9.0:1
Carburetion	4-BBL	4-BBL	2-BBL

*325 with Turbo Hydra-Matic

Capacities. 20 gallons in the gas tank, 16.2 quarts in the radiator. Oil capacity is 4 quarts, 5 with filter.

Transmissions
Standard. Fully synchronized heavy-duty 3-speed with Hurst floor shifter. Ratios are: 2.42, 1.61 and 1.00. 4-speed or Turbo Hydra-Matic are required with 360-hp Force-Air Induction System engine.

Also available. Fully synchronized 4-speed with Hurst shifter in two versions: Close ratios are: 2.20, 1.64, 1.28, 1.00. Wide-ratios are: 2.52, 1.88, 1.46, 1.00.

Turbo Hydra-Matic. Ratios are: 2.48, 1.48 and 1.00.

Axle Ratios

Engine	Transmission	Standard	Also Available				
350 hp	3-speed	3.23	3.08	3.42	3.91	4.33*	4.66*
	4-speed (close ratio)	3.91	3.42	4.33*	4.66*		
	4-speed (wide ratio)	3.42	3.08	3.23	3.42		
325 hp	Turbo Hydra-Matic	3.08	3.23	3.42	3.91	4.33*	4.66*
360 hp	4-speed (close ratio)	4.33	3.42	3.91	[illegible]		
	Turbo Hydra-Matic	3.42	3.91	4.33*	4.66*		
290 hp	Turbo Hydra-Matic	2.56	2.78	3.08			

*Dealer-installed. Not recommended for city or highway use.

Steering. Manual with recirculating ball gear. Standard ratio is 24:1. The power unit is 17.5:1.

Suspension. Heavy-duty coil springs, shocks and front and rear stabilizer bars.

Brakes. Self-adjusting. Power front discs available.

Features. Built-in Combustion Control System keeps the carb air at a constant temperature. Wide-oval, Red-Line, nylon-cord tires standard, with whitewalls available. Strato-bucket seats standard, with sports console available. Distinctive 4-4-2 grille, hood, emblems and G.T. stripes.

GS 400

Engine	Standard
Horsepower	340 @ 5000
Torque	440 @ 3200
Type	V-8
Bore and Stroke	4.04 x 3.90
Displacement	400
Compression Ratio	10.25:1
Carburetion	4-BBL

Capacities. The gas tank holds approximately 20 gallons. Oil capacity is 4 quarts, 5 with filter. The radiator holds 16.17 quarts (16.87 with air conditioning).

Transmissions
Standard. Fully synchronized 3-speed. Ratios are: 2.42, 1.61, 1.00.

Also available. 4-speed with Hurst floor shifter, also fully synchronized in all forward speeds. Ratios are: 2.20, 1.64, 1.28 and 1.00.

Super Turbine. Column-mounted. Ratios: 2.48, 1.48, 1.00 (in "D" range).

Axle Ratios

Engine	Transmission	Standard	Also Available	
340 hp	3- or 4-speed	3.42	3.64	3.91
	Super Turbine	2.93	3.42 3.91	3.64

Steering. Manual with recirculating ball gear. Standard overall ratio is 28.6:1. Power steering is 20.9:1.

Suspension. Heavy-duty coil springs, shocks and stabilizer bar are standard.

Brakes. Self-adjusting finned aluminum drums with cast-iron liners up front, finned drums in the rear. Power front discs are available.

Features. Chassis is all-new for 1968—including a wheelbase shortened 4 inches for greater maneuverability. Features of the new suspension system are a wider front track for quicker handling response and flatter cornering, a new rear geometry designed to reduce road shock and a heavy-duty rear axle for longer, more trouble-free operation.

The more you look, the more our mark of excellence means.

GM
MARK OF EXCELLENCE

All illustrations and specifications are based on latest product information available at time of printing. The right is reserved to make changes without notice in colors, materials, equipment, specifications and models, and also to discontinue models. Some models illustrated or described contain optional, extra-cost equipment. General Motors Corporation, Detroit, Michigan.

***MOTOR TREND:* NOVEMBER '67 AND *CAR CRAFT:* DECEMBER '67**

Buick Division

Should only strong, steely-nerved men be permitted to drive this '64 Wildcat?

Buick Motor Division

The only reason we raise this question is because we're talking about the toughest, meanest, most impatient Wildcat Buick's ever bred. The one with the optional-at-slight-extra-cost Super Wildcat engine. It's Buick's top output V-8 (if you know your engines, nuff said), and here's some inside dope on what makes it so "super." Horsepower—360 at 4400 rpm; displacement—425 cu. in.; compression—10.25:1; torque—465 ft.-lbs. at 2800 rpm; plus a couple of 4-bbl. downdraft carbs. To keep pace with this all fired up V-8, we suggest either the new, instant response Super Turbine 400 automatic or our 4-on-the-floor synchro. Now, do you think you're the "Super Wildcat" type? Find out—at your Buick dealer's. Drive the Wildcat—

above all, it's a Buick

Sports lovers of the world, unite... let's all go Wildcat-ing!

Face it—if you're the rocking chair, watch-it-on-TV type, forget the wild, wild '64 Buick Wildcat. But if you like your action furious and first-hand, Wildcat is for you! You can bark your signals to a regular 325 hp V-8 formation, or really take to the air with a 340* or 360* hp passer. Three scat-back transmissions add to your fun: 3-speed synchromesh; 4-speed synchro stick shift on the floor*, or Buick's new trigger-quick Super Turbine 400 automatic* (very sparing with gas, too!). Four new models: 4-dr. hardtop; 2-dr. sport coupe; 4-dr. sedan; convertible. Give one a workout; see why we say...

*Optional at extra cost.   Buick Motor Division

above all, it's a BUICK!

Buick '65 Buick

An almost impossible thing happened to Riviera on the way to '65. It got even better.

Better? Sure. Flip on the lights—you'll see. The grille over the lights automatically folds away. Inside is better also. Like a den. Wood-covered console. Wood-grained shift control knob. Wood panel on the door. Even a wood-grained steering wheel if you desire. The fireplace is up front, right under the hood, where the mighty 401 cu. in. V-8 rests. Start the engine and you fire up 325-hp. You can make your Riviera even sportier this year, with the Riviera GS packages. (One of which is a firmer suspension. A new "gyro-poise" roll control stops corkscrewing—makes for an unbelievably smooth ride.) Read all about the Gran Sport in this year's edition of the catalog, now on your Buick Dealer's newsstand.

Wouldn't you really rather have a Buick?

Here's the nicest thing anybody has ever written about the Riviera. Horsepower: 325 @ 4400. Torque: 445 @ 2800. Compression ratio: 10.25 to 1. Displacement (cu. ins.): 401. Carburetion: 4-barrel. Transmission: Super Turbine. Rear axle ratio: 3.23.

Buick Motor Division • General Motors Corporation

Buick Motor Division

Son of Gun.
The Skylark Gran Sport.
400 cu. in./325 bhp.

Ever prodded a throttle with 445 lb-ft of torque coiled tightly at the end of it?

Do that with one of these and you can start billing yourself as The Human Cannonball.

A floor-shift, all-synchro 3-speed; heavy-duty suspension; low-restriction dual exhausts; oversize, 7.75 x 14 tires; and a high-performance spread of axle ratios—from 2.78 to 3.73:1.

From the makers of the big-bore, 360-bhp Riviera Gran Sport.

The slightly smaller caliber Skylark GS.

Something between a regular Skylark and the Loch Ness Monster.

The Buick Skylark
Gran Sport

Buick '65 Buick

We changed the Wildcat a lot this year. And you may never be the same again yourself.

There it is. Our Wildcat. '65 version. Consider. None of those cars that flash down the straightaway is prettier than this. So why leave all your fun at the track? The engine has 325-hp. And there's even more for the asking. One of our brutes has 340-hp. Each of the horses comes to a full gallop at 4400 rpm. A four-barrel carburetor makes sure they're fed properly. Another thing. The automatic transmission—a Buick specialty. You can specify the Super Turbine—so sensitive, it responds about as soon as your mind delivers the impulse. And, oh yes, the suspension. No corkscrewing. Buick's new "gyro-poise" roll control sees to that. Plenty of silence, though. Each of the 8 rear bushings is specially tuned. Just like you'd tune your sports car. Say. Wouldn't it be fun to drive one of these babies to Riverside?

Wouldn't you really rather have a Buick?

When you ask for the Wildcat, this is what you can specify:

Engine: Super Wildcat	Carburetion: 2, 4-barrel
Horsepower: 360	Transmission: Super Turbine (automatic)
Torque: 465 @ 2800	or 4-speed synchromesh (manual)
Compression ratio: 10.25 to 1	Rear axle ratio: 3.07 (automatic)
Displacement (cu. ins.): 425	3.42 (manual)

Buick Motor Division • General Motors Corporation

The old grey Buick ain't what she used to be.

There was a time when maybe we didn't build your kind of car.

Times have changed.

There are Buicks coming off our drawing boards these days that would utterly destroy your faith in the established order of sporting machinery.

Tuning is what does it. Not just the engine. The whole car. What we do is take the basic elements of a car—performance, ride, handling, and styling—and tune each to the other so they work together as a balanced unit.

The prime example of our new way of doing things is the 1966 Riviera GS. It's one of our three new Gran Sports (the other two being the Wildcat GS and the Skylark GS.) Designed as a sports coupe—in the fullest sense of the term—it not only had to look the part but it also had to go, ride, and handle in sporting fashion. And, being a Buick, it had to do all this smoothly, quietly, and with a high degree of creature comfort.

Fitted under its long hood is a 425-cubic inch engine with no less than 340 horsepower and 465 lb-ft. of torque. (Which gets laid down on the road via a

limited-slip differential with a choice of three axle ratios—3.23, 3.42, and 3.58:1.) To give you some small idea of our obsession with how well the engine is put together, we even go so far as to pump hot oil into it under pressure to check for leaks. It all feels rather like you had the world's largest precision watch up front. What it feels like when you open the throttle, however, is something else.

That takes care of moving in a straight line. But since interesting corners are the stuff that serious drivers wouldn't care to live without, we've given the Riviera GS a pretty capable suspension system. It's soft enough to smother any rough stuff you might care to throw under it. Yet, because of the suspension geometry and heavy-duty springs and shocks we've used, it's stiff enough at the same time to give you that sporting handling we were talking about a couple of paragraphs back.

If you're more than normally serious about your driving, something else we've got for the Riviera GS ought to please you: an extra-quick 15:1 power steering gear that you can order. (Now that we mention it, the power steering unit itself is standard; the car doesn't come any other way. As a matter of fact,

the Riviera GS' standard equipment list reads like most other cars' extra-cost options.)

Pikes Peak the wrong way. Now for the final part of a sporting machine: the brakes. The power-assisted system on the Riviera GS is made up of 12-inch finned aluminum drums on the front, 12-inch finned cast iron drums on the rear. We tested them by attacking Pikes Peak from the wrong direction, so to speak. Downhill. In Drive range. Over and over and over again.

The power train. Ride and handling. And styling. All tuned to each other. The tuned car.

Anything else you'd like to know? Instruments? A full complement—needles and numbers and dials and all. Seats? You've a choice. Bench seats and bucket seats are standard. Then there's a special notch-back seat you can order that converts from three-across to semi-buckets.

We've heard it said that the perfect car doesn't exist. Well, then, may we offer you the closest thing?

1966 Buick. The tuned car

There are Buicks that would rattle your faith in the established order of sporting machinery. The Skylark GS, for one.

A tachometer is available.

Chromed-steel 14-inch wheels are available. Choice of 7.75 x 14 red-line or whitewall tires at no extra cost. Axle ratios: 2.78, 2.93, 3.36, 3.55, 3.90, 4.30:1 (special order). Positive Traction is included with all performance axles, at extra cost.

The following safety equipment is standard on all Buicks: 2-speed electric wipers and windshield washer; padded dash; padded sun visors; back-up lights; shatter-resistant rear-view mirror; outside rear-view mirror; and front and rear seat belts (which we sure wish you'd buckle).

Notch-back seats that convert into semi-buckets are standard. Bucket seats are available.

The standard engine. Bhp—325 @ 4400. Torque—445 lb-ft @ 2800.

More engine. Extra cost. Bhp—340 @ 4600. Torque—445 lb-ft @ 3200. Carburetion—Quadrajet 4BBL.

Floor-shift all-synchro 3-speed standard. Automatic and close-ratio 4-speed are available.

Heavy-duty springs, shocks, stabilizer bar, and frame are standard. Metallic brake linings and a rear stabilizer bar are available, dealer installed.

**1966 Buick.
The tuned car.**

A howitzer with windshield wipers.
The new Buick Skylark Gran Sport.
400 cu. in./325 bhp.

There is mounting evidence that our engineers have turned into a bunch of performance enthusiasts.

First they stuff the Wildcat full of engine. Then the Riviera Gran Sport. And now this, the Skylark GS, which is almost like having your own, personal-type nuclear deterrent. We've just turned it loose on our dealers. (See the Buick dealers run.)

Aside from all those cubic inches and horses and 445 lb-ft of torque, just what is this thing

that our engineers have unleashed?

It's a pretty sophisticated suspension package, for one thing: Heavy-duty springs and shocks, plus a stabilizer bar that's about twice as stiff as the normal Skylark's. Axle wind-up is snubbed by heavy-duty upper control arm bushings.

It's also a floor-shift 3-speed, with all forward gears synchronized. Dual exhausts. A reinforced convertible frame to handle all that extra torque. 7.75x14 tires. All standard equipment.

Want to go the 4-speed route? There's a close-ratio unit available. Axle ratios? They read like this—2.78, 3.08, 3.23, 3.36, 3.55, and 3.73:1.

Well, there's some of the evidence. Performance enthusiasts, that's what they are.

More power to them.

The Buick Skylark
Gran Sport

Your father never told you there'd be Buicks like this.

'67 Buick GS-400. Engine: V-8. Bore & Stroke: 4.040 x 3.900. Horsepower: 340 @ 5000. Max. Torque: 440 lbs/ft @ 3200 rpm. Compression Ratio: 10.25:1. Carburetion: Single, 4bbl. Suspension: Front — Coil Spring and Ball Joint. Rear — Coil Springs. Steering: Recirculating Ball Nut. Wheels: 14-6.00 "JK". Tires: 7.75 x 14. Fuel Capacity: 20 gallons. Transmission type and final drive ratio: Manual 3-speed 3.36. Available are Manual 4-speed 3.36 and Automatic 2.93. Brakes: Duo-Servo. Available are Front Disc brakes. All GM safety features are standard.

GM

BUICK MOTOR DIVISION

LIFE: FEBRUARY '65. WHAT A DESCRIPTIVE STATEMENT FOR A MUSCLE CAR—A HOWITZER WITH WINDSHIELD WIPERS!

GS-400 comes with a 400-cubic-inch, 4-barrel, 340-hp., V-8. If you like a responsive car, we're talking your language.

Buick makes all kinds of cars because there are all kinds of people in this world. So we thought we'd cater to the person who truly gets a thrill out of driving. The GS-400 is our contribution to his hobby.

The springs and shocks are heavy-duty jobs. We also put in a stabilizer bar. The way it handles is hard to describe. You have to experience it firsthand.

All '68 Buicks have the full line of General Motors safety features as standard equipment. For example, an energy absorbing steering column and outside rear view mirror. Wouldn't you really rather have a Buick?

GM

BUICK MOTOR DIVISION   MARK OF EXCELLENCE

Introducing automobiles to light your fire.

From Buick. 1970. The GS. The GS455. The Skylark Sport Coupes.
They're what you've been asking for, right?
Automobiles to really light your fire.
Sweeping, sporty lines. And plenty of performance.
The GS455 (on the right) equipped with a Stage I performance package, has a big 455 cubic-inch 360 horsepower engine with a high-lift cam and a 4-barrel carburetor which breathes through real air-scoops to increase performance. Plus a low backpressure dual exhaust system.
Four on the floor or a three-speed automatic transmission are available. It's up to you.
The GS (on the left) looks sporty, is sporty. Bucket seats are available. And an instrument panel a spaceship would be proud of.
Plus a cooling system that should never overheat and a radio antenna built into the windshield.

And wide-tread fiberglass belted tires. That means more traction and longer wear.
Altogether lots of features to excite you.
But maybe it's the name Buick, with all the goodness and confidence that goes with the name, that lights your fire.
Whatever it is, The Gran Sports and Skylark Sport Coupes from Buick have it.
See the 1970 Buick Light Your Fire Cars.
And light your fire.

Now, wouldn't you really rather have a

1970 Buick.

A sport machine to light your fire.

Get acquainted.
With a car just for you.
The GS 455 Convertible. From Buick 1970.
A machine to spark excitement. And light your fire.
It's sleek, sporty and powerful.
A 455 cubic inch V8 is standard. With four-barrel carbs that breathe through real air-scoops to increase engine performance. Power to carry you along while you chase a strong wind. Say, 350 horsepower.
A 3-speed transmission is mounted on the floor. It's standard. Four on the floor is available. Synchronized in all forward gears. A 3-speed Turbo-Hydramatic is available, too. It's your decision. All are great.
Fiberglass belted tires that are standard on all new Buicks give improved traction during braking, cornering and acceleration; significant increase in tread life; and substantially superior resistance to road hazards. Side guard beam construction is just one of the many features designed for added protection.
The inside story? All comfort and good looks. Beginning with an all vinyl interior. Bucket seats, if you want them. Full carpeting. A control console that's as beautiful as it is functional.
See it.
See all the 1970 light-your-fire Buicks.
Strike up an acquaintance.
This year, Buick will light *your* fire.

Wouldn't you really rather have a **Buick.**

1971. Buick introduces a new set of values.

1971 Buick Riviera GS.

The things people expected out of a performance car a few years ago aren't the same anymore.

They want more than emblems in return for their money. They want more value.

And value is what has led more people to Buick's performance cars every year. A whole new set of values await you in your dealer's showroom now.

Our new Riviera GS is the ultimate in an American luxury performance car. Its styling alone will set a trend. But you want more than that. And we want to give you more.

The Riviera engine.
The new Riviera GS features a big 455 cubic-inch V-8 engine designed to run clean and smooth. We put in improvements like a new time-modulated carburetor choke that will give quicker warm-ups and a more consistent fuel mixture. And we've even added new, exclusive nickel-plated engine exhaust valves for smoother engine operation and longer valve life.

The transmission.
A specially calibrated 3-speed Turbo-Hydramatic 400. The shift lever can be mounted on an available between-the-seats console that is slanted toward the driver for ease of operation.

Suspension and handling.
New, longer wheelbase with improved AccuDrive directional stability system. Full-perimeter frame. Heavy, side-guard beams for added protection. A four-link rear suspension, specifically engineered fiberglass belted, white wall tires, heavy-duty springs and shocks, stabilizer bars and heavy-duty suspension bushings will give you ride and handling without peer. Positive traction differential (3.42 axle ratio standard).

The interior and braking.
More room inside. Even in the trunk. Driver cockpit includes new control center designed around driver for ease and convenience. New brakes have a unique valve that proportions braking force front to rear to help give you quick, smooth, straight-line

stops. Standard equipment includes power front disc brakes, more nimble variable-ratio power steering and, of course, automatic transmission.

MaxTrac. Another Buick first.
We introduced MaxTrac for 1971. And you can order it for the Riviera. Listen to what it does. If you're on the ice or in the snow or in the rain, MaxTrac helps give you cat-like handling ability. A miniature on-board computer does it by controlling the power to the rear wheels to reduce slipping on slick surfaces.

One last point. Study a new Riviera GS in person at your Buick dealer's. Only a Buick Dealer can offer you our new set of values. And we want you to test them against your values. We say we build cars that are something to believe in. So, ask a lot of questions. Until there is only one question left.

Wouldn't you really rather have a Buick.

Something to believe in.

Chevrolet Division

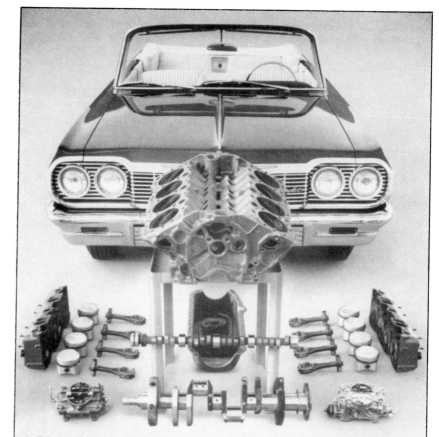

if YOU LIKE PLAYING WITH BLOCKS, TRY THIS. With Chevrolet's Turbo-Fire 409 V8* block you can build to great heights. Say, 340 hp. 400 hp. Or, with the ingredients shown here, 425 hp. All three use the same block. Looks like the Rock of Gibraltar with 409 cubic inches of tunneling punched in it.

For the 425-hp 409 we add all those lovingly machined, cast and forged items above. Twin 4-barrel carburetors. Impact-extruded pistons. Forged steel connecting rods and five-main-bearing crankshaft. Cast alloy iron camshaft. And two heads fitted with lightweight valves. Mechanical valve lifters. Along with things we didn't show—header-type exhaust manifolds, dual exhausts, special clutch and heavy-duty radiator and suspension, among others. For the tamer 340- and 400-hp 409's, we use tamer bits and pieces here and there.

You can tuck a 425-hp Turbo-Fire 409 V8 into any '64 Chevrolet Biscayne, Bel Air, Impala or Impala Super Sport. And choose low gear ratios of 2.56:1 or 2.20:1 with the 4-speed all-synchro shift*. With the 2.20:1 gear ratio you can get 4.11:1 or 4.56:1 Positraction High Performance axle ratios*. Isn't playing with blocks fun?... Chevrolet Division of General Motors, Detroit, Michigan.

*Optional at extra cost

CHEVROLET

MOTOR TREND: MARCH '64 AND *POPULAR MECHANICS:* MAY '64

CHEVELLE IS THE CAR

THAT'S MADE BY THE PEOPLE

WHO MAKE THE CORVAIR AND CORVETTE—Meet the Chevelle Malibu Super Sport. Chevelle is Chevrolet's dapper new package—115-inch wheelbase, separate perimeter-type frame, supple Full Coil suspension, and crisp, tasteful styling. Malibu Super Sport is the series, very strong on elegance, that charges Chevelle with a flavor you can trace right back to the Corvair and Corvette. In a word, sporting. It includes bucket front seats, all-vinyl interior trim, special instrumentation (oil and water temperature gauges and ammeter), and Super Sport wheel disks, trim and identification. Chevelle's performance options* include all-synchro 4-speed shift, Positraction and sintered-metallic brakes. And a 283-cubic-inch 220-hp V8 with 4-barrel carburetion and dual exhausts. Malibu Super Sports come in Coupe or Convertible versions. Both seem like sports cars until you start piling people and luggage into them. . . . Chevrolet Division of General Motors, Detroit, Michigan.

CHEVROLET

*Optional at extra cost.

YOU COULDN'T GET AN AUTOMATIC IF YOU TRIED—Which leaves you holding a stick shift. A happy fix to be in; Spyders respond best to brisk stirring motions with the right hand—either 3- or 4-speed* Synchro-Mesh. And no wonder, with a 150-hp Turbocharged Six behind you and a 6,000-rpm tach before your eyes.

Some things the Spyder gives you that others don't: special brushed chrome instrument cluster with manifold pressure and cylinder head temperature gauges plus the tachometer. Special trim and interior appointments. Chromed accents in the engine compartment. And options* such as Positraction and wire wheels.

For those who just can't live without an automatic, Powerglide* can be had in the Monza, 700 and 500 series. Not the Spyder, though; that's strictly a case of stick with us and you'll go places. Chevrolet Division of General Motors, Detroit, Michigan. *Optional at extra cost

CORVAIR MONZA SPYDER by CHEVROLET **CHEVROLET**

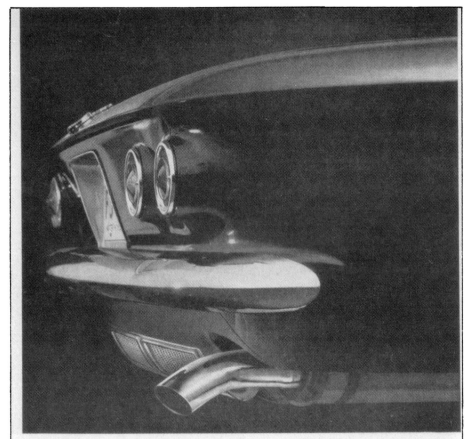

FROM THE TOP OF THE FAMOUS TURBOCHARGER, OVERLOOKING THE AIR-COOLED ENGINE ROOM, WE BRING YOU THE EXHAUSTIVE MUSIC OF CORVAIR MONZA SPYDER AND THE FLAT SIX! Sometimes a big mouth pays off. ◇ The Corvair Monza Spyder's tailpipe has a wider diameter than other Corvairs and most sports cars. It helps performance by more efficient exhausting of gases from the 150-hp Turbocharged Spyder engine. ◇ So it's practical. But we don't kid ourselves. It looks good. And it makes a throaty growl that pleases people with a feeling for such things. ◇ We don't kid ourselves about the rest of the Corvair Spyder either. It pleases people for the same reasons as the tailpipe. Practical design that means effective performance. ◇ Like any machine that does its job well, the Corvair Spyder looks right. And feels right. And works right. ◇ And sounds right. . . . Chevrolet Division of General Motors, Detroit, Michigan.

CORVAIR MONZA SPYDER by CHEVROLET

Just a minute! That's a '64 Corvette Sting Ray those two deserted to go perch on an everyday old rock and gaze at the piney woods! Ah well, love is seldom rational. Saner souls would harken to Corvette's windswept '64 styling, clean as the Sport Coupe's new one-piece rear window. They'd take to that dressed-up interior—new simulated walnut-rim steering wheel, new instrument faces, redesigned center console, an interior ventilator in Sport Coupe models to boost air circulation. People with both feet on the ground would hoist them aboard to sample Corvette's quieter, smoother ride; the muffled thunder of a V8 in one of four versions up to 375 hp*; or the joys of a new 4-speed manual transmission*, improved standard 3-speed or Powerglide automatic*. Clear thinkers know there are two Corvettes, the Sport Coupe above and the Convertible, plus a long list of comfort, convenience and performance options. No use telling all this to that Sweet Young Thing and her swain. Anyway, *you're* the one that we—and your Chevrolet dealer—are really interested in. . . . Chevrolet Division of General Motors, Detroit, Michigan.   *OPTIONAL AT EXTRA COST

'64 CORVETTE STING RAY BY CHEVROLET

IF THE '63 CORVETTE STING RAY WAS SO GOOD,   WHY DID WE CHANGE IT FOR '64?

Almost nothing is so good it can't be improved—and the '64 Corvette Sting Ray proves it.

That slippery aerodynamic shape is smoother. A broad sweep of glass gives the Sport Coupe's rear window better visibility. The cockpit enjoys new touches, from a simulated walnut-rim steering wheel to the Sport Coupe's interior ventilator that boosts air circulation.

Corvette's ride is as taut as ever. Suspension refinements give it supple new comfort in city driving. We shut out road noise and shock with extra sound-deadening materials, new body and transmission mounts. And kept Corvette's roar alive with a choice of V8's from 250 up to 375 hp*. Added a smoother new 4-speed shift* (plus quieter standard 3-speed and optional-at-extra-cost Powerglide) and new ratios.

We rested on our laurels with 4-wheel fully independent suspension and features like fully retractable headlights. Kept both Sport Coupe and Convertible models while spicing up both comfort and performance options.

All these changes make Corvette an even better car for '64. What better reason to change it?

Chevrolet Division of General Motors, Detroit, Michigan.

'64 CORVETTE STING RAY

CHEVROLET

*Optional at extra cost.

'65 Chevrolet
Impala SS Coupe

'65 Chevelle
Malibu SS Coupe

'65 Corvair
Corsa Sport Coupe

'65 Chevy II
Nova SS Coupe

Chevrolet just invented the High-Performance Coupe. Four of 'em for '65.

The all-new Chevrolet wraps super-sudden performance in candy-apple luxury. The Corvair is so new—from nuance to nuts and bolts—that it's a different driving experience. The Chevelle doesn't hold back on anything but the cost. And the Chevy II has been turned into the most powerful tightwad in town!

Looks alone put the 1965 Chevrolet at the head of the class. But that's just the start of the story. Inside, outside, top to bottom, it's a new kind of car. Lower. Longer. Solider. Sleeker. Absolutely luxurious. And you can order just the kind of performance you want, clear up to 409 cubic inches of storming V8. Yep. Four-o-nine.

Meanwhile, goodies, from the ground up. New chassis, new suspension, new body, and features out the exhaust pipe. Curved glass side windows, 15 exterior colors, 8 interiors, front bucket seats in the Super Sport. The inside's as rich as the outside; it's the most luxurious Chevrolet we've ever built.

'65 Corvair

Wait'll the guys who always wait till next year see this. A completely new rear suspension puts the handling on a par with the new international styling. Quicker steering, sharper shift linkage, bigger brakes, and wider tread add to the cat-quick response of rear engine and 4-wheel independent suspension. And for the Corsa, you can order up to 180 horsepower. *Turbo-Charged.*

That's right, Corsa. The car's so sharp, there's now a whole new top-of-the-line series. But throughout the line, you get more room inside, hardtop styling outside and all-around engineering excellence underneath. And there are seven models of the little dear to choose from!

'65 Chevelle

Last year's success story gets a new scenario — we made enough changes in the '65 Chevelle to make it feel like another whole new car from Chevrolet. New ride, new style, and an engine that'll turn your train of thought around — in case you weren't a Chevelle convert last year, now you can order up to 300 hp of soul-cleansing V8.

All of which is wrapped up in a Fisher body with extra insulation, and hung on a new ride that's as smooth and quiet as ice-skating.

Twelve Chevelles to choose from, including Super Sports that are the epitome of everything. And wait'll you try on traffic in its handy size.

'65 Chevy II

If you need proof that this one is a swinger, try it with the 300 hp club. That's right. You can specify a '65 Chevy II with a 327-cubic-inch V8 that puts out 300 bhp. And when you do, you've specified yourself one thrilling automobile.

Underlying it, though, are those wonderful things that've made Chevy II such a tightwad these past years. A battery-saving Delcotron generator. Self-adjusting brakes. Rust-resisting rocker panels. The works.

Let your Chevrolet dealer show you how the 1965 Chevy II's turned into the most exciting tightwad in town. . . . Chevrolet Division of General Motors, Detroit, Michigan.

Irresistible model shown, '65 Chevrolet Impala Sport Coupe

Irresistible force—in an irresistible object
'65 CHEVROLET 409

Order a Chevrolet and ponder some irresistible choices, too.

Like our 409-cubic-inch V8 — which we'll tuck under any '65 Chevrolet at your request. (You could tuck it under Mount Rushmore and all that molten torque would make itself known.)

For '65, the 409 comes in two powerful forms: 340 hp (4-barrel carburetor, hydraulic lifters, 10.0:1 compression ratio) and 400 hp (aluminum 4-barrel, mechanical lifters, 11.0:1 compression ratio). Both have a larger, more durable clutch. And you can specify Delcotronic full-transistor ignition for either.

For the 409, we offer 409-style equipment: you can order 4-Speed Synchro-Mesh, Positraction, metallic brake linings and with the 340-hp version even special front and rear suspension.

The 409 makes the switch to the bigger, heftier '65 Chevrolet like it was born there. Leaving you with one problem—deciding which Chevrolet to put it in.

Don't you wish you had more problems like that?

Chevrolet Division of General Motors, Detroit, Michigan

The 1955 Chevrolet V8 revised everyone's idea of what a production engine can do. Here we go again, Charlie.

TURBO-JET 396 V8

Every once in a while, in engine design, something special happens.

Technological advancement, and pure research, and engineering skill all happen to reach the same peak at the same time. The result is an engine that stands head-and-shoulders above all the rest, that clearly exceeds what the public can ordinarily hope for.

That's what happened with the Chevrolet 265-cubic-inch V8 of 1955, which became the 283, and on which the 327 is based. Everyone knows about those great engines.

And that's what happened with this one. You're going to see a lot of it.

The official name is Turbo-Jet 396 V8.

A new generation of engines begins right here.

396 cubic inches. 4.094 x 3.76 bore and stroke. 325 bhp at 4800 rpm, with 410 lb-ft of torque at 3200 rpm. From hydraulic valve lifters and one 4-bbl. carburetor. There's also a 425-horsepower version. (That's 1.073 hp per cubic inch in specific output.) Either is available in any Impala model.

This new power comes from very high volumetric efficiency, from a particularly advanced head design. Separately mounted rocker arms allow individually located valves, inlet ports, exhaust ports and precisely right combustion chamber design for remarkably good breathing characteristics. The engine breathes well, reacts quickly, and will provide durability of the sort that people have come to expect from Chevrolet.

Just try one, and see how we've understated the case. Chevrolet Division of General Motors, Detroit, Michigan.

Shown below—the neatest squelch of all, the Chevelle Malibu SS Coupe

350-hp CHEVELLE by Chevrolet, the perfect squelch

That's a potent squelch to all those others who keep talking about lions, tigers and such.

A 350-hp squelch goes into any '65 Chevelle you specify. It's that big blue-jowled 327-cubic-inch V8 of song and story, fortified with an extra helping of brute in the form of 11.0:1 compression ratio, big 4-bbl. carb, dual exhausts and 360 ft.-lbs. of torque

at 3600 rpm. With *hydraulic lifters.*

Then, too, you can order a 4-speed fully synchronized transmission. A beefier special front and rear suspension package. Sintered-metallic brakes. Positraction with 3.31:1 axle ratio. And an electric tach.

All this performance would go great in a heavyweight. Just run your imagination over what it does for the

welterweight Chevelle. Not to mention the silencing effect on all those tigers and tamers.

But why rub it in? That's your privilege. Happy squelching.

Chevrolet Division of General Motors, Detroit, Michigan

TURBO-JET 427 V8

do not tease

'66 Chevrolet Impala SS Coupe—new standard safety package includes outside rearview mirror. Always check it before passing.

Poke the gas pedal of this new Chevrolet Turbo-Jet V8 and you get action. A full 427 cubic inches of it.

Its advanced design, with tilted valves and deep-breathing ports, sees to that.

Say you choose to cage it in that bucket-seated Impala SS above (it's

available in 18 other Chevrolets too). You can order it with hydraulic lifters and an output of 390 hp. Or you can order a version with special-performance camshaft, solid lifters — and 425 hp.

Either way, you get higher rate front and rear springs, heavy-duty

shocks all around and 8.25 x 14 tires as part of the Turbo-Jet 427 package.

Sound like a lot of machine? As any road will show you; it's the most.

SS 396 Sport Coupe with front and rear seat belts standard. One of eight safety features we put there for you to use. So do.

Now that you mention it, yes, it does look lean and hungry..

This is an SS 396, a Chevelle that's swallowed a snootful of Turbo-Jet V8—396 cubic inches of it—with ratings of 325, 360 or 375 horsepower. The 325 rating is standard; the other two you have to specify because they cost extra. But it bears mentioning at this point that the 375-horsepower job endows the SS 396 with a power-to-weight ratio of 9.4 to 1. And that, performance fans, is hardly what you'd call unimpressive.

Of special interest, too, is the fact that every SS 396 swings right from the factory with stiffer springs and shocks, a bigger front stabilizer bar, special frame reinforcements and a set of red stripe tires on wide-base wheels.

Know what? You're beginning to look a bit lean and hungry yourself. Do drive an SS 396 at your Chevrolet dealer's.

Performance The Chevrolet Way GM

SS 396: More than just a straight-line machine.

Personally, we don't like the idea of a car that goes like a bird when the road's like a ruler, and then turns chicken every time it has to change direction. What's more, we don't think you do either. Be assured, we gave every SS 396 an engine — a 325-hp 396-cu.-in. Turbo-Jet V8, with 360- and 375-hp versions on order. That wasn't all. We gave it a suspension, too.

Stiffer coil springs and shocks at all four corners came first. Next, a stiffer anti-sway bar at the front and special frame reinforcements at the back. Then a set of 7.75 x 14 red stripe tires and a fully synchronized 3-speed transmission with floor-mounted shift.

By the time we were finished, we knew we had your kind of machine; a machine that you could use to demonstrate the techniques of safe precision driving to others. The final touch was to paint the grillework black and add two businesslike scoops to the hood. After all, this was a machine with a purpose. What we did was give it a purposeful look.

'66 CHEVELLE SS 396 by **CHEVROLET** CHEVROLET

Chevelle SS 396. And the SS doesn't stand for "Standing Still."

Nosiree. Any time we take a trim package like Chevelle and equip it with a 396-cubic-inch Turbo-Jet V8, the effect is anything but static. 325 hp is standard; 360 costs a bit extra, as does 375, which is tops. They all swing though. Some just more than others.

But then we take this same specially powered Chevelle, give it stiffer springs and shocks, red stripe

tires and a floor-operated 3-speed, and—voila!—you've got handling that'll send you in search of the nearest winding road.

Finally we add a hood with two sinewy bulges in it and a jet black grille, just for looks. Temptation just struck, eh? Find out what an SS 396 can mean to you at your Chevrolet dealer's.

Exhilarating The Chevrolet Way

super hooded Super Sport SS 427

Gentlemen, we have before us one very special automobile: Chevrolet's new SS 427. That big bulging hood? We'll level with you. It's there to tell the world that there's something very special underneath: a 427-cubic-inch 385-horsepower Turbo-Jet V8 with porcupine heads, angled valves, dual exhaust and 4-barrel carb.

Special springs, shocks and stabilizer bar are part of the package. So are special markings and red stripe tires. You can add 4-speaker stereo, front fender lights, set-and-forget air conditioning, special instrumentation, whatever you like. SS 427: just the ticket for the sporting man who likes some room to move around in.

SS 427 Sport Coupe: a swashbuckling new species of Chevrolet

Chevrolet gives you that sure feeling

We brag right out on the grille

But shucks, it's nothing any red-blooded American car wouldn't do if it had a set of specs like ours. Take a look.

The Turbo-Jet 396 V8 is standard with 325 horsepower. So are the stick shift, fat red stripe tires on 14 by 6 rims and special handling package of oversize stabilizer bar and special springs and shocks.

The SS 396 looks special, too, with louver-styled hood and black rear body panel. Oh, and there are SS 396 emblems, including the one in the center of that big black grille.

From there on it's just you and the catalog, with choices like a 350-horsepower version of the 396 V8, front disc brakes, Superlift shocks, 4-speed stick shift or the 3-speed Turbo Hydra-Matic, console and lots more. Take your pick.

'67 Chevelle

Chevelle SS 396 Sport Coupe with four-way hazard warning flasher standard for your added safety.

CHEVROLET GM
MARK OF EXCELLENCE

Well done . . . with everything

Pile on the goodies and build your El Camino into the sweetest two-seater ever to make the scene. Add anything from vinyl roof above to broadloom below. Play it cool with air conditioning, tach, power windows and the like. Power it the way you want—from two Sixes and five V8's ranging up to 350 horses. And trigger it with one of four manual or two automatic transmissions.

When you're through, you'll have to check the sticker to know it's not an SS 396 inside. Yet outside, you'll have a hardworking hauler that'll pull its freight—up to half a ton. You select the sensational—Chevy provides the safety elements. Items like a new dual master cylinder brake system, new GM-developed energy-absorbing steering column and many others. See your Chevy dealer for details. . . . Chevrolet Division of General Motors, Detroit, Michigan.

CHEVROLET

El Camino

Deuces wild!

Talk about a winning hand! Three deuces to a full-house 427, the Turbo-Jet V8's got it, cold. And that's precisely what Corvette offers, among other things, in the new '67 Sting Ray. In fact, you can order it two ways: 400 horsepower with hydraulic lifters or 435 horses with solid lifters and a real special performance camshaft.

On the other hand, you traditionalists can still get the 427 V8 with a big four-barrel on top, putting out 390 horses. The whole works comes with that well-known Corvette independent rear suspension, 11¾-inch disc brakes all around, new 1967 styling touches and comforts galore. And it has safety features like the GM-developed energy-absorbing steering column and seat belts with pushbutton buckles, standard.

Take the base 300-horsepower Turbo-Fire 327 V8 or order any of the other four engines available. Decide on the extras, like AM-FM radio, you can add. Choose the standard three-speed or Powerglide or the four-speed gearbox you can order. Shuffle up the equipment the way you want it, and deal yourself a Sting Ray.

'67 Corvette

Corvette Sting Ray Sport Coupe with passenger-guard door locks standard for added safety

GM

CHEVROLET

'67 Corvette

Corvette Sting Ray Convertible with GM-developed energy-absorbing steering column, padded sun visors and windshield washer standard.

GM

Good second hand car.

Go ahead. Match the Corvette Sting Ray against the second hand. Put it through its paces the way you think a car like this one ought to be tried. Then come talk to us about sports cars.

Tell us of another sports car with Corvette's combination of comfort, convenience and pure performance.

Tell us of another sports car you can tailor so exactly to your desires—five engines, three transmissions, axle ratios from here to there and back again. And there are two different models. Mix to suit yourself.

Show us another luxury sports car—even at twice Corvette's price—that can stop a watch the way the Sting Ray can. Go ahead. Tell us.

If you can.

CHEVROLET

CAR AND DRIVER: JANUARY '67. THIS IS AN UNUSUAL AD FOR A CORVETTE. ITS NORMAL 'SELL' OF A REFINED SPORTS CAR IS SWITCHED TO EMPHASIZE THE RAW POWER-EQUIPMENT IT CAN POSSESS AS A MUSCLE CAR.

CAR AND DRIVER: DECEMBER '66

"If you ask me, the best GT/sports car over 3000cc is Corvette."
—6,815 readers of Car and Driver magazine

In the 1967 *Car and Driver* Readers' Choice Poll, 6,815 automobile aficionados chose Corvette as the best GT/sport machine over 3000cc. Quite an honor, when you consider Corvette was in competition with the greatest marques of Europe.

Not really surprising though, when you consider the long list of Corvette attributes. Like four-wheel ventilated disc brakes, an exclusive independent suspension system, V8s with up to 435 horsepower on order and more posh

than you'd expect to find even in a GT car.

What else can we say, when almost seven thousand car buffs name ours as the world's best in its class, except to compliment them on their good taste?

Corvette

Corvette Sting Ray Convertible

CHEVROLET | GM
MARK OF EXCELLENCE

Meet the masked marvel.

Meet Camaro. Masked because it carries Rally Sport equipment with hideaway headlights. A marvel because it's an SS 350: telltale domed hood, rally stripe and Camaro's biggest V8.

Over 3,200 pounds of driving machine nestled between four fat red-stripe tires, an SS 350 carries the 295-horsepower 350-cubic-

inch V8. So you know it's some other kind of Camaro.

For a suspension, it has special high-rate springs—coil in front, single-leaf in back—and stiffer shocks at all four corners. And with its exceptionally wide 59" tread, we assure you an SS 350 handles the way a sporting machine should.

And for your added safety,

every Camaro—be it SS 350 or not—comes with such protective conveniences as the GM-developed energy-absorbing steering column, dual master cylinder brake system with warning light, folding front seat back latches and shoulder belt anchors. Try one on at your Chevrolet dealer's. It's a ball-and-a-half.

GM
MARK OF EXCELLENCE

Command Performance

Camaro By Chevrolet
CHEVROLET

Nova SS

Chevelle SS

Impala SS

Camaro SS

Chevrolet Sports Dept.

We'll bet you didn't know that nobody makes as many different kinds of sports models as Chevrolet does.

What's nice about this is that you can come to just one place, Chevrolet's Sports Department, and sample anything from a family-size Impala to a couple-size Corvette.

And, as you can see, we don't reserve the performance and handling glories for coupes alone. Chevrolet convertibles can also be outfitted with engines up to 427 cubic inches, tach and 4-speed, taut suspension and domed hood. With *complete* Super Sport equipment.

To put together one good performance model is no trick. But to build as many different kinds as you see here—ah, now that's our department. Main floor, at your Chevrolet dealer's.

CHEVROLET Be smart. Be sure. Buy now at your Chevrolet dealer's.

GM
MARK OF EXCELLENCE

How much Camaro you want depends on how much driver you want to be.

Top:
Camaro-about-town. The sport coupe. Buckets. Carpeting. Fully synchronized 3-speed. Very civilized Six. Safety features like dual master cylinder brake system with warning light. Especially nice for wife-types.

Center:
Country-club Camaro. Rally Sport with hideaway head-lights and standard V8, 210 hp. Add custom interior, Powerglide, console, wheel covers, vinyl roof cover, stereo tape system. Decorate right front seat suitably.

Bottom:
Camaro the Magnificent. SS convertible, now available with 396 cu. in., 325 hp! Bulging hood, striped nose, red stripe tires all come. You order the 4-speed, front disc brakes, Positraction and such. At your Chevrolet dealer's.

 Command Performance CHEVROLET Camaro

GM MARK OF EXCELLENCE

Aerodynamic duo

Front: Camaro SS Sport Coupe. Rear: Corvette Sting Ray Coupe.

GM MARK OF EXCELLENCE

They're two of a kind. The fantastic, low-slung Corvette Sting Ray. And Camaro, The Hugger, the only car that comes even close. In styling, in handling, in performance. Both are aerodynamic from nose to deck, with Astro Ventilation, full door-glass styling, bucket seats, refined suspension and 327-cu.-in. standard V8s. You can order Vettes all the way up to 435 hp in a 427-cu.-in. Turbo-Jet V8. Camaros score almost as high: Cubes — 396, Horses — 325. Corvette's a tough act to follow. Buckle up a Camaro and see what we've done for an encore.

Camaro '68 CHEVROLET Corvette

Tough act to follow.

We raised the curtain on Corvette 15 years ago. It has enjoyed the role as America's only true production sports car ever since. Unchallenged. With that lean aerodynamic profile and credits like four-wheel disc brakes, a fully independent suspension system and V8 choices that deliver up to 435 horsepower, it's no wonder. Try one.

Corvette Sting Ray Coupe

Encore!

Then try Camaro. You'll get plenty of Corvette excitement. From the way Camaro looks to its road-hugging ride to its Astro Ventilation to V8s you can order all the way up to 325 horsepower. How do you follow an act like Corvette? Camaro. The Hugger. Produced and directed by Chevrolet.

CHEVROLET

Camaro SS Coupe

Corvette Sting Ray Convertible and Camaro SS Convertible.

Camaro hugs the road with the best of them.

If you've ever driven a Corvette Sting Ray, you know what handling's all about. About as precise and steady and smooth as they come, right? Never a question *who's* driving *what*. Trouble was, after one ride in a 'Vette nothing else quite measured up. Not until Camaro came along. If you've never driven "The Hugger," you're in for a big surprise. From the way it sticks to the pavement to the way it straightens a curve, you know this one's got Corvette's sporting heritage. Go on! Let a '68 Camaro do its stuff. Even if you've never driven a Corvette.

'68 Camaro **CHEVROLET** Corvette

Be smart! Be sure! Buy now at your Chevrolet dealer's.

It'd be a big mover on looks alone.

It's domed. It's striped. It's got bulges on its bulges. It's SS 396, boss of the Quick-Size Chevelles. But don't let all the niceties fool you. Underneath, it's got everything you need for your kind of driving. 396 cubic inches, beefed-up shocks and springs, wide oval treads, the whole thing. With credentials like that, you could get along nicely without the glittering goodies. You *could*, but why play it down when you're living it up?

Chevelle SS 396

Be smart. Be sure. Buy now at your Chevrolet dealer's. **CHEVROLET**

Chevelle SS 396 Sport Coupe

Closest thing to a Corvette yet.

Special order Z/28 and you get a Camaro that comes on like Corvette... for a lot less.

Dual exhausts with 2¼" diameter pipes and deep tone mufflers.

3.73 rear axle. (Ratios up to 4.88 available when you specify Positraction.)

Big, bold stereo rally stripes. (No mechanical function, but having great psychological value.)

Air spoiler available on request.

Special suspension system, including multi-leaf rear springs with bias-mounted shocks.

15" x 6" wheels and E70 x 15 special nylon cord "Wide Tread GT" high-performance tires.

Limited production 302-cu.-in. V8. 4.0 bore, 3.0 stroke. 11.0:1 compression ratio. 290 rated bhp at 5800 rpm. 290 rated torque at 4200 rpm. Carburetion: 1x4 Holley rated 800 cfm mounted on special tuned aluminum manifold. Special cam. Solid lifters. Curb weight: 3220 lb.

Heavy-duty radiator. Temperature-controlled fan with dual pulleys for fan and water pump.

4-speed and power disc brakes for you to order.

21.4:1 quick-ratio steering. 17.9:1 fast ratio also available.

The Z/28 CAMARO **CHEVROLET**

SPORTS ILLUSTRATED: MAY '68 AND *MOTOR TREND:* MARCH '68

CAR AND DRIVER: MAY '68

The "convertible" coupe

Look, it's the 1968 Corvette Sting Ray Coupe: sleek, snug, sporty. Look again. Now, with the roof panels off, it's open to the sun, the sky, the air. This "convertible" feature is standard on the new Sting Ray Coupe, as are hidden headlights, concealed wipers, rear-deck spoiler and a cockpit that's impeccably comfortable yet utterly functional. Standard, too: fully independent suspension, four-wheel disc brakes, 300 hp and Corvette's taut, precise sports-car handling. Sting Ray for 1968 at your Chevrolet dealer's.

'68 Corvette by Chevrolet

CHEVROLET

Removable roof sections stow behind seat, along with the detachable glass rear window. Opened up, Corvette's a "convertible." Buttoned up, it's a coupe. More than ever, it's one-of-a-kind.

GM
MARK OF EXCELLENCE

Did you expect anything less from The Leader?

Anything less than an astonishingly beautiful sports car seven inches longer and nearly two inches lower, with windshield wipers concealed by a power-operated cowl, rear deck spoiler and high-backed bucket seats. Anything less than Astro Ventilation, a new air-intake and pressure-relief system.

Anything less than four-wheel disc brakes and fully independent suspension.

Anything less than V8s you order up to 435 hp. Anything less than new security features like side marker lights and many more.

The '68 Corvette Sting Ray.

What else would you expect from Chevrolet?

'68 Corvette

Chevy II Nova SS

The equal to cars known for their looks. The equal to cars known for their road-holding rides. The equal to cars known for their performance. The equal to cars known for their quietness.

The very low-priced Nova is a great way to stay equal with people who, for some reason, spend a lot more for a car. So, be smart. Be sure. Buy now at your Chevrolet dealer's.

Nova, the great equalizer

from Chevrolet CHEVROLET

1968 Chevelle SS 396, Camaro SS, Corvette Sting Ray Convertible. You can buy a 1968 car anywhere, but you'll have to see your Chevy dealer to buy the new ones.

Chevrolet stays in first place for a lot of reasons...here're three for a start

Triple-threat performance from The Leader for 1968! *Balanced* performance, in a selection of sizes and models made for the most demanding enthusiast. More axle ratios to choose from, new transmission availability, new comforts like Astro Ventilation, new safety features like energy-absorbing front seat backs.

CHEVELLE SS 396: So smooth, so quiet, so luxurious that a little old lady could drive it and never know that it's the king of the mid-size cars. Sport coupe or convertible, the basic machine has a new frame, wider tread front and rear, refined rear suspension and styling that'll knock your eye out. Start from there and add the other features you want—anything from rally wheels and Turbo Hydra-Matic 3-speed automatic transmission to stereo tape and air conditioning —and you just made every other car on the street ancient history.

CAMARO SS: There's a 350-cubic-inch V8 for the man who just wants the best in town, a 396 for the one who won't settle for anything but the best there is. Improved rear suspension helps put all the power on the road, too. We'll surround your engine with a coupe or convertible body, red stripe wide-oval tires, give it a special hood and special SS markings; and you'll know instantly why "The Hugger" is so far ahead of its field.

CORVETTE STING RAY: Everybody's automotive advertising has a lot of performance and excitement and startling innovations these days, but Chevrolet just puts it in the cars—like this one. One look tells you it's the far-out-front style leader! The convertible is available with soft top, hardtop, or both. It has its own special disappearing headlights and Hide-A-Way windshield wipers, a selection of five V8 engines, ranging from the standard 300 hp to a 435-hp 427 you can order. It's beautiful and it's tough. It's probably the first good reason you've ever had for getting rid of your old one.

'68 CHEVROLET

Nova SS Coupe with Turbo-Jet 396 V8

GM
MARK OF EXCELLENCE

Toughest block on the block

Nova moves with two big V8's for its SS version: one with 350 hp and the other with 375.
Both Turbo-Jet 396's feature four-barrel carburetors, molybdenum-inlaid piston rings, forged steel cranks, aluminum bearings and alloy steel connecting rods.

The ultimate setup offers still more: mechanical lifters, a special cam and a mammoth Holley carb. Compression ratio is an ultra-high 11:1.
And, of course, Chevrolet doesn't just plunk in one of these without setting up a welcoming committee.

Multi-leaf rear springs, dual exhausts, large ring-and-pinion gears and a high-capacity clutch come with these V8's. So do wide ovals.
Nova SS: a quick looking coupe you can order with the toughest block on the block.

CHEVROLET
NOVA SS

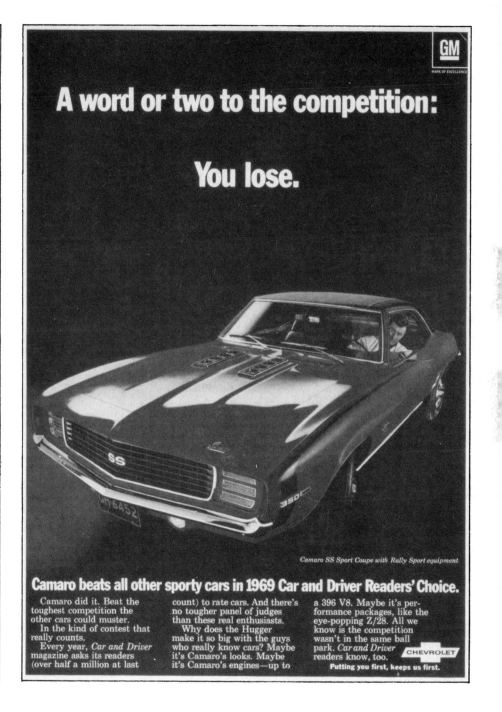

GM
MARK OF EXCELLENCE

A word or two to the competition:

You lose.

Camaro SS Sport Coupe with Rally Sport equipment.

Camaro beats all other sporty cars in 1969 Car and Driver Readers' Choice.

Camaro did it. Beat the toughest competition the other cars could muster.
In the kind of contest that really counts.
Every year, Car and Driver magazine asks its readers (over half a million at last

count) to rate cars. And there's no tougher panel of judges than these real enthusiasts.
Why does the Hugger make it so big with the guys who really know cars? Maybe it's Camaro's looks. Maybe it's Camaro's engines—up to

a 396 V8. Maybe it's performance packages, like the eye-popping Z/28. All we know is the competition wasn't in the same ball park. Car and Driver readers know, too.

CHEVROLET
Putting you first, keeps us first.

We've got a mean streak.

Z/28 Camaro.

The '69 Z/28: So ominous it goes by its code name.

Cubic Inches: 302.

Standard equipment: mechan-ical lifters, high-performance cam and an aluminum intake manifold under a massive Holley 4-barrel.

Underneath: multi-leaf rear springs and heavy-duty shocks.

New for '69 are special white lettered tires on 15 x 7-inch-wide wheels and a Hurst shifter for the 4-speed.

To complete the setup, just add the new 'Vette-type 4-wheel power disc brakes.

By now you know the mean streak isn't just painted on—it's built in.

One more thing. People are bound to ask what the Z stands for.

Tell them "Zap!"

Putting you first, keeps us first.

1970 Chevelle SS 396.

It's getting tougher and tougher to resist.

The standard V8 has been kicked up to 350 hp.

A new air-gulping Cowl Induction Hood awaits your order.

You can also order your choice of a floor-mounted 4-speed or the 3-range Turbo Hydra-matic.

Under that lean and hungry look is a lean and agile suspension. F70 x 14 white-lettered wide oval treads. 7"-wide mag-type wheels. And power disc brakes.

Your mission is to infiltrate your Chevy dealer's and escape with this car.

It will go willingly.

Putting you first, keeps us first.

CHEVROLET On The Move.

In ten seconds, your resistance will self-destruct.

'69 Camaro SS Sport Coupe with RS equipment and new Corvette Coupe

We'll take on any other two cars in the magazine.

Camaro SS, plus Rally Sport.
Black grille.
Undercover headlights with built-in water jets to clean them.
Up to 325 hp on order.
Sport stripes.
Special hood.
Power disc brakes.
Seven-inch rims and wide oval tires made very obvious with raised white lettering.
Head restraints.
New Hurst-linkage 4-speed available.

Can't be driven when steering column is locked.
Usually seen in the company of people who can tell the real article from an imitation.
Known as "The Hugger."
Kin to Corvette.
Corvette, 'Vette, Stingray and other sassy names.
Unusually powerful looking hood.
Morocco-grain vinyl on instrument panel.
New map pockets.

Wider 8-inch wheels.
New assist grips on the doors.
Six bucket seat colors.
New concealed door handles.
Built-in headlight washers.
The driver of this car is always ready with 350 cubic inches of new standard V8.
Other cars, if we were you, we'd drive on the other side of the street.
Way on the other side.

CHEVROLET

Putting you first, keeps us first.

Camaro SS Convertible with Rally Sport equipment and new air intake hood.

Why is the Camaro the pace car again? Because it's *the Hugger.*

Camaro has been named the Official Pace Car in the Indianapolis 500 for the second time in three years— a 50-year record! If you haven't driven the Hugger, take a hint from the guys at Indy. Maybe they know something you don't.

Camaro SS has what it takes. Again this year, it'll lead the pack at Indy.

Engine choices start with a 300-hp 350-cu.-in. V8 and run up through a 325-hp 396-cu.-in. job. There's even a new hood you can order with a super scoop intake that opens on acceleration, ramming cooler air into the engine for more power.

This Hugger offers the widest tread of any sportster at its price. It comes on strong with wide oval tires on 14 x 7-inch-wide wheels and a beefed-up suspension.

The transmission is a special 3-speed floor shift. For those who want still more, there's a 4-speed available with a Hurst shifter.

Indy's tough. So's Camaro SS.

When it comes to pacesetting, Camaro knows its way around.

Putting you first, keeps us first.

The Sleeper Awakes

'69 Chevy Nova SS. Up and at 'em!
Louvers on the front fenders, a bulging hood and a throbbing exhaust note let people know this one's no imitation.
Backing up a standard 300-hp V8 is a muscular foundation: special suspension, an extra-tough clutch, red stripe wide ovals on 7" wide wheels, a special 3-speed and power disc brakes.
The '69 Chevy Nova SS, the car that woke up swinging.

CHEVROLET

Putting you first, keeps us first.

Chevelle SS 396 Sport Coupe

There's a fine line between pure sport and pure luxury.   It's called Chevelle.

Out-and-out sports cars are often thought to be exciting but undisciplined.
On the other hand, luxury automobiles sometimes earn the undeserved reputation of being sluggish and unresponsive.
Is it possible to combine the best of these extremes, while completely eliminating the negatives? Happily, yes.
Chevelle can offer the stimulation of a 396-cubic-inch V8 together with the serenity of a full coil ride on computer selected springs.
And family-size roominess with needle-sharp handling. And a surprisingly rich look with a price that's not too rich for your blood. Beginning to get the idea?
A visit to your Chevrolet dealer's will make Chevelle all the more appealing. Put your sales resistance to the test.

CHEVROLET

Putting you first, keeps us first.

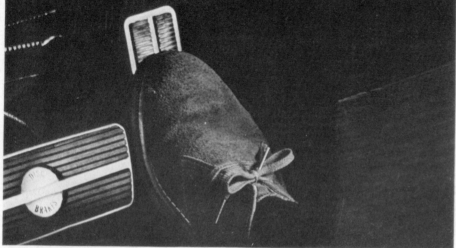

insert foot...

open mouth

Camaro SS Sport Coupe with Rally Sport equipment and Super Scoop hood.

Camaro's new Super Scoop.
Step on the gas and it steps up performance.

We really put our foot in it this time. Brought out a new Super Scoop hood you can order for Camaro SS and Z/28. It opens on acceleration and socks cool air to the carburetor for more power.

Camaro's got a lot of other scoops, too. It hugs the road with the widest tread of any sportster at its price.

It's the only sportster with computer-selected springs.

Bucket seats, Astro Ventilation, full door-glass styling and wall-to-wall carpets are all standard equipment.

With the SS version, you get all this *plus* a big V8, wide oval tires, power disc brakes and a special 3-speed with floor shift.

Your Chevrolet dealer's got the whole story on how the Hugger scoops the competition. Stop in.

See for yourself.

And step on it.

CHEVROLET

Putting you first, keeps us first.

New Camaro Z28

GM
MARK OF EXCELLENCE

Separates the men from the toys.

Remember when you were a kid and you put a lot of trick stuff on your bike to make it look like something it wasn't?

A lot of so-called "sporty cars" still operate that way.

But not this one.

The new Camaro Z28 is as good looking underneath as it is on top.

With a 360-horse Turbo-Fire 350 V8. And with a Hurst shifter that comes along for the ride when you order the 4-speed.

Then there's the suspension that lets you feel the road without feeling the bumps. And the quick ratio steering. And the special wheels with the F60 x 15 tires. And on, and on, and on.

But don't just take our word for it. Pick one up at your Chevy dealer's Sports Department and take it for a road test.

You'll see we're not kidding around.

CHEVROLET

Putting you first, keeps us first.

New Corvette Stingray Coupe

GM
MARK OF EXCELLENCE

Handle with driving gloves.

Some cars you have to handle with kid gloves. Not so with Corvette.

Because under that sleek hull is a sports car capable of handling any road you'd care to put before it.

Behind fat F70 x 15 tires are disc brakes all around. And an advanced fully independent suspension. That glues Corvette down to roads most other cars just can't come to grips with.

Under that long stretch of hood: a standard

300-hp V8. Or order the 350-, 370-, 390- or 460-hp engine. All are backed up by a 4-Speed shift and Positraction rear axle.

And to help you keep tabs on all this, there's an instrument panel that reads out like Apollo 13.

Big tach. Ammeter. Oil pressure gauge. Running light monitors—the works.

Corvette. Go ahead and try one on a road. It fits like a glove.

Putting you first, keeps us first.

Other cars wish the Chevelle SS 396 would hold still long enough for them to catch up.

Other cars wish the 1970 SS 396 hadn't added those 25 more horses to boost its standard V8 to 350 hp.

Other cars wish the SS 396 didn't offer you that new air-gulping Cowl Induction Hood.

Other cars wish the SS 396 didn't offer a 4-speed or a 3-range Turbo Hydra-matic transmission.

And other cars wish the stock SS 396 didn't give you power disc brakes, beefed-up suspension, F70 x 14 white-lettered wide ovals and 7"-wide sport wheels.

Aren't you glad other cars don't have anything to say about it?

On the move.

Chevelle SS 396. Other cars wish we'd keep it this way.

MOTOR TREND: OCTOBER '69. WHAT IMAGINATION CHEVROLET HAD! TYING DOWN ITS 396 CHEVELLE WAS A GREAT WAY TO DRAMATIZE WHAT A HAIRY BEAST IT POSSESSED WITH THIS MODEL.

'70 Corvette. What else.

Here it is. It's not really a whole lot different looking. But in 17 years, we've never changed it just to change it.

And there's one thing that hasn't changed at all.

The Corvette idea.

It's still a car that's built for the person who drives for the sheer excitement of it. For the driver who enjoys the true feel of the road.

Yet, it's still a car you can drive at 10 mph in a traffic jam.

It's still a car you can swing out to the beach in. Or pull up in front of a theater with your girl dressed to the teeth.

No, it isn't a hard-core sports car. There are too many nice things about it.

No, it isn't a luxury car. It was made to perform. And it does just that.

No, it's not the smoothest riding car you'll find. But then again, it won't rattle your bones.

What it is is a new Corvette. It's refined for '70. The 4-Speed is standard. So is tinted glass. There are even a couple of new engines. All the way up to the 460-hp Turbo-Jet 454.

But if we know you, you'll find out all that for yourself.

We just want you to know it's here. And it's one of those few cars that aren't something else.

Putting you first, keeps us first.

See it, Feb. 26th. At your Chevrolet Sports Dept.

CHEVROLET

GM
MARK OF EXCELLENCE

Corvette.
Everything you need is standard except the gas.

In 1953, we set out to build an American sports car because there wasn't one. Little did we know that 19 years later it would still be the only production sports car made in this country.

That's our Corvette. A classic. A legend. A car with as good a reputation as any car in the world.

Like all great cars, Corvette's price might make you stretch your budget a little. But like all great cars, you get a lot for your money. We think you get the *most* for your money in Corvette.

The list of standard equipment is impressive and extensive. A 4-Speed fully synchronized transmission. A 350-cubic-inch V8 with a 4-barrel carb. Disc brakes at all four wheels. Fully independent suspension all the way around. Positraction rear axle.

Full instrumentation including tach, ammeter, oil pressure gauge and temperature gauge.

The list goes on through carpeting, hidden windshield wipers, pop-up headlights and Astro Ventilation.

The point is that Corvette's standards aren't bare necessities. Along with all the excitement, they're the things most people want in a sports car. You might like to order air conditioning, an AM/FM/Stereo radio, leather seats, and a few other extras, but there just aren't too many things you can add to Corvette. When you buy a Corvette, about everything you need is standard . . . except the gas. And even that is no lead, low lead or regular.

Chevrolet

Corvette Convertible with extra-cost hardtop at Great Smoky Mountains National Park.

There's so much to see, make sure you're around to see it. Buckle up.

GM
MARK OF EXCELLENCE

Chevrolet. Building a better way to see the U.S.A.

Have you noticed how legends tend to improve with time?

Corvette, America's only true production sports car for the past 21 years, a legend in its time and yours, now has a handsome new impact-absorbing rear end with a resilient urethane cover. Other 1974 improvements include new exhaust resonators and tail pipes to help soften the sound, new air conditioning outlets for improved air distribution, a wider rearview mirror inside, new color choices inside and out, and a new "Gymkhana" suspension you can order. If you've wanted a Corvette since you were a kid, you've waited long enough.

CHEVROLET MAKES SENSE FOR AMERICA. Chevrolet

A new look.

Same fine feel.

Front discs standard.

Sport Coupe

With Camaro, you can be practical.
Or go bananas.

Z28

Type LT interior.

Deck stripes.

Sport mirrors.

Special Z28 wheels.

If you can restrain yourself when it comes time to order the extras, you can move into a handsome 1974 Camaro Sport Coupe for less money than you might imagine.

That's one approach. Approach "A" we'll call it.

There's also Approach "Z", The renowned Camaro Z28 package. All the basic good things plus a 350 V8 with 4-barrel, a dual exhaust system, special sport suspension, Positraction rear axle, sport mirrors, F60-15 white-lettered tires and more. If you *really* want to go bananas you can add spoilers and those bold new Z28 hood and deck stripes.

(There's a third approach, comfortably in between: Camaro Type LT with its sumptuous interior and other elegant touches.)

Camaro. The way it looks is the way it goes.

Building a better way to see the U.S.A. **Chevrolet**

Oldsmobile Division

Police needed it... Olds built it... Pursuit proved it!

Put this one on your WANTED list!

OLDSMOBILE 4-4-2

4-BARREL CARBURETOR!
4-ON-THE-FLOOR!
DUAL EXHAUSTS!

Now ready to put more muscle and hustle into *your* everyday performance needs! The Olds **4-4-2** —brand new action-tailored F-85 package—delivers 310 h.p. and 355 lb.-ft. of torque from its 4-barrel Jetfire Rocket V-8! Makes life still more exciting with a floor-mounted 4-speed synchromesh transmission, track-tested Red-Line tires, dual exhausts and heavy-duty chassis components—all part of the package!* Ask for details on the all-new **4-4-2**—available in any F-85 V-8 model except station wagons.

Additional special-duty options also available at extra cost.

GET THE FULL STORY!
See your
Local Authorized Oldsmobile
Quality Dealer!

GO OLDS WHERE THE ACTION IS!

OLDSMOBILE DIVISION · GENERAL MOTORS CORPORATION · QUALITY BUILDERS OF THE NINETY-EIGHT, STARFIRE, SUPER 88, DYNAMIC 88, JETSTAR I, JETSTAR 88, F-85

MOTOR TREND AND *HOT ROD:* JULY '64. IS NOTHING SACRED? EVEN THE HOT RODDERS WEREN'T SAFE ANY LONGER ONCE THE POLICE STARTED BUYING 4-4-2 MUSCLE CARS.

Dig the new Olds 425-cu.-in. SUPER ROCKET V-8 ENGINE!

Here's half the picture

Here's the other half

You don't build a hairy mill like this one by looking over your shoulder. You start from scratch. Absolute. Sweat off pounds and bulk with special iron alloys and casting techniques. Add sinew with a forged crank that takes its thrust on the center bearing. The precision of integrally-cast valve guides. Lightweight rocker arms for better lubrication. A wedge-shaped combustion chamber with more potent compression. That's Oldsmobile's new 425-cubic-inch Super Rocket—available in 300-, 310- and 360-bhp., including a regular-gas version.

The 1965 Olds Dynamic 88 with a Super Rocket V-8 tucked under its hood! This powerhouse-on-wheels flattens hills like they were going out of style. Loafs along at turnpike speeds with inches of reserve action under the throttle. Strong claims? You bet they are! And your nearby Olds Dealer is prepared to turn you into a real believer. Make a pit stop soon and pick up the keys to a Dynamic 88 for a remarkable discovery: The whole world isn't standing still when you're bossing a Super Rocket—it only *seems* that way! Oldsmobile Division • General Motors Corp.

'65 OLDS
The Rocket Action Car!

sedate it ain't

400 CID V-8. Full 115-inch wheelbase. Heavy-duty springs, shock absorbers, shaft. Sway bars, front *and rear*. High-performance axle. Dual exhausts. Beefed-up wheels. White-Line or wide-oval Red-Line tires. Bucket seats. Louvered hood. Higher oil pressure. They're all standard goodies at one modest price. Available also, if you wish—Rocket Rally Pac, UHV ignition, superstock wheels, front disc brakes and the like. Put one into action and you'll agree: 1967 Olds 4-4-2 is the sweetest, neatest, completest anti-boredom bundle on rubber!

ENGINEERED FOR EXCITEMENT...TORONADO-STYLE!

Obey Laws Drive Safely. Olds thinks of your safety, too, with GM-developed energy-absorbing steering column that can compress on severe impact up to 8¼ inches; with four-way hazard warning flasher; outside rearview mirror; dual master cylinder brake system; plus many other safety features—all standard!

GM
MARK OF EXCELLENCE

What are those funny things under the bumper?

Air scoops, that's what. Snagging cool air for Oldsmobile's new performance-boosting Force-Air Induction System. It's now available for the first time on all three Cutlass S models (a similar performance package is offered on Cutlass Supreme and F-85 coupes).

Though Cutlass S has plenty of other good things going for it, too. Here's what the specs look like when you equip it with the Force-Air Induction System:

ENGINE
Type	Rocket V-8
Bore x stroke, inches	4.057 x 3.385
Displacement, cubic inches	350
Compression ratio	10.25-to-1
Bhp	320 at 5800 rpm
Torque, lb.-ft.	390 at 4000 rpm
Carburetion	Specially calibrated Quadrajet 4-bbl.

System includes dual air scoops, ducts and hoses; dual-intake air cleaner; extra-large intake and exhaust valves with spring dampers; special high-lift camshaft; special crankshaft vibration damper; specially calibrated distributor; dual exhaust system.

COOLING SYSTEM
Heavy-duty radiator, viscous-drive fan clutch, 6-blade aluminum fan, heavy-duty water pump.

DRIVE TRAIN
Transmission	Heavy-duty, fully synchronized 3-speed floor shift with Hurst Competition Shifter
Clutch	Heavy-duty, 10.5-inch diam.
Rear Axle	3.91-to-1 heavy-duty performance type with h.d. shafts, bearings, differential gears.

Available: 4-on-the-floor (close- or wide-ratio, with Hurst Shifter).

CHASSIS and BODY
Suspension	Four-coil-spring with front stabilizer bar.

Available: Rally Sport Suspension (h.d. springs, shocks, front stabilizer bar).
Steering ratio	24-to-1

Tires	7.75x14"

Blackwall (Std.), Whitewall (available). F70x14", Nylon-Cord Wide-Oval Red-Line Tires are also available.

ALSO AVAILABLE
Anti-Spin Differential. Simulated-wire wheels. Super Stock Wheels. Radial-Ply Whitewalls. Rocket Rally Pac. G.T. pin-striping. Bucket Seats (std. in Convertible). Sports Console. Custom Sport Steering Wheel. Stereo tape player. Others.

GENERAL
Wheelbase	112"
Overall length	201.6"
Overall width	76.2"
Overall height	52.8"
Curb wt. (lb.) Holiday Coupe	3487
Tread	front 59.0", rear 59.0"

SAFETY
And all the new GM safety features are standard, of course.

Olds Cutlass S

DRIVE A YOUNGMOBILE FROM OLDSMOBILE

recreation center

Meet Oldsmobile's new four-wheeled fun machine—swinging 4-4-2! Specs: 400 CID V-8. 115-inch wheelbase. Heavy-duty springs, shock absorbers, shaft. Performance axle. Sway bars, front *and* rear. Dual exhausts. Beefed-up wheels. White-line or wide-oval red-line tires. Buckets. Carpets. Louvered hood. All standard at one modest price. Includes dual master cylinder brake system, full list of important safety features. Can also be equipped with Rocket Rally Pac, UHV ignition, superstock wheels, front disc brakes, console, tach, ski rack and the like. That's Olds 4-4-2—sweetest move on rubber. Make it your move. At your Olds Dealer's.

ENGINEERED FOR EXCITEMENT...TORONADO-STYLE!

OBEY LAWS DRIVE SAFELY

Olds thinks of your safety, too, with GM-developed energy-absorbing steering column that can compress on severe impact up to 8¼ inches; with four-way hazard warning flasher; outside rearview mirror; dual master cylinder brake system; plus many other safety features — all standard!

Olds 4-4-2: Here's what's behind the reputation.

ENGINE

Type	Rocket V-8
Bore x stroke, inches	3.87 x 4.25
Displacement, cubic inches	400
Compression ratio	10.5-to-1
Bhp	350° at 4800 rpm
Torque, lb.-ft.	440 at 3200 rpm
Carburetion	4-bbl.
Exhausts	Dual

Built-in Combustion Control System provides constant carb air temperature.

Availabilities: Force-Air Induction System. 360 bhp at 5400 rpm. Teams with close-ratio 4-on-the-floor transmission or Turbo Hydra-Matic.

Cruising package: Includes 400-CID V-8 with 2-bbl. carb, 290 bhp, 9-to-1 compression, Turbo Hydra-Matic, 2.56-to-1 axle.

°325-hp Rocket 400 V-8 with 4-bbl. carb and 10.5-to-1 compression ratio teams with Turbo Hydra-Matic.

DRIVE TRAIN

Transmission....Fully synchronized, heavy-duty 3-on-the-floor with Hurst Shifter

Availabilities: 4-on-the-floor (close- or wide-ratio with Hurst Shifter) or Turbo Hydra-Matic floor shift.

Prop shaft...............Heavy-duty

Axle ratios....2.56-to-1 up to 4.66-to-1

Availabilities: Heavy-duty axles (H.D. shafts, bearings, differential gears), 3 ratios.

CHASSIS

Suspension..........Heavy-duty. Includes heavy-duty springs and shocks, front and rear stabilizers.

Steering ratio................24-to-1

Wheels...........Heavy-duty 14-inch with extra-wide rims

Tires...........F70 x 14", Nylon-Cord Wide-Oval Red-Lines

OTHER AVAILABILITIES

Power front disc brakes. UHV Transistorized Ignition. Anti-Spin Differential. Rally Stripes. Rally Pac (clock, tach, engine gauges). Sports console. Custom Sport Steering Wheel. Simulated-wire and Super Stock Wheels. Special wheel discs. Others.

GENERAL

Wheelbase	112"
Overall length	201.6"
Overall width	76.2"
Overall height	52.8"
Curb wt. (lb.) Holiday Coupe	3670
Tread	front 59.0", rear 59.0"

SAFETY

All the new GM safety features are standard, including energy-absorbing column, seat belts for all passenger positions.

CARS Magazine names Olds 4-4-2 "Top Performance Car of the Year."

DON'T THROW AWAY THE LUMBER. YOU'LL NEED IT TO CRATE UP AND CART OFF THE COMPETITION. OLDS 4·4·2 W·30

W-30 is more than just a great machine. It's a labor of love.

Every moving, breathing part in its engine is individually selected. And matched. And fitted. To extremely close tolerances.

If a part isn't exactly right? It gets the thumb!

The good doc is just as vehement about handling. No 4-4-2 (W-30 or otherwise) gets out of the laboratory without heavy-duty underpinnings—and stabilizer bars front and rear.

If you've been looking for the one that's got everything, now you know where to find it.

ENGINE

Type . . . . . W-30 Rocket V-8 (available)	
Displacement, cubic inches 400	
Bhp . . . . 360 at 5400 rpm	
Torque, lb.-ft. . . . . 440 at 3600 rpm	

Bore x stroke, inches . . . . 3.87 x 4.25	
Compression ratio 10.5-to-1	
Combustion chamber volume, min. allowable . . . . 79.64 cc	
Min. deck clearance 0.002	
Carburetion . . . . Quadrajet 4-bbl.	
Throttle dia.	
Primary 1.375	
Secondary 2.250	
Camshaft duration	
Intake . . . . 328°	
Exhaust . . . . 328°	
Overlap . . . . 108°	
Total valve lift	
Intake 0.475	
Exhaust 0.475	

Valve diameter	
Intake 2.0625	
Exhaust 1.625	
Tappet type . . . . Hydraulic	
Max. valve spring pressure	
Closed . . . . 128 lbs.	
Crankshaft journal diameter	
Mains 3.00	
Connecting rods 2.50	
Firing order 1-8-4-3-6-5-7-2	

W-30 system includes 26.2-sq.-in. dual front air scoops; wide-throat dual air ducts; dual intake air cleaner; minimum combustion chamber volume; separated center exhaust ports for optimum tuning; streamlined, individually branched exhaust manifold; high-overlap cam; low-friction bearings; dual hood paint patches; and low-restriction dual exhausts.

Standard engines. A 400-cu.-in., 350-hp Rocket V-8 with heavy-duty 3-speed manual. A 400-cu.-in., 325-hp version with Turbo Hydra-matic 400.

DRIVE TRAIN

Transmission . . . . Fully synchronized, heavy-duty 3-on-the-floor with Hurst Shifter. Available: 4-on-the-floor with close- or wide-ratio Hurst Shifter, or Turbo Hydra-matic 400. Special W-30 Turbo Hydra-matic 400 (with high-performance converter, high-rpm shift points, and firmed-up shifts) or close-ratio included with W-30.

8 axle ratios 2.56-to-1,	

2.78-to-1, 3.08-to-1, 3.23-to-1, 3.42-to-1, 3.91-to-1, 4.33-to-1, 4.66-to-1. Availability depending on engine choice.

CHASSIS

Suspension . . . . Heavy-duty. Includes heavy-duty springs and shocks, front and rear stabilizers.

Steering ratio 24-to-1	

Available: 17.5-to-1 with power.	
Wheels . . . . . . Heavy-duty 14-inch with 6-inch rims.	
Tires . . . . F70x14", polyester-cord wide-oval red-lines (or whitewalls).	
Available: F70x14" fiberglass-belted wide-oval red-line or wide-oval black-wall with raised white letters.	

GENERAL

Models . . Holiday Coupe, Sports Coupe, Convertible	
Wheelbase . . . . 112"	
Overall length . . . . 201.9"	
Curb wt. (lb.) Holiday Coupe 3675	
Tread . . . . . front 59.0", rear 59.0"	

SAFETY

New GM safety features are standard, including seat belts for all passenger positions, and new ignition, steering and transmission lock on steering column.

HOT ROD AND *CAR CRAFT*: DECEMBER '68. TWO PAGES FROM AN EIGHT-PAGE AD FOR THE 1969 DR. OLDSMOBILE W-MACHINES.

GM
MARK OF EXCELLENCE

Built like a 1¾-ton watch.

We hover over every 1969 Oldsmobile like a mother hen. But when we get to the 4-4-2, we become downright fanatical.

Critical parts in this precision machine are individually selected. And matched. And fitted. To extremely close tolerances. If a part hasn't got it, it gets the thumb.

Sure, it takes time. But you wind up with a great timepiece.

ENGINE

Type .... Rocket 400 V-8
Bore x stroke, inches ...3.87 x 4.25

Displacement, cubic inches 400
Compression ratio 10.5-to-1
Bhp ....350* at 4800 rpm
Torque, lb.-ft. .....440 at 3200 rpm
Carburetion ....4-bbl.
Exhausts ....Dual
*325-hp Rocket 400 V-8 with 4-bbl. carb and 10.5-to-1 compression ratio standard with Turbo Hydra-matic 400.
Availabilities: Force-Air Induction System (W30). 360 bhp at 5400 rpm. Teams with close-ratio 4-on-the floor transmission or Turbo Hydra-matic 400.
All 4-4-2 engines for 1969 feature individually branched exhaust manifolds for improved tuning and increased performance through entire drive range.

DRIVE TRAIN

Transmission ....Fully synchronized, heavy-duty 3-on-the-floor with Hurst Shifter
Availabilities: 4-on-the-floor (close- or wide-ratio with Hurst Shifter) or Turbo Hydra-matic 400.
8 axle ratios .... 2.56-to-1, 2.78-to-1, 3.08-to-1, 3.23-to-1, 3.42-to-1, 3.91-to-1, 4.33-to-1, 4.66-to-1. (Availability depending on engine selection.)

CHASSIS

Suspension ...Heavy-duty. Includes heavy-duty springs and shocks, front and rear stabilizers.
Steering ratio 24-to-1
Wheels ....Heavy-duty 14-inch with extra-wide rims
Tires ....F70x14", Nylon-Cord Wide-Oval Red-Lines

GENERAL

Wheelbase ....112"
Overall length ....201.9"
Overall width ....76.2"
Overall height ....52.8"
Curb wt. (lb.) Holiday Coupe ...3675
Tread ....front 59.0", rear 59.0"

SAFETY

GM safety features are standard, including seat belts for all passenger positions, and new ignition, steering and transmission lock on steering column.

The 1969 Olds 4-4-2
Make your escape from the ordinary.

SNARLS SOFTLY
AND CARRIES A BIG STICK...

GOOD YEAR

Awesome is the word for it.

You roll up to the light next to the cocky-looking guy in the supercar.

He gives it a couple of blips ... then looks you over.

And you watch the creeping horror of realization hit him.

"That's more than a 4-4-2 ... it's a '69 Hurst/Olds!"

Guys do funny things then.

Some start looking for something under the seat.

Some blow their nose 'til the light changes.

Most just look out the other window and try to pretend they never really blipped at all.

That's half the fun of owning a '69 Hurst/Olds.

The other half is the solid joy of punching that big Hurst Dual/Gate Shifter up through the gears ... feeling those 455 cubic inches grab you ... all to the genteel accompaniment of the silkiest snarl you ever heard. That, sir, is awesome!

SPECIFICATIONS—'69 HURST/OLDS

☐ 455 Cu. In. modified Rocket V-8. Special heads, cam and distributor. ☐ Performance-modified Turbo Hydra-Matic. ☐ Hurst Dual/Gate Shifter and Console. ☐ Force Air Induction. ☐ Power Front Disc Brakes. ☐ Goodyear G60-15 Polyglas™ tires on special 7 inch wheels. ☐ Custom hood scoop, racing mirrors and rear deck spoiler. ☐ Custom paint, striping and H-O emblems. ☐ Air Conditioning, optional.

See your Olds dealer soon. This is a limited-production custom special from Hurst.

HURST / OLDS

Hurst
Performance
Research, Inc.
Subsidiary of Hurst Performance, Inc.
Ferndale, Michigan 48220

INTRODUCING...

OLDS RALLYE 350

Dr. Oldsmobile scores again with a new action look— and a price that says "Let's Go!"

It's an all-new action look. From the wheels up. From the price down. Olds Rallye 350. Just plain beautiful—to look at, drive, and price.

A 4-barreled, air-inducted V-8 makes it run. A 4-4-2 developed suspension makes it handle. And about every action/appearance item you can think of (scoops, stripes, blacked-out grille, yellow-coated bumpers and wheels, etc.) makes it the boldest scene-stealer that ever toured Main Street. And you can order it with a rear-deck spoiler.

The coupe that could win car-of-the-year honors on looks alone is at your Olds dealer's now. Olds Rallye 350.

WHAT IT'S GOT: 350-cu.-in., 4-bbl. V-8 with air-induction ● Special Sebring Yellow paint with sport stripes (sides and rear) ● New urethane-coated bumpers ● Blacked-out grille ● Fiberglass hood with functional air scoops, wide paint patches, chromed hood tie-downs ● Rear bumper specially notched for flared dual exhausts ● Heavy-duty FE2 suspension with front and rear stabilizer bars ● Super-wide G70 x 14" bias-belted blackwalls on styled, Sebring Yellow sports wheels ● Custom-sport steering wheel with leather-like, non-slip grip ● Sports-styled outside mirrors, left side with remote control ● Rally 350 decals on rear-quarter panels ● 3.23:1 axle ratio ● Olds Rallye 350 option is available on three models—F-85 Sports Coupe and Cutlass S Holiday or Sports Coupe.

POPULAR HOT RODDING: MARCH '70. DR. OLDSMOBILE— THE MAD SCIENTIST OF THE AUTO INDUSTRY. SOME OF DR. O's PERFORMANCE COMMITTEE MEMBERS WERE: ELEPHANT-ENGINE ERNIE, SHIFTY SIDNEY AND WIND-TUNNEL WALDO.

When the good Doc first put his 455-powered 4·4·2 on the road, he figured he had a pacesetter.

Now it's official!

OLDSMOBILE OFFICIAL PACE CAR
442

The motion-minded folks at Indy have just named 4-4-2 the official pace car for this year's classic.

It's easy to see why. Its standard V-8 has a pace-setting 455-cu.-in. displacement. Nobody in its class offers more. Its valve system is revolutionary, featuring positive valve rotators for more efficient performance, longer engine life. Its special suspension with front and rear stabilizers? Fast becoming the most imitated in the business.

Ready to set a pace of your own? See your Olds dealer and test-drive a 4-4-2 or other Olds. You'll find that great performance runs in the family.

OLDS 4-4-2 SPECS

Engine type	H.C. Rocket V-8
Displacement	455 cu. in.
Bhp	365 at 5000 rpm
Torque, lb.-ft.	500 at 3200 rpm
Bore x stroke, in.	4.125 x 4.250
Compression ratio	10.50-to-1
Combustion chamber volume, min. allowable	91.72 cc
Min. cyl. head vol.	69.75 cc
Min. deck clearance	.002 below
Carburetion	Quadrajet 4-bbl
Camshaft duration Intake/exhaust (Sync)	294°/296°
Camshaft overlap Intake/exhaust (Sync)	68°
Total valve lift Intake/exhaust	472
Valve diameter (Max.) Intake	2.077
Exhaust	1.630
Brakes	9.5" drums
Transmission	Full sync h-d 3-on-the-floor, Hurst Competition Shifter
Axle (Sync)	3.08 ratio
Exhaust system	Full duals
Suspension	FE2
Has h-d springs, shocks, rear control arms, plus stabilizer bars front and rear	
Wheels	H-d 14" with 7" rim
Tires	G70
bias-belted with white stripe	
Strato Bucket Seats	Std.
Lightweight fiberglass hood, functional scoops, big hood stripes, chromed hood tie-downs, and low-restriction air cleaner (W25), available.	

Oldsmobile 4·4·2

Beneath that air-scooped, fiberglass hood rumbles as large a V-8 as ever bolted into a special-performance, production automobile.

Olds 4-4-2: The complete Escape Machine. The name of the game is cubic inches. 4-4-2 packs 455 of them, standard! But this V-8 is more than big. It's revolutionary. It features Olds' exclusive Positive Valve Rotators for smoother, more trouble-free performance. Something else that's news—the 4-4-2 suspension with front *and* rear stabilizers. The imitators are popping up faster than you can say "me too." The special hood? It's part of the new W-25 package you can order. Do so—while you're still young enough to enjoy it!

Oldsmobile: Escape from the ordinary.

Meet the 1972 Olds 4·4·2, 4·4·2, 4·4·2, 4·4·2!

Now you can get 4-4-2 four great ways. And that includes a new, low-priced way! (You're welcome.)

How can we do it? Easy. We've come up with a great new 4-4-2 Sport/Handling Package. And you can order it on four Cutlass models – the Cutlass Supreme Convert, way back there. The Cutlass Hardtop and Cutlass S Coupe, next in line. And that gorgeous Cutlass S Hardtop, front and center. All different. All great.

Here's what the 4-4-2 Package includes: FE2 suspension with heavy-duty front and rear stabilizer bars, wide 14 x 7" wheels, louvered hood, special 4-4-2 grille, hood and body paint stripes, 4-4-2 identification. And you can order a Hurst Competition Shifter, if you like.

Engine choice? That's a whole new ball-game, too! A spirited 350-cube 2-barrel V-8 is standard. But you can order a 350 4-barrel. Or a 455-cubic-incher with 4-barrels, flared dual exhaust outlets, and a specially sculptured rear bumper. Or order our top package, the W-30 with a dual-intake fiberglass hood and a factory-blueprinted 455 Cold-Air V-8!

The point is this: Now you can "pack up" and go 4-4-2 in more ways than ever. And you can do it for less! Go do so – at your nearest Olds dealer's.

OLDSMOBILE
ALWAYS A STEP AHEAD

Pontiac Division

*For the man who wouldn't mind riding a tiger
if someone'd only put wheels on it—Pontiac GTO*

This piece of machinery is something our Engineering Department slipped a motherly big Pontiac 389-incher into and named the GTO.

It comes in hardtop, sports coupe and convertible form, based on the Le Mans—only sleekened down some and fitted with a special set of red-circle high-performance tires.

The looks you can see for yourself. The big deal is under the hood: 325 bhp at 4800 rpm and 428 lb-ft of torque at 3200 rpm. That's just the standard 4BBL engine. There's also a version with 348 bhp* at 4900 rpm and 428 lb-ft of torque at 3600 rpm. *optional at extra cost.

This one does deep-breathing exercises through a 3-2BBL setup. Both make bad-tempered noises through dual pipes. As illustrated above, pairs of exhaust splitters on each flank, just behind the rear wheels, are available dealer installed*.

A 3-speed transmission is standard, stirred by a Hurst shifter on the floor. Extra-cost variations include an automatic with shift on the column . . . an all-synchro 4-speed on the floor . . . or a choice of any one of them sprouting out of a console.

Give yourself a blast of tonic. Sample one of these here big pussycats.

PONTIAC MOTOR DIVISION • GENERAL MOTORS CORPORATION

I wouldn't stand in the middle of the page if I were you...
It's a Pontiac GTO!

If you insist on reading at a time like this—that's a 6.5 litre Gran Turismo Omologato aimed right at you, 325 bhp @ 4800 rpm with 1-4BBL. It may have an optional 3-2BBL setup* with 348 bhp, look lively! As it goes by, notice the nylon red-circle tires and dual exhausts. Listen to the standard 3-speed trans-mission with Hurst shifter going through the motions. Or, the fully synchronized 4-speed* on the floor. Or, the auto-matic*—you can't tell from here. It may even have a console*. Like every GTO, it has heavy-duty springs, shocks and stabilizer. Quick, get off the page!

*Optional at extra cost.

the GTO makers—Pontiac
PONTIAC MOTOR DIVISION • GENERAL MOTORS CORPORATION

Hands off the grab bar, Charlie, you're tearing out the dash!

The faint *shoosh* of a seat being depressed. The metallic click of seat belts. A 12-volt starter rasps briefly, followed by a vast convulsion as things mechanical happen in a big way under the hood. The left front fender rises, then falls back again as torque prematurely shows its hand. A rumbling boom as of distant thunder. Dust sets to swirling suddenly in the path of a pair of downward point-ing exhaust pipes. Someone has just prodded one of our 421's into fire-in-the-nostrils, show-me-a-road-any-road life. There are three such engines. Meet them:

Engine	Bhp @ rpm	Torque @ rpm	Displ., cu. in.	Carburetion	Compression Ratio
Trophy 421	320 @ 4400	455 @ 2800	421	1-4BBL	10.5:1
Trophy 421	350 @ 4600	454 @ 3200	421	3-2BBL	10.75:1
Trophy 421 HO	370 @ 5200	460 @ 3800	421	3-2BBL	10.75:1

the 421 makers—Pontiac
PONTIAC MOTOR DIVISION • GENERAL MOTORS CORPORATION

A couple of terrible things just happened to our competitors.

Pity the poor men who turn out other brands of cars and then have to look at something like our '64 Catalina 2+2, say we happily. (Not that looks are everything, you understand, but you don't catch us hiding Pontiac's power team under a ho-hum body.)

The 2+2 commences proceedings with a high compression 283-horse 389-incher for the 4-speed box (267 bhp with Hydra-Matic), but there's nothing to stop you from playing footsie with one of our three 421-inchers*. Take your pick—320, 350 and 370 bhp at your command. Standard transmission is a choice of 4-speed or Hydra-Matic, with the shift in a central console.

There are two of these cars—sports coupe and convertible—both with bucket seats and both with their own individual interior styling.

Considering the range of options and accessories we've got, no two 2+2's need be alike. Know just the kind of car you want? Put it on paper for your Pontiac dealer and we'll turn it into metal.

Ask us what's new with Le Mans (and every Tempest) for '64 and we'll pour you an earful.

Take engines: the standard plant is now an in-line 6 of 215 inches and 140 horses—and there's a duo of 326-inch V-8s* at 250 and 280 horses.

Frame?—It's a new swept-hip perimeter Pontiac type. Suspension?—Pontiac-type 4-coil, independent front, 4-link rear.

Options?—Tempest is a Pontiac, right? And Pontiac is noted for its options, right? So naturally, there's everything from a 4-speed* for both 6 and V-8s to a limited-slip differential* with a staggering array of no-extra-cost axle ratios.

Anything else? Not much, unless you count bigger brakes . . . longer, 115" wheelbase . . . larger gas tank . . . new steering gear . . . curved side glass . . . and so on. And on. (And on.)

*optional at extra cost

Both by the Builder of the Wide-Track Cars

155

How to tell a real tiger from a pussycat:

Drive it.

Two seconds behind the wheel of a Pontiac and you know unquestionably you're in tiger country. You realize right away there's more to being a tiger than just bucket seats, carpeting, and sleek upholstery. There's Wide-Track handling, say. And availability of a six or two rambunctious V-8s in the LeMans. And a snarling 335-hp GTO or its 360-hp, slightly hairier, cousin. Get out and drive a tiger!

**Quick Wide-Track Tigers
Pontiac LeMans & GTO**

our Thing.

Standard equipment: Engine—389 cu. in., 335 bhp, 4BBL; dual exhausts, low-restriction mufflers, lightweight resonators; declutching fan; chromed low-restriction air cleaner, rocker covers, oil filler cap; 3-speed with Hurst shifter; heavy-duty springs, shocks, stabilizer bar; choice of premium 7.75 x 14 red-circle nylon tires or same-size rayon whitewall tires; 14 x 6JK wide-rim wheels; bucket seats; full carpeting; custom pinstriping.

Extra-cost performance equipment: Engine—389 cu. in., 360 bhp, 3-2BBL, with factory-installed mechanical linkage on stick shift jobs (Code 802); all-synchro 3-speed with Hurst shifter (Code 743); wide- and close-ratio 4-speeds with Hurst shifters (Code 744 and 778); Safe-T-Track limited-slip differential (Code 701); axle ratios—3.08, 3.23, 3.36, 3.55, and 3.90:1, factory installed; 4.11 and 4.33:1, dealer installed; metallic brake linings (Code 692); extra-stiff springs and shocks (Code 621); 20:1 quick steering

(Code 612); 17.5:1 power steering (Code 501); tachometer, ammeter, oil pressure and water temp gauges (Code 504); high-performance transistorized ignition (Code 671); competition-type steel wheels (Code 691); exhaust splitters (Code 422); custom sports steering wheel (Code 524); heavy-duty radiator (Code 432); to be continued in our special GTO/2+2 performance catalog, free at any Pontiac dealer's.

Wide-Track Tiger—Pontiac GTO

NATIONAL GEOGRAPHIC: **MAY '65**

HOT ROD: **NOVEMBER '64 AND** *MECHANIX ILLUSTRATED:* **DECEMBER '64**

421 cubic inches standard equipment. Pontiac 2 + 2.

You read that right. Hulking under the 2 + 2's hood is our whacking great 4BBL 421. Horsepower—338. Torque—459 lb-ft. Blam!
Other standard equipment:
new all-synchro manual 3-speed with Hurst floor shift
heavy-duty springs and shocks
dual exhausts
chromed air cleaner and rocker covers
bucket seats
full carpeting
custom pinstriping and like that.

You're the 4-speed type? Order the all-synchro Muncie unit with a close-ratio gear set.
For stab-and-steer men there's a new 3-speed automatic you can lock in any gear. Turbo Hydra-Matic. No lag, no lurching, no surprise shifts. Just straighten right leg, wind tight, move lever. Repeat. Make small noises in your throat. Attaboy, tiger!
There are two 2 + 2's—a hardtop and a convertible. And two other engines to stuff in them—356 and 376 bhp, both breathing through 3-2BBL.
Decisions, decisions.

335 horsepower standard equipment. Pontiac GTO.

Just a friendly little 389-inch saber-toothed pussycat. Gas-works—one 4BBL. Torque—431 lb-ft. One of these at a fast idle sounds like feeding time at the zoo.
Other standard equipment:
manual 3-speed with Hurst floor shift
heavy-duty springs, shocks, stabilizer bar
dual exhausts
chromed air cleaner, rocker covers, oil filler cap
7.75 x 14 red-circle nylon tires
bucket seats
custom pinstriping and like that.

There are three GTO's—a hardtop, a sports coupe, and a convertible.
Except for new looks, more power, and a few dozen other things you can have like an all-synchro 3-speed; new instrument package (oil pressure/water temp/ammeter, plus tach); and a 3-2BBL engine that churns out 360 bhp, with mechanical carb linkage installed at the factory on stick shift jobs, the GTO hasn't changed a bit from last year.
After all, how can a tiger change its stripes?

Wide-Track Tigers

Have new tigers. Need tamer.

Apply any Pontiac dealer.

PONTIAC MOTOR DIVISION · GENERAL MOTORS CORPORATION

You can get a set of five big, full-color action shots of the GTO and 2+2—suitable for framing—see details below.

A flying machine for people who can't stand heights.

The object in the foreground is a Pontiac 2+2. It's what you might call a sudden automobile. Meaning that if it had started accelerating when this sentence began, you would now be feeling enormous pressure on your abdomen. Bucket seats and full carpeting are standard. So are a Hurst floor shifter, 3-speed fully synchronized transmission, heavy-duty springs and shocks, and lots more. The moving force is a 421-cubic inch V-8 with 338 hp. Still more pressure can be applied with the optional 356 and 376 hp versions of the same powerplant. The line forms outside Pontiac dealers for flying tiger rides.

Pontiac will send you a set of five huge 26" x 11½" full-color reproductions of the famous Wide-Track Tigers in action just like the one above—along with a complete set of specs and tune-up tips—and they're suitable for framing. Send 25¢ to cover handling and mailing to Wide-Track Tigers, P.O. Box 988B, 196 Wide-Track Blvd., Pontiac, Michigan. _(No stamps please.)_

Quick Wide-Track Tigers—Pontiac 2+2 and GTO

Pontiac Motor Division • General Motors Corporation

You don't know what a real tiger is   until you hear this GeeTO Tiger growl.

Roaring up a growl by cutting in the quad on the 335-horse job or opening up the triples on the 360 isn't the only charge you get from owning a GTO. Try handling a wicked curve with one and you will never look at those so-called sports cars again.

Same goes for the interior. All that carpeting and bucket seats make those expensive foreign machines look positively drab. Then there's the chrome-plated air cleaner, chrome-plated rocker covers, pinstriping, an all-synchro 3-speed Hurst shifter, and a reputation as fierce as a Bengal tiger's.

If you want a taste of what it's like to own a GTO, or if you already own one and like to lullaby yourself to sleep in style, send 50¢ (60¢ in Canada) for the swingingest record you ever heard. On one side there's The Big Sounds of the GeeTO Tiger—your chance to ride shotgun with a top Pontiac test driver as he puts the GTO through its paces at the GM Proving Ground. And on the flip side, the hit that's sure to sweep the country: GeeTO Tiger! Man, that's tiger talk. Send your half dollar to: GeeTO Tiger, P.O. Box 456K, 196 Wide-Track Blvd., Pontiac, Michigan.

Wide-Track Pontiac Tiger—GTO

CAR CRAFT: MAY '65

2+2—A fistful of Pontiac!

Pontiac Motor Division · General Motors Corporation

Inventing the 2+2 was the easiest thing we've done. We started with a Pontiac, which right there put us in a league by ourselves. Then we laid on some of the Pontiac performance options we've been perfecting for years and made them standard equipment. Things like a 338-hp 421. Heavy-duty springs and shocks. Dual exhausts.

Even chromed rocker covers and air cleaner. We added bucket seats, full carpeting and custom pin-striping. Then we stuffed in a brand-new all-synchro 3-speed with Hurst floor shift as standard equipment, which means you can run up and down through the gears like a 4-speed. We made up a list of extra equipment

that you can choose from (which includes 356- and 376-hp 421's!) and sent our 2+2's out into the world. If you haven't been lucky enough to hear one growl, ask your dealer for the special 2+2/GTO performance catalog. It's almost as much fun as driving one.

Wide-Track Tiger—Pontiac 2+2

GTO stands for *Gran Turismo Omologato*. You've probably heard of it. A Pontiac in a saber-toothed tiger skin. The deceptively beautiful body comes in convertible, sports coupe, and hardtop configurations. With pinstriping. On a heavy-duty suspension system that thinks it's married to the ground. Bucket seats and carpeting. Wood-grained dash. Redlines or whitewalls at no extra cost. Chromed 335-hp 4-barrel under the hood. Fully-synchronized 3-speed on the column. Or order a heavy-duty all-synchro 3-speed or 4-speed with Hurst floor shifter. Or 2-speed auto. Or the 360-hp 3 2-BBL. There's a catalog full of options. See if you can get your Pontiac dealer to cough one up. That's the GTO/2+2 performance catalog. You'll recognize it. It vibrates.

Speak softly and carry a GTO

Pontiac Motor Division · General Motors Corporation

Standard plumbing: 421 4-BBL, 338 hp. Duals, straight-through mufflers, low-restriction resonators. Chromed low-restriction air cleaner, rocker covers, oil filter cap. 3.08, 3.23 or 3.42 rear axles. all-synchro 3-speed with Hurst. Heavy-duty suspension, buckets, carpeting. Front and rear seat belts an enthusiast will use and appreciate. Extra-cost plumbing: 421 Tri-Power, 356 and

376 hp. 4-speed with Hurst. Turbo Hydra-Matic. Extra-large diameter exhaust system, extra-heavy-duty suspension. Transistorized ignition, oil pressure and water temperature gauges, tach. Limited-slip. Heavy-duty radiator, oil cooler and battery, aluminum wheel hubs and drums, 3.73 and 4.11 rear axles and all the other items you'll see in our special GTO/2+2 performance catalog.

Pontiac 2+2. Listen! Did you hear something growl just then?

Big Brother.

Behind that appropriately ferocious split grille, there's a 428 cubic inch V-8 that releases 360 horses as fast as you can add 2 + 2. Which is one good reason why Big Brother may well make you stone your present machine.

Others include a floor-mounted, heavy-duty, all-synchro three speed, buckets, carpeting and special suspension that lets you take a curve like you were riding slots.

Of course, these things are available on all the big Pontiacs. Grand Prix, Bonneville and Catalina offer

you a power choice that ranges from a very respectable 400 cubic inch V-8 all the way up to a 376 hp Quadra Power 428. And an option list that includes everything from a four-speed stick to rally wheels. Even a hood-mounted tach.

Naturally, the GM safety package (including the new energy absorbing steering column) is standard. But why sit here reading this when you could be down at your Pontiac dealer's driving one? Big Brother is watching.

Want to watch Big Brother? And friends? We'll send you five 26" x 11" full-color pictures of 2+2, GTO and OHC Sprint, plus complete specs and decals, if you'll send 25¢ (35¢ outside USA) to: '67 Wide-Tracks, P.O. Box 880F, 196 Wide-Track Blvd., Pontiac, Mich. 48056. Please include your ZIP code.

Wide-Track Pontiac

ac Motor Division • General Motors Corporation

You can get a set of five big, full-color action shots of the GTO, 2+2 and the new OHC Six—suitable for framing. See details below.

To all the other cars from the GTO:

"What's new, pussycats?"

It takes more than a big bore V-8 on a little chassis to make a GTO. The genius of the GTO is that it's the world's greatest compromise. In its proletarian version, it's a very manageable machine. With its 4-barrel carb, standard cam, and firm but civilized suspension, your grandmother can drive it. (Front and rear seat belts are standard. Be sure to tell her to buckle them.) But if you want to start grubbing around in our parts bin and add on our three deuces, one of our close-ratio four speeds and our tach, you can turn your GTO into the famous Gee TO Tiger. Catch one. Wherever real tigers are sold.

Like to have the Wide-Track Tigers prowling your wall? Pontiac will send you five ready-to-frame, 26" x 11½" full-color reproductions of the famous GTO, 2+2 and new OHC Six in action just like you see above—plus a full set of factory specs on all three, plus five GTO emblem decals. Just send 25¢ (35¢ outside USA) to: Wide-Track Tigers, P. O. Box 888A, 196 Wide-Track Blvd., Pontiac, Mich. 48053.

(No stamps please.)

3 Wide-Track Tigers—2+2, GTO and OHC Six

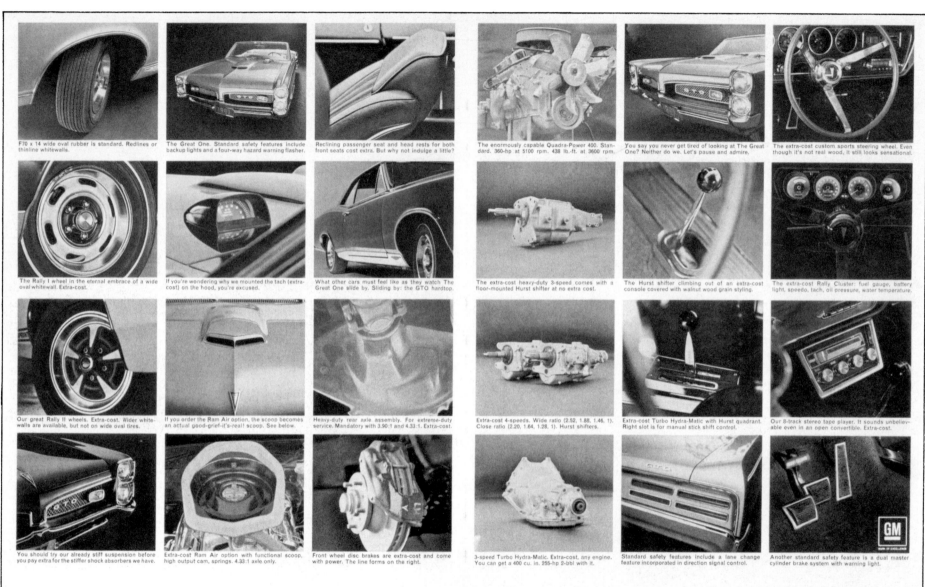

F70 x 14 wide oval rubber is standard. Redlines or thinline whitewalls.

The Great One. Standard safety features include backup lights and a four-way hazard warning flasher.

Reclining passenger seat and head rests for both front seats cost extra. But why not indulge a little?

The enormously capable Quadra-Power 400. Standard. 360-hp at 5100 rpm. 438 lb.-ft. at 3600 rpm.

You say you never get tired of looking at The Great One? Neither do we. Let's pause and admire.

The extra-cost custom sports steering wheel. Even though it's not real wood, it still looks sensational.

The Rally I wheel in the eternal embrace of a wide oval whitewall. Extra-cost.

If you're wondering why we mounted the tach (extra-cost) on the hood, you're excused.

What other cars must feel like as they watch The Great One slide by. Sliding by: the GTO hardtop.

The extra-cost heavy-duty 3-speed comes with a floor-mounted Hurst shifter at no extra cost.

The Hurst shifter climbing out of an extra-cost console covered with walnut wood grain styling.

The extra-cost Rally Cluster: fuel gauge, battery light, speedo, tach, oil pressure, water temperature.

Our great Rally II wheels. Extra-cost. Wider white-walls are available, but not on wide oval tires.

If you order the Ram Air option, the scoop becomes an actual good-grief-it's-real! scoop. See below.

Heavy-duty rear axle assembly. For extreme-duty service. Mandatory with 3.90:1 and 4.33:1. Extra-cost.

Extra-cost 4-speeds. Wide ratio (2.52, 1.88, 1.46, 1). Close ratio (2.20, 1.64, 1.28, 1). Hurst shifters.

Extra-cost Turbo Hydra-Matic with Hurst quadrant. Right slot is for manual stick shift control.

Our 8-track stereo tape player. It sounds unbelievable even in an open convertible. Extra-cost.

You should try our already stiff suspension before you pay extra for the stiffer shock absorbers we have.

Extra-cost Ram Air option with functional scoop, high output cam, springs. 4.33:1 axle only.

Front wheel disc brakes are extra-cost and come with power. The line forms on the right.

3-speed Turbo Hydra-Matic. Extra-cost, any engine. You can get a 400 cu. in. 255-hp 2-bbl with it.

Standard safety features include a lane change feature incorporated in direction signal control.

Another standard safety feature is a dual master cylinder brake system with warning light.

Pontiac GTO

Now you know what makes The Great One great.

Pontiac Motor Division

Want 8 car pictures for your wall, complete specs and decals? Send 25¢ (35¢ outside U.S.A.) to: '67 Wide-Tracks, P.O. Box 888F, 196 Wide-Track Blvd., Pontiac, Mich. 48056. Please include your ZIP code.

CAR CRAFT: DECEMBER '66 AND *CAR AND DRIVER:* FEBRUARY '67

Anything our light heavyweight can't handle

Firebird HO. The HO on that sleek machine above means High Output. And what that means is a 326 cu. in. 285-hp V-8 with dual exhausts that blow the sweetest music this side of Sebring. A column-mounted 3-speed is standard, but you can order 3 or 4 on the floor. Also an automatic. Bucket seats? Of course. Your choice of hardtop or convertible. The stripes mean what they say.

Firebird 400. Below. Those scoops hide 400 cubes of chromed V-8 that churns out 325 hp. It's hooked to a 3-speed stick and lashed to special sports suspension. A 4-speed (or our 3-speed Turbo Hydra-Matic) is extra cost, but the wide-oval redlines are standard. So is the GM safety package (on all Firebirds). Leave it to Pontiac to do it right. **Two of Pontiac's Magnificent Five**

our heavyweight can.

Pontiac Motor Division

Picture this. We'll send you six 24" x 13½" full-color pictures of Firebird 400, Pontiac 2 + 2, GTO and OHC Sprint, plus complete specs and decals. Send 25¢ (35¢ outside USA) to '67 Wide-Tracks, P.O. Box 880F, 196 Wide-Track Blvd., Pontiac, Mich. 48056. Include your ZIP code.

Others have caught on. But they haven't caught up.

Imagine, for a moment, that you are in charge of designing an answer to the GTO. And that this has been your task since The Great One first rumbled into reality, sending shock waves through your offices.

Each year you've sent your answer into the streets. And, each year, seen it change into something merely mediocre alongside GTO's Hurst shifter, bulging hood scoops and Wide-Track. And, this year, humiliated by an incredible new kind of bumper.

And just when you're getting the hang of its extra-cost Ram Air (yours will surely out-GTO GTO next year), you find Pontiac has improved theirs. With a new high-lift cam, larger swirled exhaust valves, new freer breathing combustion chambers.

When the Car of the Year is improved even before the year is over, can your car ever catch up? Pontiac Motor Division

The Great One by Pontiac

Anxious for 5 color pictures, specs and decals of the Great Wide-Tracks? Don't be. Send 30¢ (50¢ outside U.S.A.) to: '68 Wide-Tracks, P.O. Box 888B, 196 Wide-Track Blvd., Pontiac, Michigan 48056

Our almost Great One.

350 cubic inch H.O. V-8, 320 hp, 380 ft. lb. torque, 4-bbl Quadrajet. All wrapped up in that nifty Tempest Custom captured above. And even after you add things like our 4-speed stick, Hurst shifter and handling package, the price is still right down there in your ball park. As we said, not quite a GTO. But then, what is?

Pontiac Tempest Custom H.O.

Anxious for 5 color pictures, specs and decals of the Great Wide-Tracks? Don't be. Send 30¢ (50¢ outside U.S.A.) to: '68 Wide-Tracks, P.O. Box 888A, 196 Wide-Track Blvd., Pontiac, Michigan 48056

We'd like you to meet one of the most active members of our Break Away movement. GTO!

Pontiac's Great One has never been one to meddle with mediocrity. Ever since our enthusiastic "men in white" launched this splendid specimen back in 1964, it's been breaking away from the pack with grand sincerity. And continues to do so.

Behold our convertible version for 1969. All that you see is truth. Deep bucket seats. Console with standard, floor-mounted, 3-speed shift, and our standard, 350-horsepower, Quadra-jet V-8. If you want something more, ask about GTO's other V-8 possibilities—up to a 400-cubic-inch Ram Air.

You want a lesson in road handling? GTO is ready with all the right answers. With sports-type springs and shocks, specially tuned to The Great One's modus operandi. Or just stand there and look at the car that runs as great as it looks. With the same chip-, fade- and corrosion-proof front nose, that elated you last year. GTO. Our prime example of getting there first with the most. Go ask for a check ride.

The year of the great ▼ Pontiac Break Away

**Pontiac Firebird H.O.
350 cu. in.
Quadra-jet 4-bbl.
H.D. Suspension
320 hp.**

Now let us tell you about our Heavyweight.

You see it on the right. Our 400. Heavyweight of Pontiac's Magnificent Five Firebirds for 1968.

Along with its heavy-duty but newly obliging suspension (asymmetrically mounted multiple leaf rear springs and wide-ovals) there's a heavy-duty 3-speed with Hurst shifter. All standard. And augmented by a 330-hp, 400-cu.-in. V-8 with 430 ft. lbs. of torque and Quadra-jet. Or you can select the new 335-hp H.O. engine, or a 335-hp Ram Air with functional scoops.

But don't think we'd surround you with all that exuberance and neglect elegance. Any Firebird can be ordered with knitted (just like mom used to make) vinyl upholstery. And picture windows (no side vents), carpeting, and simulated wood grain styling on dash are standard. And with every Firebird you get GM's many safety features. Like seat belts, safety armrests, and side-mounted marker lights.

Now, any guess why we decided to call them the Magnificent Five—again?

GM MARK OF EXCELLENCE
Pontiac Motor Division

Announcing
Pontiac's new pony express.   Firebird Trans Am.

Back when the Chisholm Trail was considered an expressway, you needed 335 horses to haul the mail. We figure you still do. So Firebird Trans Am's got 'em. Stabled under oversized hood scoops in 400 cubic inches of Ram Air V-8. A heavy-duty, 3-speed box hitches them to a 3.55:1 rear axle and fiber-glass-belted tires. Wells Fargo rides again!

Sound like Trans Am is strictly for wide-open spaces? Take it through a mountain pass. Heavy-duty shocks and springs, 1" stabilizer bar, power front disc brakes and variable-ratio power steering make Trans Am our version of a quarter horse.

But you can probably guess all that by looking at it. Trans Am's engine-air exhaust louvers, rear-deck airfoil, black textured grille, full-length blue stripes, leather-covered steering wheel and special I.D. provide fair warning that this is no ordinary mount. It's Pontiac's new pony express. And that's about as far from ordinary as you can get.

Shown above are some of the many available Trans Am features. See your Pontiac dealer. Pontiac Motor Division.

**MOTOR TREND: JUNE '69. THIS MARVELOUS AD SHOWS
THE VERY FIRST TRANS AM.**

GM
MARK OF EXCELLENCE

Pontiac Motor Division

The Judge can be bought.

For a lot less bread than a lot of those so-called performance cars, we hasten to add.

Surprised? The Judge is full of them.

Like a *standard* 366-horse, 400-cube Ram Air V-8 with Quadra-jet carb. Coupled to a *standard* 3-speed, fully-synched, manual gearbox. Stirred by a *standard* Hurst T-handle shifter.

Those big, black, fiber-glass belted tires? *Standard* too. Same as the mag-type wheels. The 60" airfoil. The custom black grille. And the blue-red-yellow striping.

True. Money will get you most of the equipment on some other car. But you'd be getting short-changed. Because you'd still have some other car. Not a special GTO from Pontiac. The Judge. It's a steal.

Four color pictures, specs, book jackets and decals are yours for 30¢ (50¢ outside U.S.A.). Write to: '69 Wide-Tracks, P.O. Box 888A, 196 Wide-Track Blvd., Pontiac, Michigan 48056.

CAR AND DRIVER: MARCH '69 AND MOTOR TREND: APRIL '69. DID SAMMY DAVIS JR.'S ROUTINE OF "HERE COMES DA JUDGE" ON THE OLD TV PROGRAM CALLED LAUGH-IN, HAVE ANY INFLUENCE ON PONTIAC NAMING THIS GTO, THE JUDGE?

Born great.

Did you expect less? Shame! This is The Judge. And The Judge claims Pontiac's great GTO as its closest of kin.

Which explains The Judge's bump-proof Endura snoot. And the bulging hood scoops which can be opened or closed from the driver's seat. And the very unspongy springs and shocks. And the Morrokide-covered front buckets. And the no-nonsense instrument panel.

Now, if you want to think of The Judge as Billy's kid brother, OK. Just keep in mind that the family resemblance only goes so far.

You see, The Judge comes on with a 60" air foil. A custom grille. Big, black fiber glass belted tires. Special mag-type wheels. Blue-red-yellow striping. And name tags (like the wild one below) inside and out.

Keep in mind also that this baby performs like nobody's kid brother. Not with a standard 366-hp, 400-cube V-8 and Ram Air. Or a 370-horse Ram Air IV, if you so order. Either couples to a fully synchronized 3-speed with a Hurst shifter. Or order a close-ratio 4-speed. (Little old ladies might even order Turbo Hydra-matic.)

No sir. The kid brother hasn't been born yet that's greater, or tougher than The Judge.

THE JUDGE *A special GTO by Pontiac*

Four color pictures, specs, book jackets and decals are yours for 30¢ (50¢ outside U.S.A.). Write to: '69 Wide-Tracks, P.O. Box 888A, 196 Wide-Track Blvd., Pontiac, Michigan 48056.

Pontiac Motor Division

EQUIPMENT
Standard: Rear-deck airfoil · Front air dam · Striping · Special mag-type wheels · Blacked-out grille · G70—14 black fiberglass-belted tires · Special "The Judge" emblems · Front stabilizer bar—1⅛" · Rear stabilizer bar—⅞" · Firm ride and handling package
Available: Variable-ratio power steering · Hood-mounted tachometer · Power front disc brakes · 7-blade thermostatic fan · Limited-slip differential (Safe-T-Track) · Heavy-duty battery · Rally gauges · Custom sport steering wheel · Formula steering wheel · Radios —AM, AM/FM, AM/FM with stereo, multiplex · Stereo tape player

STANDARD RAM AIR
Displacement .... 400 cu. in.
Horsepower .... 366 @ 5100 rpm
Torque .... 445 lb.-ft. @ 3600 rpm
Bore & Stroke .... 4.12 x 3.75
Deck Clearance .... .023
Compression Ratio 10.5:1
Chamber Volume .... 66.27 cc
Carburetion .... Quadra-jet, 4-bbl.
Exhaust .... Performance duals
Valve Lifters .... Hydraulic

RAM AIR TRANSMISSIONS
Standard 3-speed Heavy-duty
Make .... Muncie

Shifter .... Hurst
Available 4-speed Wide-ratio
Make .... Muncie
Shifter .... Hurst
Available 4-speed Close-ratio
Make .... Muncie
Shifter .... Hurst
Available 3-speed Turbo Hydra-matic
RAM AIR AXLE RATIOS
Standard 3.55
With Air Conditioning 3.23
Available .... 3.90 & 4.33

AVAILABLE RAM AIR IV
Displacement .... 400 cu. in.
Horsepower .... 370 @ 5500 rpm
Torque .... 445 lb.-ft. @ 3900 rpm

Bore & Stroke .... 4.12 x 3.75
Deck Clearance .... .023
Compression Ratio 10.5:1
Chamber Volume .... 69.12 cc
Carburetion .... Quadra-jet, 4-bbl.
Exhaust .... Performance duals
Valve Lifters .... Hydraulic limited travel with manual transmission

RAM AIR IV TRANSMISSIONS
Standard 4-speed Close-ratio
Make .... Muncie
Shifter .... Hurst
Available 3-speed Turbo Hydra-matic
RAM AIR IV AXLE RATIOS
Standard 3.90
Available 4.33

After a few moments of respectful silence, you may turn the page.

The Judge: a special GTO from Pontiac.
(We take the fun of driving seriously. Very seriously.)

3 individual color pictures of Pontiac performance cars, specs, book jackets and decals are yours for 40¢ (60¢ outside U.S.A.). Write to: '70 Wide-Tracks, P.O. Box 888, 196 Wide-Track Blvd., Pontiac, Mich. 48056.

5 individual color pictures of our '69 Break Away Squad, specs and decals are yours for 30¢ (50¢ outside U.S.A.) Write to: '69 Wide-Tracks, P.O. Box 888F, 196 Wide-Track Blvd., Pontiac, Michigan 48056.

The Graduate.

We'll grant you two wheels are better than none. But look what happens when Firebird swoops onto the scene. If it's our 400 version.

You won't believe how this one handles. Don't let the smoothness fool you. New rear axle, new load rates on our multi-leaf rear springs and a set of sticky wide-ovals (mounted on 7-inch rims) put new shine on Firebird's cornering reputation. A 400-cubic-inch, Quadra-jet V-8 attached to a 3-speed, heavy-duty transmission, stirred by a Hurst, is your standard power setup. But there's also our two-scoop Ram Air IV that you can order with a 4-speed hand shifter or with 3-speed Turbo Hydra-matic, if you just tell your dealer.

Obviously, all that genius is below decks. Topside, Firebird comes on with all-new looks. Inside, new comfort. With wider, more heavily padded bucket seats wrapped in Pontiac's own woven vinyl. Also, an all-new highly readable instrument panel.

Hood tach, front disc brakes, variable-ratio power steering, polyglas-cord, wide-tread rubber . . . all that great Pontiac stuff . . . will practically let you build your own Firebird . . . if you want to.

And that's a liberal education in itself.

Firebird 400 by Pontiac

The Wide-Track Family for '69: Grand Prix, Bonneville, Brougham, Executive, Catalina, GTO, LeMans, Custom S, Tempest and Firebird. Pontiac Motor Division

(We take the fun of driving seriously.)

The quick way out of the little leagues.

Every year Pontiac's hard-nose gets tougher on upstarts.

Not that we go out of our way to humble amateur performers. We just take the fun of driving very seriously.

Like engines. GTO's standard is a 350-horse V-8. But this year there's a high-torque 455-cube V-8 to order, as well as two Ram Airs. So someone's bound to get his feelings hurt. Letting you order a new, low-restriction, exhaust should be the final blow.

Sorry, guys. But this is the big league. And it's time to make a cut.

The Humbler.

(We take the fun of driving seriously.)

Any licensed driver is eligible to participate.

In the beginning of tomorrow. Which is where it's at when you take your seat in the 1970 Firebird Trans Am.

The stick is from Hurst. And it controls a wide-ratio 4-speed transmission. Just right for making the 400 Ram Air V-8 do what you want it to.

You'll know exactly what it's doing, too. Thanks to the tach, speedometer, voltmeter and oil, water and fuel gauges set in that engine-turned aluminum instrument panel.

The thick wheel is our 14" Formula version. It goes directly to the extra-quick, variable-ratio power steering. You have to feel it to believe it.

Outside, the Trans Am is all function. An air dam under the Endura bumper and a spoiler at each wheel will help keep the car aerodynamically stable. Cooling air, that goes to the engine, is vented through two side air extractors. Preventing air buildup in the engine compartment. All these

good things are standard. And combined with the rear spoiler, they create a downward pressure of 50 lbs., both front and rear. At turnpike speeds.

Trans Am. It's our ultimate Firebird.

The Firebird Formula 400 is enough to be anyone else's ultimate car. It develops 430 lb-ft of torque from the standard 400 V-8. Order Ram Air, and those twin fiberglass scoops allow cold air to be rammed into the four-barrel carburetor.

Like every Firebird, the Formula 400 has front bucket seats. Bucket-type seats in the rear. Front and rear stabilizer bars help give a flatter ride.

Trans Am or Formula 400. Only Pontiac could build them. So naturally they're only at your Pontiac dealer's. Better get over there. If you want in on the beginning of tomorrow.

Firebird. New, even for Pontiac.

In case you haven't noticed, Pontiac's '73 Firebirds are here.

We build four different kinds. For people who take driving excitement seriously. The question is... how serious do you want to get?

Trans Am: As serious as they come.
It's the red one above. See how serious it is? Everything functional. The spoilers spoil. The air dams dam. That's why a lot of folks rank it as the best performing Yank on the road.

A 455-cubic-inch, 4-bbl. V-8 with a 4-speed manual transmission is standard. And there's a new Super

Duty 455-cubic-inch V-8 available.

No, the giant bird on the hood isn't functional. It's not standard, either. You have to order it. But...!

Formula: Two scoops, three flavors.
The two scoops you can see on the hood above. The flavors are a 350 V-8, a 400 V-8, a 455 V-8. Order the Formula 'Bird as you see fit.

The new interior is all business.

So are the standard front disc brakes and the handling package you can order.

While the scoops look tough, the toughest part of any Firebird is the front bumper. It's made of Endura to help fight dents and dings. And it's been reinforced this year to make it stronger.

Esprit: Can a sports car be luxurious?
Esprit wipes out all doubt. The new bucket seats, the new cloth or all-vinyl upholstery, the new instrument panel and door trim are as plush as you'll find in many a luxury car.

The ride's almost that plush, too.

Basic Firebird: What we didn't sacrifice for price.
This is our easiest to own Firebird.

You still get molded foam bucket seats; loop-pile carpeting; High-Low ventilation; the Endura bumper; a strong, double-shell roof that absorbs sound; Firebird's futuristic styling and outstanding handling.

That's our way with sports cars. Are you ready to get serious?

GM
MARK OF EXCELLENCE

Buckle up for safety.
Pontiac Motor Division

The Wide-Track people have a way with cars.

1974 Pontiac Firebirds.

Part engineering.
Part soul.

There's something about a 1974 Firebird you won't find in any fact sheet or spec book.

Because it's something you can't weigh or measure or touch. It's something you have to feel.

We call it soul.

Take the '74 Formula Firebird for example. Any spec sheet will tell you it comes with a 350, 400 or 455 V-8. A floor-shifted 3-speed trans. Performance dual exhausts. Hood scoops. Front disc brakes. And front and rear stabilizers. A very impressive list of features.

But no feature list can explain what it's like to drive a Formula 'Bird. Gauges set so you can read them at a glance. Controls positioned so they seem like they're extensions of your arms and legs. Response so quick it almost anticipates your commands. And an overall driving experience that makes it hard to suppress a toothy grin.

That's the soul of a Firebird.

The '74 Firebird Trans Am is even better. Because what we know about performance driving, we make standard on Trans Am.

A 400 4-bbl. V-8. 4-speed trans. Power front disc brakes. A limited-slip axle. Full instrumentation. F60—15 tires on 7" Rally II wheels.

A shaker hood. A complete entourage of functional air dams, extractors, deflectors and spoilers.

And enough soul to make Trans Am the ultimate Firebird.

Anybody can appreciate Firebird's engineering. To appreciate the soul, you have to love driving cars as much as we love building them.

PONTIAC GM
Pontiac Motor Division

The Wide-Track people have a way with cars.

More Great Reading

Chevy Spotter's Guide 1920-1980. Nearly 1,200 illustrations of Chevrolet cars and trucks for the enthusiast. 136 pages, softbound.

Ford Spotter's Guide 1920-1980. A great 136-page reference of Ford autos and trucks. Over 1,100 illustrations, softbound.

Chevy Super Sports 1961-1976. Exciting story of these hot cars with complete specs and data. 178 pages, 198 illustrations, softbound.

Illustrated Ferrari Buyer's Guide. Features all street production models 1954 through 1980. 169 pages, over 230 photos, softbound.

Ferraris For The Road. Lavish pictorial coverage of Ferrari's production models. In the Survivor's Series. 126 pages, 269 photos, many in color.

Lincoln and Continental: The Postwar Years. Interesting historical information through 1980. 152 pages, 226 illustrations.

The Ford Agency: A Pictorial History. The complete story of Ford's Dealer network. 131 pages, 260 period photos, softbound.

The American Car Spotter's Guide 1940-1965. (Revised). Greatly enlarged edition—almost 3,000 illustrations. 358 pages, softbound.

American Car Spotter's Guide 1966-1980. Giant pictorial source with over 3,600 illustrations. 432 pages, softbound.

Oldsmobile: The Postwar Years. 280 fine illustrations help tell this exciting story. 152 pages.

Pontiac: The Postwar Years. One of America's most exciting makes is covered in this factual story. 205 pgs. 222 photos.

The Cobra Story. Autobiography of Carroll Shelby and Cobra production & racing history through 1965. 272 pages, 60 photos.

Make Money Owning Your Car. Down-to-earth analysis on beating high depreciation and interest costs of car ownership. 179 pages, 96 photos.

Buick: The Postwar Years. Comprehensive history of a styling and engineering leader. 166 pages, 157 photos.

The Production Figure Book For U.S. Cars. Reflects the relative rarity of various makes, models, body styles, etc. Softbound, 180 pages.

Shelby's Wildlife: The Cobras and Mustangs. Complete, exciting story of the 260, 289, 427 and Daytona Cobras plus Shelby Mustangs. 224 pages, nearly 200 photos.

Auto Restoration From Junker to Jewel. Illustrated guide to restoring old cars. 292 pages, 289 illustrations, softbound.

Chrysler and Imperial: The Postwar Years. Year-by-year account through 1976. 216 pages, 488 photos.

Motorbooks International
Publishers & Wholesalers Inc.
Osceola, Wisconsin 54020, USA